D0744195

THE FRENCH RIGHT AND NAZI GERMANY
1933-1939

THE FRENCH RIGHT
AND NAZI GERMANY
1933-1939
A Study of Public Opinion

BY

CHARLES A. MICAUD

OCTAGON BOOKS

A DIVISION OF FARRAR, STRAUS AND GIROUX

New York   1972

Reprinted 1964

by special arrangement with The Duke University Press

Second Octagon printing 1972

OCTAGON BOOKS

A DIVISION OF FARRAR, STRAUS & GIROUX, INC.

19 Union Square West

New York, N. Y. 10003

LIBRARY OF CONGRESS CATALOG CARD NUMBER: 64-28555

ISBN 0-374-95586-7

Printed in U.S.A. by

NOBLE OFFSET PRINTERS, INC.

NEW YORK 3, N. Y.

TO

N. B. M.

FOREWORD

WHEN PRECISION instruments are lacking, a study of public opinion is inevitably exposed to the danger of willful or involuntary deformation on the part of the interpreter. Two conditions appear essential if the margin of error is to be reduced to acceptable limits, thus qualifying such an inquiry into peoples' minds to enter the realm of the respectable social sciences. These requisites are a first-hand knowledge of a nation's institutions, political make-up and psychology, and an objective viewpoint.

The first condition was partly fulfilled by years of observation and study in France; the second by my coming to America some seven years ago and here acquiring a more detached and undoubtedly clearer picture of a very complicated scene. This experience permitted valuable comparison of the French and American reactions to the growing menace of war and placed me in the privileged position of being at once well acquainted with and personally remote from the political passions which have played such a dominant role in the history of contemporary France.

I wish to acknowledge my deep gratitude to Professor Lindsay Rogers, not only for his advice and for the valuable material he put at my disposal, but for his help in making possible my graduate studies at Columbia University. I wish to express my appreciation to Dr. W. R. Dittmar, also of Columbia University, for his useful criticism and assistance. Most especially I thank my wife, Nancy Bradley Micaud, for her invaluable help and encouragement. I am also grateful to Bowdoin College for a teaching fellowship that has given me the time to accomplish this long and absorbing work.

C. A. M.

CONTENTS

Foreword.   vii

Introduction.   3

TRADITIONAL NATIONALISM IN ACTION

  I. The Right: Ideology and Foreign Policy.   12

 II. Defense of the *Status Quo:* 1933-1935.   24

III. Answers to a Challenge: The Stresa Front and
      the Soviet Pact.   37

FROM TRADITIONAL NATIONALISM TO NEO-PACIFISM

 IV. Pro-Italian Policy: "Sanctions Mean War!".   52

  V. Opposition to the Franco-Soviet Pact: February, 1936. . .   67

 VI. Remilitarization of the Rhineland:
      "Above All, No War!".   85

FROM NEO-PACIFISM TO APPEASEMENT

 VII. Spain and the International Civil War.   108

VIII. The *Anschluss*   133

  IX. Munich.   161

BACK TO RESISTANCE?

  X. The Four Power Diplomacy.   190

 XI. The End of the Truce.   206

Conclusion.   222

Appendix.   233

Bibliography.   238

Index.   249

ABBREVIATIONS

JO. Ch.   *Journal Officiel de la République Française,*
               Chambre des Députés, *Débats Parlementaires*

JO. S.   *Journal Officiel de la République Française,*
               Sénat, *Débats Parlementaires*

RP   *Revue de la Presse*

BJ   *Bulletin du Jour*

S. I. A.   *Survey of International Affairs,* Arnold Toynbee

C. G. T.   *Confédération Générale du Travail*

P. S. F.   *Parti Social Français*

P. P. F.   *Parti Populaire Français*

THE FRENCH RIGHT AND NAZI GERMANY
1933-1939

INTRODUCTION

THE PURPOSE of this study is to follow the evolution of the foreign policy of the French "Right" in terms of the growing menace of Pan-Germanism from the advent of Adolf Hitler to power until the outbreak of the second World War.

The term "Right" describes that section of the French people which has never quite reconciled itself to the ideals of the French Revolution.[1] The word "Right" has been preferred to "Bourgeoisie," since many bourgeois belonged to the Left, and many nonbourgeois to the Right; to "Conservatives," since the Extreme Rightists were actually revolutionaries; and to "Nationalists," since the Right had a common political and social philosophy of which nationalism was only one element.

Traditionally the foreign policy of the Right contrasted with the conciliatory pacifism of the Left in its distrustful vigilance and hostile attitude toward Germany, and in its determination after the war to stop any attempt to revise the peace treaties, by force if necessary. Between the years 1933 and 1938, however—that is, between the advent of nazism and the Munich agreement—there took place a complete change in the foreign policy of the majority of the Right as well as in that of the Left: the nationalist Right began to preach pacifism, and the pacifist Left to urge resistance. "The reversal of these attitudes . . . ," wrote M. Pierre Brossolette in *L'Europe Nouvelle* shortly before Munich (August 20, 1938), "has been of a prodigious suddenness. . . . And so it is that today one can see the most serious organs of the Right speak of a 'Leftist bellicism,' while the Left returns to the Right their old accusation of being 'in the service of Germany.'"

The author's purpose is to fathom and to explain this reversal of the Right's position in foreign affairs from an anti-German policy of integral defense of the *status quo* of the peace

[1] For a definition of the Right, see pp. 12 ff.

treaties to the acceptance of German expansion in Central and Eastern Europe.

Public opinion since the World War has become for all governments an increasingly important factor in the determination of foreign policy. Today most people believe that, by having their own ideas on international affairs, they are actually playing their part in the making of history; and the sum of these individual opinions has resulted in a tremendous force that every state, democratic or totalitarian, has had to recognize and deal with. In France the intensity of public interest in what used to be the domain of a few experts resulted in a state of affairs contemptuously described by the old-school specialists of foreign policy as *"la diplomatie de place publique,"* and undoubtedly played an essential part in the great political game in Europe from 1933 to the present war. A well-controlled and therefore apparently united public opinion was a tremendous asset in the hands of the dictators, while the divisions and strifes in the democracies were a major element of weakness.

This study does not attempt to estimate the role of public opinion in France, or to measure, for example, the degree to which the passive attitude of the French Government toward the remilitarization of the Rhineland in March, 1936, was determined by the pressure of an apathetic public opinion. Its aim is rather to try to understand the elements that formulated the foreign policy of the Rightists and caused them to play the part they did in the tragedy of France.

It may be objected that the restriction of this inquiry to the Right will give a distorted picture of French public opinion as a whole; but since the foreign policies of both Right and Left during this period were closely linked to domestic politics, and since the attitude of the Right was deeply influenced by the changes in the attitude of the Left, it will be found that a study of the former necessarily reflects at least the general outlines of the latter.

It may also be objected that there is no reason for a limitation to the conservative section of the French people, since most observers have agreed that at the time of Munich the Left was just as adept as the Right in turning out good "appeasers" of Germany. This superficial view, however, the present study will attempt to disprove.

This inquiry lies on dangerous ground, where sweeping generalizations and indignant condemnations may be tempting. It must enter not only into the political ideas of the Right but also into their fears and prejudices if the problem is to be approached in its true perspective with some degree of accuracy. Instead of simply condemning the leaders of the Right as fools or traitors and dismissing their arguments as proof that they were either the dupes or the creatures of German propaganda, we should rather attempt to find the main trends of opinion at the Right, to place the arguments in their factual and ideological background, and to group them according to their relative importance in an effort to get nearer the real motives behind the reversal of their foreign policy.

In spite of the importance of public opinion in contemporary history, most scholars have been hesitant in facing its study, fearing that it would be vague, elusive, and necessarily unscientific. "Public opinion is one of these vague terms which elude precise definition. In its common use it refers to the composite reactions of the general public, but, as a rule, the only tangible evidence of those tendencies is to be found in the opinion of the more influential leaders."[2] It is through the medium of these "leaders of opinion" that we shall endeavor to reach the considerable body of opinion at the Right which showed interest in foreign affairs and in turn influenced the policies of the government.

The most important and articulate leaders of French Rightist opinion were to be found in the press and in Parliament, although others existed in the field of literature, in the administration, the clergy, the army, the universities, and business.

[2] E. M. Carroll, *French Public Opinion and Foreign Affairs, 1870 to 1914* (New York, 1931), p. 4.

As for the chiefs of authoritarian groups, like Colonel de la Rocque or M. Jacques Doriot, they had of course real authority over their large followings and quasi-dictatorial power over the political thinking of an important section of opinion.

The role of Parliament, especially of the Chamber, as interpreter and guide of public opinion is quite evident. More than the senators, who were not the direct representatives of the people and whose influence on foreign policy was secondary, the deputies played an important part both in interpreting and shaping the public's attitude toward Nazi Germany. The debates on foreign policy were infrequent, however, and during the long intervals between them only the press discloses what were the currents of thought.

The role of the press as interpreter and molder of opinion is far more controversial than that of Parliament; for it has been accused of such venality as to make one doubt its value as an expression of public opinion. But contrary to the popular belief that the French newspapers were generally in the hands of dishonest owners who offered the hospitality of their columns to the highest bidder, the present writer contends that they may be considered a fairly good barometer of Rightist opinion as well as the most important instrument in directing trends of thought.

Unlike the American press, which on the whole pretends to give an uncolored presentation of news, every French paper openly defended a definite political viewpoint, and each had its faithful following. While the French press was not an exactly scaled map of public opinion, since the Left was not represented in proportion to its strength, the dailies and periodicals, nevertheless, gave a good cross-section of Rightist views. The *journaux d'information,* or *Grande Presse,* were mainly profit-making enterprises attempting to gain and keep as large a public as possible, although maintaining definite political preferences. "The popularity of a paper being achieved by agility at espousing the currents of opinion," admitted M. Thibaudet, "one may say that these papers follow public opinion even more than they make it."[3] The *journaux d'opinion,* on the other hand, put the emphasis on politics rather than circulation, and had a smaller clientele of the most politically-minded citizens.[4] They had to cater to their public, "which expects to be told what it thinks better than it would say it itself. Without this agreement with a multitude of unknown people," wrote M. Alain, the philosopher of Radical-Socialism, "the paper dies."[5] M. Julien Benda also declared that "if the papers presumed to teach lessons to their public, the latter would boycott them immediately. . . . The public today has the profound feeling of its power, and the papers will be its valets or will not exist."[6] The literary periodicals also had a political character; most of the important ones belonged to the Right or even the Extreme Right. The various political views were thus clearly presented, and a relatively accurate picture of Rightist opinion may be formed from the very partiality and diversity of the press.

In this connection it is noteworthy that the average reader was content with following only one paper, which best reflected his own political outlook. This confirms the thesis that each paper represented a definite social or political group. "It is *de bon ton* to read a certain paper; to be a member of a certain party, of a certain religious confession, of a certain profession justifies one in reading this one (rarely those), and in disdaining, despising or detesting the others. . . . Thus we come back to our starting point, that is, that the press reflects the social state of the country fairly exactly."[7]

By this limitation to one paper, however, the general public

---

[3] *La République des professeurs* (Paris, 1927), p. 159.

[4] Cf. Pierre Frédérix, *Etats des forces en France* (Paris, 1935), pp. 158-159. In some cases both types were combined in papers with the popular appeal of the former and the proselytism of the latter, as the pro-Fascist *Le Jour* and *L'Ami du Peuple.* Another group of papers catered to definite social units, such as businessmen, Catholics, the *grands bourgeois,* while also defending a political viewpoint.

[5] *Nouvelle Revue Française,* July 1, 1935, p. 90.

[6] *Ibid.,* Jan. 1, 1937, p. 148. Cf. also Robert de Jouvenel, *La République des camarades* (Paris, 1914), p. 248, and *Le Crapouillot,* Nov., 1938, p. 49.

[7] Georges Bourgin, "Panorama de la presse française," *Encyclopédie française* (Paris, 1939), XVIII, 18-36-9. Cf. Frédérix, *Etat des forces en France,* p. 160.

exposed itself to any clever and progressive change of editorial policy, for its critical sense was dulled by lack of comparison with other competent opinions. "Except for a minority . . . most readers read only one paper, at the maximum two. . . . It necessarily follows that it will be more and more impossible to effect any critical control over the sheets read, and in particular that internal changes, following a change of proprietor, administration, board of directors, editorship—changes more or less cleverly camouflaged and rarely made wholly public— may escape the average reader . . . who progressively becomes accustomed to the relatively new tone of his paper."[8] While it seems evident that "no paper, however powerful it may be, can survive if it openly clashes with the convictions of the family of readers that constitutes its clientele,"[9] it seems equally true that a paper could gradually change its editorial policy without offending the political beliefs of its readers, and thus convert them unwittingly to a new policy. As Mr. L. W. Doob has well expressed it in his study of propaganda: "It must not be forgotten that not only are newspapers a reflection of a social *milieu* but at the same time they also try to change that *milieu*. Those two roles are actually mutually interdependent and can be separated only for the purpose of analysis."[10]

The influence of the press in shaping public opinion through the power of repetition in the editorials seems to have been considerable. In this respect a small number of news analysts and editors of the Parisian press had great authority, not only upon the general public, but also upon the better informed and more articulate section of opinion, as shown by the frequent quotation from their articles in Parliament.[11] This influence was not limited to Paris, but extended either directly or indirectly to the provinces, where papers of the capital were extensively read,[12] and where the prestige of the

---

[8] *Encyclopédie française*, 18-36-11.   [9] *Ibid.*, 18-36-10.

[10] *Propaganda: Its Psychology and Technique* (New York, 1935), p. 334.

[11] Cf. Frédérix, *Etat des forces en France*, p. 161.

[12] According to the *Encyclopédie française* (XVIII), 6,700,000 of the 10,700,000 dailies read in France were published in Paris.

dozen or so leading specialists of foreign affairs weighed heavily with the provincial editors. A study of the editorials in the Parisian press of the Right as well as of the parliamentary debates will therefore give a fairly accurate picture of at least the important trends in Rightist opinion concerning foreign policy.

The influence of this small number of editors and specialists was due even more to their talent than to the importance of their newspapers; they had their own followings and were relatively independent of the directors and owners of their papers, and in some cases they even exercised the functions of both directors and editorial writers. Their prestige and independence, besides the unquestionable honesty of some of them, refute the accusation of bribery generally brought against the French press. As for those who were undoubtedly corrupt and were more or less conscious tools of economic interests, foreign governments, and even the Quai d'Orsay,[13] their influence upon their readers was not necessarily diminished by their lack of integrity. Contrary to general belief, however, it is unlikely that big business or foreign governments were very influential in shaping French public opinion. The same divergent trends concerning foreign affairs were to be found among business leaders as among the public at large, and it is significant that while all papers of the Right were controlled by financial or business interests, they disagreed on foreign policy. This was true even of those sheets directly or indirectly under the control of the Comité des Forges, such as *Le Temps, Le Journal des Débats, L'Information,* and *Le Bulletin Quotidien.* The Comité des Forges was partly responsible for creating the pro-German Comité France-Allemagne, under the leadership of Fernand de Brinon, and for spreading the concept of a "realistic" policy toward the Reich. It is questionable, however, whether its foreign policy

[13] It is generally admitted that the Quai d'Orsay used the "Bulletin du Jour" of *Le Temps* as its mouthpiece, at least when the government in power was of the Right. Prestige and advance information were probably sufficient rewards for the paper to open its column to suggestions made by the Foreign Office.

was primarily influenced by consideration of business interests. Political and ideological motives, common to the whole Right, probably played a much more important part in determining the anti-Soviet and pro-German stand of captains of industry. As the following pages will disclose, a purely economic interpretation of the Right's attitude toward the Third Reich would be entirely misleading.

On the other hand, foreign powers presumably did make generous payments to the French press; Italy, for instance, was said to have scattered sixty million lire among a number of French dailies and periodicals at the time of the Ethiopian Affair. Yet no amount of money spent by the Russian Government would have resulted in a sudden crop of pro-Soviet articles in the reactionary papers. Foreign subsidies could have promoted policies formulated beforehand, but could not have created them.[14]

It is unlikely, moreover, that enough leaders of opinion could have been bribed or influenced to modify greatly what appeared to be general trends involving very important minorities or even majorities in both press and Parliament. An effort has been made to give special emphasis to the statements of a relatively small number of influential men, best representing a trend of opinion or a political group, and generally above suspicion as to their honesty and patriotism.

This study of public opinion will confine itself mainly to the periods of international tension from 1933 to 1939. The procedure of establishing important landmarks will permit comparison between the successive crises and will help to explain the main changes in foreign policy by placing them in the domestic as well as in the foreign picture. It was dur-

[14] The views held by the General Staff—concerning the strength of the Red Army, for example—may well have influenced the attitude of some leaders of opinion and thus indirectly that of the public. In the absence of reliable information, however, this aspect of the problem of Franco-German relations has to be dismissed. It would not be surprising if the political ideas held by army leaders colored their technical opinions. In any case the mystery of Russia's armaments permitted entirely divergent interpretations as to her military strength, both by specialists and by amateur strategists.

ing international crises, moreover, that the responsibility and influence of the leaders of opinion were the greatest; then they had to guide rather than interpret opinion. Their judgment, based on a better knowledge of the facts, should have been more farsighted and less warped by emotional reactions than that of the public at large.

PART I

TRADITIONAL NATIONALISM IN ACTION
(1933-1935)

CHAPTER I

THE RIGHT: IDEOLOGY AND FOREIGN POLICY

THE CLASSICAL division of the French electorate in two political halves called *Right* and *Left* suggests an abrupt and complete separation that did not exist in fact, for only a nuance of opinion distinguished the right wing of the Left from the left wing of the Right. The latter even took over party labels which the Left had abandoned; by 1914 all the groups which had "Gauche" in their designation—such as Gauche Radicale, Républicains de Gauche, etc.—actually sat at the Right of the Chamber.[1] This alternation recalls Macaulay's famous comparison of two parties to the fore and hind legs of a stag, each pair of legs being continually in advance of, but having its place taken by, the other pair.

The new terminology of the Rightist parties illustrated the inevitable *"Sinistrisme"* described by the political essayist Albert Thibaudet,[2] yet it did not indicate a profound transformation in political outlook. The shift toward the Left was slow, and the compact strength of the Right was a reality which overshadowed mere changes in names; even in the general elections of 1936, which saw the triumph of the Popular Front, the Rightist parties and groups still represented about 43 per cent of the total vote.[3]

[1] In the course of the Third Republic the *Journal Officiel* was obliged to stretch the conventional terminology that described the parties and groups of the Chamber as "Right," "Center," and "Left," to include the "Extreme Left" and the "Communist Extreme Left" as well. The former "Gauche" in Parliament actually became the new center, holding the balance of power, and the generic term *la Droite* or *les Droites* was usually applied to the parties and groups belonging to both the parliamentary "Center" and "Right," specifically, all those to the right of the Radical-Socialists. Hereafter, the parliamentary groups referred to as "Right" or "Left" will be distinguished from the generic terms *Right* or *Left* by quotation marks.

[2] *Les Idées politiques de la France* (Paris, 1932).

[3] In 1932 the parties of the Right ("Right" and "Center") received 4,380,717 votes out of a total of 9,579,482; in 1936, 4,202,298 out of 9,847,266. The decrease in their voting strength was only 124,409 votes from 1928 to 1932, and 178,419

This conflict between Right and Left is something a Frenchman feels rather than analyzes. It cannot be described after the World War in terms of the outworn religious issue; neither can it be described in terms of the economic question, if by this one means the struggle between capitalism and socialism, for the bourgeois Radical-Socialists defended liberal economy, while the new authoritarian leagues, at least outwardly, appeared to be anticapitalist as well as anti-Marxist.[4] The significant and lasting basis of the opposition between Right and Left should rather be found in their political and social philosophy, or as André Siegfried put it, in their "conception of life."[5] There was an ideology of the Right opposed to that of the Left, although this must of course be interpreted as meaning the attraction exercised by an ideological pole whose radiation progressively diminishes toward the outer edge, the opportunist Center.

Their respective attitudes toward the principles of the French Revolution were at the bottom of the conflicting philosophies of the two halves of France.[6] The ideals of liberty, equality, and the rights of the individual had always been challenged by the Right, which opposed to them the realistic concepts of authority, inequality, and the rights of the group above those of the individual. The Right did not believe in the *mystique du suffrage universel;* the idea of the rule of the majority was for them "a convenient convention, a working

---

from 1932 to 1936 (cf. Georges Lachapelle, *Elections législatives,* Paris, 1936, pp. ix-x). For the composition of the Chamber, see Appendix, pp. 236-237.

The peculiar French electoral system (uninominal *scrutin* with two ballots) favored alliances and gave the disciplined Left more seats in the Chamber than they would have received through a system of proportional representation. On the first ballot the elector voted for the candidate he preferred; on the second ballot he voted against the one whom he most disliked. Electors of the Left thus gave their votes on the second ballot to the Left candidate who had obtained a plurality. The aim of this *"discipline républicaine"* was to *"barrer la route au réactionnaire";* it usually succeeded.

[4] The defense of economic interests and social privileges is, however, an important element in any definition of the Right.

[5] *France: A Study in Nationality* (New Haven, 1930), p. 53; also Thibaudet, *Les Idées politiques de la France,* p. 13.

[6] A reservation must be made for including the Communist party among the heirs of the French Revolution.

hypothesis," while for the Left it was "the absolute right of number."[7]   The greater part of the Right had apparently accepted the system based upon the rule of the majority, but with mental reservations. *"La loi du nombre,"* wrote M. Lucien Romier, "is a constitutional guarantee by which the weaker are protected against the government of the stronger. . . . It represents a political compensation that frees the State from the exclusive pressure of the naturally preponderant social elements, the best armed or the best endowed." Consequently, he continued, the majority, "in spite of the frequent illusion among the demagogues, cannot defend itself alone against the *forces réelles.* . . . If the regime of the majority abuses its fictive strength, it is preparing a reaction, more or less delayed, but always effective, by the real forces."[8]   Such reasoning was at the bottom of the Right's convenient, but arbitrary, division of the nation after 1934 into the *pays légal,* represented by the Parliament and the voters, and the *pays réel,* containing the real forces of the country without whose support the government could not last.   The rule of the majority was tolerated by the Rightists only as long as it did not threaten their economic and social positions.

This divergence between the ideas of the Right and those of the Left was inherent in their respective outlooks upon life: realistic pessimism on the one hand, idealistic optimism on the other.   "The ideas of the Right," wrote M. Thibaudet, "are thought according to Nature: inequality of persons, prerogatives of personal qualities, existing social groups, among which the isolated individual is, according to the word of Comte, only a social abstraction.   The ideas considered Leftist are thought according to what ought to be. . . ."[9]

The realism of the Right may be founded upon the bourgeoisie's suspicious defense of economic interests and class prestige; their pessimism about the inherent goodness of man and

---

[7] Daniel Halévy, *La République des comités,* quoted by Thibaudet in the *Nouvelle Revue Française,* July 1, 1934, p. 92.

[8] *Le Temps,* May 8, 1934.

[9] *Nouvelle Revue Française,* July 1, 1934, p. 91.

his ability to govern himself may be partly attributed to the influence of the Catholic Church. "The Revolution considers Man as naturally good. . . . The Church considers him as naturally bad. The Revolution states the right of Man to govern himself in an equalitarian society. The Church, [states] his role and duty to govern in an unequal and hierarchic society. . . . The Revolution believes in justice on Earth, and its individualist current therefore is going to enter the socialist sea. The Church only believes in justice from on high. . . ."[10]

In practice, however, this pessimistic and realistic philosophy did not make the whole Right oppose parliamentary democracy. A distinction should be made between the *Extrémistes,* or Revolutionary Right, and the *Modérés,* or Parliamentary Right.[11] Briefly, the *Extrémistes* put the emphasis upon ideology, while the *Modérés,* who formed the great majority of the Right, stressed the economic interests of the privileged classes. As a consequence, the latter accepted political liberalism, at least outwardly, as a logical and even useful accompaniment of economic liberalism; while many did not fundamentally believe in the principles of the Revolution, they at least paid them lip service and in normal times were grateful to the Republic that gave them economic liberty in return for the concession of political equality.

At the beginning of 1934 *L'Action Française* was still the most important representative of the Revolutionary Right,

[10] Thibaudet, *Les Idées politiques de la France,* p. 251.

[11] The term *Extrémiste* as used here is not entirely synonymous with *Conservateur, Traditionnaliste,* or even *Réactionnaire,* which in French political jargon were used to designate the defenders of the traditions of the *ancien régime.* These terms are too narrow and might lead to awkward confusion. As M. Pierre Hamp remarked in the *Nouvelle Revue Française* (Feb. 1, 1936, p. 305): "Today the bourgeois State and its parliamentarianism are defended by the former revolutionaries [the Left], and attacked by the former *Conservateurs* [the Extreme Right]. . . . The *Conservateurs* proclaim themselves revolutionaries, and as a result the revolutionaries, who are opposed to them, become conservative."

Only a handful of deputies of the Right were *Extrémistes;* these were the so-called *Conservateurs,* some Independents, and the right wing of the Fédération Républicaine. In 1936 the Parti Social Français of Colonel de la Rocque had several representatives and sympathizers in the Chamber.

although the semi-Fascist leagues, especially the Croix de Feu, were soon to take the lead of the antiparliamentary movement.[12] *L'Action Française* expressed the royalist tradition as interpreted by Charles Maurras, but the other leagues were rather the heirs of the century-old Bonapartism, rejuvenated by Maurice Barrès, which was a dormant force in the bourgeoisie with greater potentialities than the aristocratic and numerically small royalist movement.

Both political movements resembled fascism in that they defended the principles of nationalism with its corollaries of dictatorship and hierarchy, but unlike fascism, the royalism of *L'Action Française* did not insist upon obtaining a forced unanimity of public opinion. As one of the theorists of authoritarian royalism, Thierry Maulnier, explained: "When the sovereignty of the State does not come from the collective will, that sovereignty can be strong without demanding and obtaining tyrannically the adhesion of all the individuals."[13] Like fascism, however, *L'Action Française,* and more especially the other leagues, criticized economic as well as political liberalism and advocated a degree of collectivism.[14]   Thus Charles

[12] In 1926 *L'Action Française* was put on the Papal Index. The other leagues began to challenge the royalist movement, since "Fascism promised more than the improbable return to the Monarchy" (D. W. Brogan, *France Under the Republic,* New York, 1940, p. 643). Many disciples of Maurras began to look for a Caesar as a substitute for a Bourbon. The famous street riots of February 6, 1934, against the parliamentary regime in general and the Leftist government of M. Daladier in particular, marked an important date in extremism in France. They crystallized and unified the opposition to parliamentary democracy, which was latent at the Right, and started the spectacular growth of the Croix de Feu. Their main result was the formation of the Rassemblement Populaire of the Leftist parties against the Fascist danger.

[13] *Revue Universelle,* March 15, 1936, p. 753.

[14] The economic theories of *L'Action Française* were first evolved by Georges Valois. He later organized *Le Faisceau,* in which he advocated a French version of the Fascist doctrines. *Les Jeunesses Patriotes,* organized in 1924 by Pierre Taittinger, deputy from Paris, *La Solidarité Française,* founded by the perfume manufacturer François Coty, and the *Francistes* of Marcel Bucard borrowed more or less heavily from fascism and National-Socialism. The last two, especially, fought liberalism and capitalism and advocated the corporate state.

From 1934 on the paramilitary formations of the Croix de Feu were a semi-Fascist, semireactionary organization with a vaguely anticapitalist economic and social program. Politically it advocated a "unanimist democracy" reached through the "reconciliation" of the French people; it flirted with the idea of a *coup de*

Maurras, after opposing Marxism as an economic system incompatible with nationalism, declared: "But socialism freed of the democratic and cosmopolitan element can fit nationalism like a well-made glove on a beautiful hand."[15] What distinguished the Extreme Right in France from Italian or German fascism seemed to be the aristocratic traditionalism and fundamental conservatism of many antidemocratic elements, and the emphasis put upon individual rather than national self-realization; this fitted the psychology of the individualistic and civilized French, as well as the character of French nationalism, which was satiated and defensive in comparison to the hungry and arrogant nationalism of Germany and Italy.

While the French Fascist leagues and *L'Action Française* represented the Revolutionary Right, in open revolt against political and even economic liberalism, with programs and methods similar to those of international fascism, it would be difficult to classify among the Extreme Right those bourgeois whose love for a strong government led slowly to an antiparliamentary attitude. Their dormant Bonapartism could manifest itself in a parliamentarian *Poincarisme* as well as in a Caesarian *Boulangisme* or a Fascist *Mussolinisme;* the

---

force, but abandoned it in 1936. At that time the Parti Populaire Français of the former Communist deputy Jacques Doriot became the main representative of French National-Socialism, while the new Parti Social Français of Colonel de la Rocque diluted its doctrines and methods in order to gain the support of the timid *bien-pensants.* See below, pp. 126 ff.

[15] *Dictionnaire politique et critique* (Paris, 1934), V, 169. The social conservatism of the Traditionalists could easily be reconciled with the collectivist element of fascism, which may well be compared to the old mercantilism of the *ancien régime.* It was accepted by them either from love of tradition or resignation to an economic revolution that would fit well with an authoritarian nationalist state. This anticapitalist revolution, however, would not be accompanied by a social revolution as in case of a proletarian upheaval, since the hierarchy of the social classes would continue whether the privileged ones conserved all or only some of their privileges. Here the question of class prestige appears essential, perhaps more so than class economic advantages, in explaining the evolution toward fascism of actually underprivileged social groups, like the white-collar workers, who preferred to keep the illusion of their social rank and prestige under a Fascist regime rather than to ameliorate their economic standards under a classless society as in Marxism.

dream of a strong man, ever recurrent in the minds of the bourgeoisie, was not necessarily entertained only by revolutionaries of the Fascist type. As M. Lucien Romier, himself a *Modéré,* expressed it:

In the bourgeois mind of France, the traditional purpose of dictatorship is to re-establish good order, bring back calm and assure tranquillity to all. . . . There is, therefore, nothing in common between the phenomena of dictatorship that one sees in foreign countries and the idea of dictatorship that is the theme today of numberless conversations of the bourgeois in our salons and on our beaches. . . .[16]

The natural opposition of the bourgeois to fascism was contemptuously described by M. Thierry Maulnier, an avowed *Extrémiste*: "For most of our Conservatives the religion of order is limited to the purely political if not *policier* domain. Order would thus consist in the maintenance of a *status quo* that would favor certain established situations and would protect the reigning economic anarchy with a good police force, to the profit of a few."[17]   The general attitude of the French bourgeoisie in 1934 was one of contempt for fascism, not so much for its dictatorial character as because of its economic doctrines.   Typical of this distinction was the statement of Professor Barthélemy, who after criticizing the Neo-Socialists for "going away from political and economic liberalism and at the same time from the spirit of the French Revolution," added: "Liberalism is not dead.   Humanity is suffering for having sinned against it. *A la rigueur le politique se commande, l'économique pas.*"[18]   It is also significant to note that fascism appeared to the *Modérés* as more likely to come from the Left, i.e., the Neo-Socialists, than from the Right:

[16] *Le Temps,* Aug. 22, 1933; see also Emmanuel Berl, *Frère bourgeois, mourezvous? Ding! Ding! Dong!* (Paris, 1938).

[17] *Revue Universelle,* Jan. 1, 1936, p. 19. "Fascism, considered by the Marxists as a force for capitalist defense, is considered by capitalism as the fruit of a kind of socializing demagogy. The Marxists fear abuses of authority in the political sphere, the capitalists expect to see it tyrannize the economic life in which they are especially interested" (*ibid.*).

[18] *Le Temps,* June 12, 1934. Cf. Abel Bonnard, *Les Modérés* (Paris, 1936), and *Sciences Politiques,* April, 1938, p. 123.

"It is from the side of the so-called Leftist parties," wrote the editor of *Le Temps,* "that there begins to appear a kind of National-Socialism that M. Léon Blum was horrified by. . . . Upon reflection, socialism is the best anteroom for fascism, the clearest way of access."[19] If fascism may be considered as both an anticapitalist and an antidemocratic nationalist revolution, the French bourgeoisie as a whole was far from being fascist in 1934.

It is difficult to delimit Rightist extremism, since to a member of *L'Action Française* the bourgeois hope for a military dictatorship would appear a sign of moderation, while to a Leftist the defenders of M. Doumergue in 1934 seemed incurable Fascists. A possible criterion may be found in the open criticism of parliamentary democracy and the advocacy of the principles of dictatorship, hierarchy and state capitalism; however, one must bear in mind that many *Modérés* were potentially authoritarian, and many authoritarians potentially Fascist.[20] The Right's admiration for Mussolini and his regime was by no means limited to the *Extrémistes.*

In foreign policy the pessimistic realism of the Right was translated in terms of militarism and nationalism. "They are convinced that as man is a sinful creature, we shall always have wars and rumors of wars, and, therefore, we must put our faith in armies, in diplomacy and in treaties—in short, in the old order condemned by the dreamers."[21]

Since the Dreyfus case, the foreign policy of the Right had been opposed to that of the Left. "Previously tame enough in its foreign policy and still imbued with *Bourgeois* Orleanism, the Right began aggressively to preach Nationalism as opposed to Internationalism and class war. . . . In its eyes the army stood for all the virtues of tradition, above all the healthy discipline which the republican equality denied, while the Church regarded war as a chastening Christian influence. This

[19] Aug. 16, 1934; also May 22, 1934; June 14, 1934; Sept. 4, 1934.

[20] Authoritarianism and fascism may be distinguished by the totalitarian character of the latter, its state capitalism and forced unanimity.

[21] Siegfried, *France: A Study in Nationality,* p. 55.

was a definite conception of life and not without its beauty, but it denied the very principles of democracy. So the Left was dragged in by a natural reaction to support the doctrine of peace and pacifism."[22]   In fact, nationalism was the most vital element in the ideology of the Right, their real religion rather than Catholicism, which was used as a discipline rather than believed in as a dogma.   It fitted well with their pessimistic and realistic philosophy and their craving for an authoritarian and hierarchical society.   In its extreme form it was represented by the integral nationalism of Charles Maurras and the Caesarism of Maurice Barrès;[23] chauvinism was its most popular and naïve expression, while a more subdued and civilized nationalism was translated into distrustful realism in foreign policy.   It was used by its high priests, not only to make the nation into an efficient fighting unit, but to "dissimulate economic and social problems"[24] and to justify the necessity for an authoritarian system of government.

The foreign policy of the Right before the World War had been based on the desire to re-establish France in her dignity as a great power; French nationalism was therefore dissatisfied and volcanic, it had to find an outlet in colonial expansion and in a dangerous policy of prestige. With Versailles, however, France was placed in the first rank of world powers, her lost provinces were returned, and she had increased her colonial empire, which was more than sufficient for her needs.   France had become a satisfied and exhausted country, interested only in the preservation of the *status quo,* a state of mind that permeated the Left[25] as well as the

[22] *Ibid.,* p. 51.

[23] Charles Maurras, *Enquête sur la monarchie* (Paris, 1925), and *Mes Idées politiques* (Paris, 1937); Maurice Barrès, *De l'Energie nationale: Les Déracinés* (Paris, 1897), *L'Appel au soldat* (1900), *Leurs Figures* (1902); also *Les Amitiés françaises* (Paris, 1903), which completes the presentation of his doctrine. Cf. W. C. Buthman, *The Rise of Integral Nationalism in France* (New York, 1939); also Marie de Roux, *Charles Maurras et le nationalisme de L'Action Française* (Paris, 1928).

[24] Henri Lefebvre, *Le Nationalisme contre les nations* (Paris, 1937), p. 68.

[25] If the Communist party is eliminated, (its foreign policy could swing from one extreme to the other with the greatest of ease), three main trends were to be found at the Left concerning France's foreign policy: the doctrinaire pacifism of the

Right, and that goes a long way in explaining the successive capitulations and the final collapse of an apparently powerful nation.

Inevitably the character of French nationalism was modified, became less aggressive, and lost its intensity in becoming passive. Wladimir d'Ormesson saw the danger of this new form of nationalism in a Europe of turbulent and dissatisfied nations: "We are on the side of the defense. It is our good fortune. But it is our danger. We perceive that danger so well that the only thing we ask is security, that is to say, the certainty of pacific stability."[26] Moreover, the reality of war had cooled off the enthusiasm of the young men of 1914; the disillusioned and pacifist literature of the postwar decade did not limit its influence to the Left.[27] To a humanitarian hatred of war could be added a realistic fear of its economic and social consequences, a lesson taught by the economic disorders that followed the war, and by the success of the Bolshevist Revolution in Russia and of the Communist party in France. This hatred and fear of war partly explained the passion for security which was characteristic of postwar French nationalism, as the desire for prestige had been before.

In the twenties and early thirties, however, this nationalism was not without strength. It manifested itself by its distrust

---

Socialists, which extended into the ranks of the Radical-Socialists; the Jacobin patriotism of a dwindling minority of the latter; and a more or less sincere and active determination to enforce collective security, found throughout the Left. Of the three trends, the first was undoubtedly the strongest, the second the weakest. As for the third, it could be regarded as the common denominator of the first two; it became more and more apparent after 1935 that collective security was only an ideal that few Leftist leaders had the courage to translate into hard facts.

[26] Le Temps, Jan. 22, 1933.

[27] Among the authors expressing bitterness and disillusionment toward the war, or simply stressing the sufferings of the common soldier, were: Henri Barbusse, Le Feu (Paris, 1916); Roland Dorgelès, Les Croix de bois (Paris, 1919); Henri Malherbe, La Flamme au poing (Paris, 1917); Georges Duhamel, Civilisation (Paris, 1923); Joseph Jolinon, Le Valet de gloire (Paris, 1923); André Thérive, Noir et or (Paris, 1930); Alain, Mars ou la guerre jugée (Paris, 1921); Drieu la Rochelle, La Comédie de Charleroi (Paris, 1934). To these must be added the anti-war series of Le Crapouillot (Histoire de la guerre, La Guerre inconnue, Les Horreurs de la guerre, Les Marchands de canons, etc.).

of Germany, its stubborn refusal to revise the peace treaties, and its hostile or skeptical attitude toward the League of Nations.[28] "For or against *rapprochement* with Germany, for or against the League of Nations, Right and Left had decided without hesitation, in pursuance of their opposed traditions of nationalism and pacifism."[29]

The Right, fearing the potential military strength of Germany, showed a dangerous inferiority complex toward that country. "[France] was a victor but she had in many ways the psychology of a defeated nation. . . . The rulers of France . . . knew that the conjunction of circumstances that had brought them safely through the ordeal was unlikely to recur. What was not achieved in the way of security now, would not be secured later. And security was what France wanted above all else."[30] Since the peace treaties had not given her satisfactory guarantees, it was essential to maintain the margin of actual military superiority that she held over Germany, as well as the advantages received at the peace conferences, and above all the territorial *status quo* of the treaties.[31] The pessimistic and suspicious realism of the Nationalists thus explained their attitude toward the question of reparations and toward the occupation of the Ruhr, their criticism of the Locarno Pact and of Briand's policy of concession, and their refusal to accept disarmament as long as the question of security was not settled.

It also explained their skeptical and distrustful attitude toward the League of Nations, whose purpose was incompatible with the ideology of the Extreme Right and whose methods did not appeal to the realistic *Modérés*. The Extreme

[28] The pet idea of the Extreme Right was still the division of Germany. Charles Maurras expressed it in his book, *Devant l'Allemagne éternelle* (Paris, 1937), pp. 302 ff., first written in 1915, and in numerous articles. Jacques Bainville and Le Grix were other advocates of the dismemberment of Germany. Most Rightists, however, were contented to keep her in the state of relative weakness established by the treaties.

[29] Pierre Brossolette, *L'Europe Nouvelle*, Aug. 20, 1938, p. 899.

[30] Brogan, *France Under the Republic*, p. 543.

[31] Cf. Arnold Wolfers, *Britain and France Between Two Wars* (New York, 1940), pp. 29 ff.

Right always criticized the democratic character of the League. M. Benda wrote of the enemies of the Geneva institution: "Above all they accept that philosophy according to which human conflicts must go on being settled in blood, man must be eternally condemned to war, his aspiration to free himself from it is only an absurd dream, the efforts that he makes to do so are inevitably doomed to failure: this philosophy they adopt because they detest the belief in the possibility of being happy, to them the great modern catastrophe, which makes the subjection of the masses more difficult from day to day."[32]

This accusation is less applicable to the *Modérés,* who criticized the inefficiency rather than the pacific purpose of the League. M. Louis Marin, President of the Fédération République, declared at a party congress in April, 1935, that they had always wanted a preventive and repressive international justice, with compulsory arbitration and assured sanctions against lawbreakers, and that it was only because these requirements had not been satisfied that they had criticized the League and advocated the necessity of alliances.[33] Although the League was considered a useful instrument for the preservation of the *status quo* in Europe, a strong army and the old-fashioned system of alliances were deemed far more efficient in restraining dissatisfied powers. The nationalist Right refused to abandon the guarantees of the peace treaties until security had been assured by a really efficacious international organization. No concession should be made to Germany until then. "The whole German policy is founded on revision, ours and that of our allies on nonrevision: one does not mix water and fire."[34]

[32] *Le Temps,* Oct. 8, 1935.   [33] *Ibid.,* April 14, 1935.
[34] Franklin-Bouillon to the Chamber, quoted by *ibid.,* Jan. 31, 1935.

CHAPTER II

DEFENSE OF THE *STATUS QUO*: 1933-1935

THE BIRTH of the Third Reich was unpleasant news for the French, but there was no consternation: Germany's preceding cabinets, those of Von Papen and Von Schleicher, had already opened the eyes of the optimists to the new anti-Weimarian spirit of military reassertion.[1] As to the pessimistic Right, their traditional distrust of Germany was far from modified by the advent of Adolf Hitler to power. Their only consolation lay in the proof that events had justified their fears, and also, perhaps, in the hope that the "Viennese house painter" would lack diplomatic skill and would inevitably rally Great Britain to the side of France.

Typical of the reaction of the Rightist press was Wladimir d'Ormesson's interpretation of National-Socialism: "Hitler's regime is controlled by two laws of attraction: state socialism, which leads to an advanced form of bolshevism, and the spirit of conquest, which leads to war." Reminding his readers of *Mein Kampf,* he declared that Germany would try to expand toward the East of Europe, and must inevitably fight France.[2]

Several aspects of the domestic policy of the Führer, such as the persecution of Jews and Catholics, and the "striking relationship between nazism and bolshevism,"[3] were condemned by the Right; but their attitude toward Nazi Germany was above all determined by the new danger created for France by the rearmament of this powerful neighbor and by the inculcation of a nationalist and bellicose spirit into her people, "a people of whom the greater part has been made

[1] M. Daladier entered upon his first premiership January 31, 1933, one day after Hitler's accession to power in Germany. The Socialists seemed more agitated by the news than the Radicals; in the Chamber on June 9, 1933, M. Daladier asked: "Who among us thinks of making the organization of peace dependent upon the nature of the regime?" (*JO. Ch.*, p. 2825).

[2] *Le Temps,* May 20, 1933.

[3] Raymond Recouly, *Revue de France,* Sept. 15, 1934, p. 339.

fanatic, the rest terrified and enslaved, all in the hands of a few
chiefs who are leading them and who will lead them wherever
they want."[4] The racial theory, "scientifically absurd, is only
a useful instrument of foreign policy, a new and particularly
virulent form of Pan-Germanism. . . ."[5] *Mein Kampf* was not
forgotten, and the pacific declarations of Herr Hitler did not
convince the skeptical Rightists. "One cannot at the same time
—especially when the German people are concerned—cultivate
an inflamed nationalism for domestic consumption and practice a reasonable policy for foreign consumption. . . . This
double game does not deceive us. We know only too well
what is being prepared under Hitler's regime. . . ."[6] For the
Right there were some good things in the Nazi movement,
especially the ending of class struggle and the "abominable
Communist demagogy. . . . But what is odious is the spirit of
violence and hate, the pride of race, the bellicose ideology."[7]

Thus National-Socialism appeared to the Right as the per-
sonification of the Teutonic spirit, the incarnation of the worst
elements of Germanism.[8] "Hitlerism did not rise up like a
monster in the Reich of 1930; it is only the most categorical
and most complete expression of the philosophy, of the morality, of the politics and of the religion of Germany. It is Germanism itself, at the end of a long evolution: it contradicts
nothing of the thoughts or aspirations that have been appearing
for centuries, and especially since the Romantic period, among
this nation in perpetual childbirth, whose undoubted ambition

[4] *Ibid.*, p. 340.

[5] René Pinon, *Revue des Deux Mondes*, June 15, 1933, p. 954.

[6] *Le Temps*, May 18, 1933.   [7] *Ibid.*, May 27, 1933.

[8] A few young intellectuals at the Extreme Right seem to have admired nazism
from the beginning and to have preached the idea of direct conversations with
Germany. M. Drieu la Rochelle wrote in the *Nouvelle Revue Française* (March 2,
1934) of his admiration for the "moral strength" of fascism, whose foundations
were a "disposition for sacrifice" and socialism. "My confidence in the future
of socialism comes from the spectacle the Fascist countries are giving today." It
seems, however, that more young intellectuals of the Right were attracted by the
dynamism and romanticism of nazism than by its socialism. M. d'Ormesson sadly
admitted in *Le Temps* (Aug. 19, 1933): 'It sometimes happens in the singular
times in which we live that violence is revered by the intellectuals even more than
by the strong-arms. . . . Our authors therefore find some kind of heroic attitude
in the German revolution that captivates them."

is to have a planet for itself alone. Hitler has never been anything but the sonorous voice of Germanism."[9]

Faced with this threat, the Right were determined to oppose either disarmament without definite guarantees of security, or any attempt to revise the territorial *status quo* of the peace treaties.

The order established at Versailles was soon challenged, however, by the proposal of the Four Power Pact. In the form in which the idea was presented by Signor Mussolini in March, 1933, the "Big Four," France, Italy, Great Britain, and Germany, were to constitute a *directoire* for the peaceful revision of the treaties—at the expense of other nations. Il Duce and Prime Minister MacDonald were to assume the roles of honest brokers between France and Germany.

The French counter-proposal eliminated the possibility of imposing revision upon the smaller nations, and insisted that the negotiations proceed within the framework of the League; it rendered the original proposal innocuous by suggesting that the four powers should "meet to consult and not to decide. They stipulate only when they themselves are exclusively concerned."[10]   Yet even in its modified form the Four Power Pact drew down the universal anger of the Nationalists.[11] If France should put her hand in the machine, warned the pro-Fascist *L'Ami du Peuple,* "next the arm, then the body would be dragged in."[12] "If the pact has lost its principal objections," wrote René Pinon, "it is at least useless, but . . . it will keep the mark of the original idea of which it was born. In the eyes of Germany and Italy, it was destined to prepare the revision of the treaties. We will limit ourselves, they will say, to establishing the procedure that could eventually be utilized to this end. But that is too much! Establishing a procedure means familiarizing the idea that it will be used. We do not

[9] Max Hermant, "Pente naturelle du Germanisme," *Revue de France,* July 15, 1934, p. 238.

[10] *Le Temps,* June 11, 1933; also, *ibid.,* BJ and RP, May 30, 1933.

[11] *Ibid.,* RP, March 28 through April 5, 1933, and June 9, 10, 11, 1933.

[12] *Ibid.,* RP, June 9, 1933.

see the advantage that France can gain from this."[13] Similarly in the Chamber the pact was violently criticized by the Rightist speakers MM. Franklin-Bouillon, Jean Fabry, and Louis Marin as dangerous because it "contains potentially the revision of the treaties and the disarmament of France."[14] While Premier Daladier recognized the possibility of treaty revision, as "no treaty is eternal,"[15] and while the whole Left, with few exceptions, voted for the pact, the majority of the Right opposed it even in its modified form.[16] *Le Temps,* in the "Bulletin du Jour" of April 5, professed surprise that sections of the Left, "which have always appeared hostile to the system of separate agreements and action limited to a few powers only . . . should so readily subscribe to this dangerous formula of a regular directory of the four principal powers." The rights of third powers, the article continued, would be sacrificed, and France would find herself isolated from her present allies.

Certain reversals are disconcerting when it concerns the fundamental principles of contemporary policy. It would be inconceivable . . . that one should think of profoundly modifying the traditional role of France in the international field. . . .

The most elementary prudence demands that we do not leave a policy of collaboration, of solidarity, and of responsibilities equitably divided, which finds its justification in the spirit of the League of Nations; . . . outside the League we could only make a leap into the unknown.

Thus the Right, paradoxically, appeared to defend against the Left the principle of collective security, i.e., the *status quo* of the peace treaties, which according to them was threatened by the application of the Four Power Pact.

[13] *Revue des Deux Mondes,* June 15, 1933, p. 957.

[14] Franklin-Bouillon, *Le Temps,* June 11, 1933. Although a leader of the Gauche Radicale, he was a Rightist in foreign policy.

[15] *JO. Ch.,* April 6, 1933, p. 1930.

[16] On April 6, the motion of lack of confidence in the government's foreign policy, specifically directed against the signing of the Four Power Pact, was approved by the Right with 80 for, 51 against, and 38 abstentions (*Le Temps,* April 8, 1933). On June 10 the majority of the Right voted against a motion of confidence in the general policy of the government: 126 against, 36 for (including 15 Démocrates Populaires) (*ibid.,* June 11, 1933).

The first international crisis created by the Nazi regime came a few months later, on October 14, 1933,[17] when the German Government decided to withdraw from the League of Nations and the disarmament conference. This action, which was accompanied by protestations of peaceful intentions, and followed, shortly afterward, by a proposal for direct Franco-German *rapprochement*,[18] aroused great emotion in the French press. *Le Temps* solemnly stated in an editorial (October 16): "A vast conception of the organization of Europe and of the world is shaken. The dream of an international democracy . . . is fading farther and farther away. National security must be assured first of all in the chaos of these disillusions." The departure of Germany from the League, however, modified the function of that institution in the eyes of many Rightists: instead of being considered as a potential instrument for the revision of the treaties, the League came more than ever before to be seen as a useful agency for the preservation of the *status quo*. Its new usefulness was emphasized by C. J. Gignoux, who wrote on the first day of the crisis in *La Journée Industrielle:* "Since yesterday evening some have seen in this bold adventure the condemnation to death of the League of Nations. Yet it is perhaps now that it has its greatest role to play."[19]

While Germany's withdrawal from the League did not in itself appear to be a mortal sin to many of the Right—they had never shown great love for the Geneva institution as such—they nevertheless criticized the defiant attitude of the German Government, which, by opposing the community of nations, had made clear its intentions to rearm and to demand the revision of the treaties. "This is the fine result of the ten years of that absurd policy that began at Chequers, was pur-

[17] M. Daladier was still premier, with Paul-Boncour as foreign minister; he was replaced by Sarraut on October 26, with Paul-Boncour remaining at the Quai d'Orsay. In September and October, France believed she could count on the support of Great Britain (Sir John Simon on October 14 rallied to the support of the thesis of security first, and disarmament by steps), but the apologetic reaction of the MacDonald Cabinet to Germany's coup was a bitter disillusion.

[18] See Fernand de Brinon's interview with Hitler, *Le Matin*, Nov. 22, 1933.

[19] *Le Temps*, RP, Oct. 16, 1933. Cf. *ibid.*, Oct. 17, 24, 1933.

sued at Locarno and Thoiry, and has just died at Geneva. And now will Europe remain dumbfounded, or will she find the force to understand and act?"[20] The most radical position against Germany was taken by Pertinax in *L'Echo de Paris;* he suggested that the Council of the League of Nations meet and put into force paragraph 7 of Article 15 of the Covenant. "No one doubts at this time," he added, "that the conflict between Hitler's regime and the powers attached to the maintenance of the treaties is fatal. To lose time is to give Germany the feeling of impunity and push her on to new coups, especially in Austria, to perhaps irreparable coups."[21] There was a similar reaction in the Chamber: M. Mandel asked for the application of Article 213 of the Versailles Treaty,[22] and the other speakers of the Right, MM. Jean Fabry, Franklin-Bouillon, de Lasteyrie, and Louis Marin, furnished specifications concerning German rearmament and advocated a policy of firmness based on alliances and a strong army.[23]

The subsequent proposals of the German Government brought up two important issues: that of direct *rapprochement* between the two countries, and the question of the limitation of the army of each nation to three hundred thousand men. Apparently only two Rightist newspapers, *Le Jour* and *Le Matin,* which remained in the vanguard of those advocating a direct understanding, gave their support to the German proposal for conversations between the two governments. *Le Matin* published an anonymous article on November 14 entitled "The Crossroads of the Three Ways," which reviewed the three possible roads for France to follow: the road of force, the road of direct conversations, and the road of Geneva. "We have seen only too well where the third road has led," concluded the writer. "And since it is too late to take the

[20] *Journal des Débats* (*Le Temps,* RP, Oct. 16, 1933). The position taken by André Tardieu was typical: "Inertia in the face of a Germany openly rebellious towards the treaties and heading towards war would be filled with dangers that spring to one's eyes. But philippics of tribune and press not based on an exact knowledge of our resolves and of those of other governments would only aggravate these perils" (*La Liberté,* in *Le Temps,* RP, Oct. 18, 1933; also Oct. 17, 1933).

[21] *Le Temps,* RP, Oct. 17, 1933.

[22] *Ibid.,* Nov. 16, 1933.   [23] *Ibid.*

first road—that of force—since it is repugnant to our sentiments, to our traditions, to our ideal of peace, why not try
the second—that of direct conversations with Germany?"[24]

Evidently here was at least the beginnings of a movement
toward direct *rapprochement* with Germany, comprising both
some "realistic" pacifists at the Center[25] and some admirers of
the Nazi regime at the Extreme Right.[26] M. Jean Schlumberger noticed the beginning of this *chassé croisé* between the
respective positions of Right and Left:

. . . it is the Leftist papers, defenders of Franco-German rapprochement, which have most insinuatingly stifled or suppressed the sensational appeals of Hitler to France. And it is at the Right that
with amazement one begins to perceive voices (timid as they may
still be), expressing alarm that after so many lost occasions we risk
letting this last chance escape tragically. . . .[27]

The great majority of the Rightist press, however, was
opposed to a direct understanding, which was interpreted as
signifying the abandonment by France of her allies in Eastern
Europe.[28] "If a country plays the comedy of offering another
peace and fraternity on condition that the treaties be destroyed,
it is using a procedure that resembles the bargain offered by
those who demand your purse or your life,"[29] wrote *Le Journal
des Débats,* in criticism of the anonymous article published in
Le Matin a few days before; and in *L'Agence Economique et
Financière,* M. Henri Bérenger asked: "Could Germany im-

[24] Cf. *ibid.,* RP, Oct. 17, 1933; also Oct. 18, Nov. 14, 19, 1933.

[25] The most important advocates of *rapprochement* at the Center were Jean
Piot of *L'Œuvre,* Pierre Dominique and Emile Roche of *La République,* Dubarry
of *La Volonté,* Jacques Kaiser, Vice-President of the Radical-Socialist party, Henry
Pichot and Jean Goy, presidents of war veteran organizations.

[26] The most outspoken advocates of direct *rapprochement* among them were
Fernand de Brinon (see his *France-Allemagne, 1918-1934,* Paris, 1934), Georges
Suarez (*Les Hommes malades de la paix,* Paris, 1933), Louis Bertrand, and Stanislas
de la Rochefoucault. To the papers of the Extreme Right sympathetic to a bilateral
agreement with the Reich (*Le Jour, Le Matin*), must be added *L'Ami du Peuple,*
whose pro-Fascist proprietor and editor, François Coty, published in November,
1933, an article entitled "Avec l'Allemagne contre les Soviets." Cf. Elizabeth
Cameron, *Prologue to Appeasement* (Washington, 1942), p. 23.

[27] *Nouvelle Revue Française,* Jan. 1, 1934, p. 145.

[28] *Le Temps,* RP, Nov. 15, 16, 1933.

[29] *Ibid.,* Nov. 16, 1933; also see *L'Ordre, L'Echo de Paris (ibid.).*

agine that France would lack memory and judgment to that point? To give the Third Reich elbow room to fortify and arm itself against the East while according us tranquillity on the Rhine, except for the Saar—that is what they demand of France in return for the 'peace' of M. Hitler. No, thank you."[30] An article in *Le Temps* on November 19 by M. d'Ormesson presented the pros and cons and resumed the attitude of the majority. After remarking that Germany had just broken with the League in a "frenzied explosion of supernationalism," he exclaimed: "And it is at this very moment that they speak of direct conversations tête-à-tête between France and Germany. We have witnessed many follies during the last twenty years. I do not know whether we have seen a greater one. . . ." He then analyzed the so-called advantages of a direct *rapprochement* as presented by its advocates. "But exactly what is meant by these magic words: direct Franco-German conversations?" His answer was that of the majority of the press: "No illusions! What Germany means by direct negotiation with France is a group of measures that are *all* to the benefit of Germany, without counterpart, without concrete advantages of any sort for us. We could not accept most of these measures without agreeing to a veritable capitulation. And this capitulation would very quickly be transformed into constant pressure, into vassalage, for the essential characteristic of Germany is never to be satisfied."[31]

The real meaning of direct Franco-German conversations was thus clearly brought out, and the great majority of the Rightist press was firmly opposed to an agreement with the Third Reich at the cost of German expansion in the East. The Right's insistence upon the maintenance of the territorial *status quo* of the treaties was exemplified by M. René Pinon. After criticizing the English and the Italians bitterly for their revisionist attitude, he went so far as to advocate a policy of integral resistance to Germany even if British opposition were provoked:

[30] *Ibid.*, Nov. 15, 1933.
[31] See also D'Ormesson in *Le Temps*, Nov. 19, 25, Dec. 2, 1933.

If the Franco-English alliance—which France wishes with all her ardent desire for peace—should have as a counterpart . . . the revision of the treaties and the destruction of the Europe that emerged from our common victory, we should reject it. . . . We ardently hope not to have to choose between England and Continental stability: if we are obliged to do so, our choice is made."[32]

An equally firm stand was adopted by the Rightists toward the German proposal for the limitation of both the French and the German armies to three hundred thousand men each. The sincerity of this overture was not credited: "There is no other explanation for Germany's *coup d'éclat* [her departure from the League] than the will of this power to continue her rearmament, already begun in violation of the military clauses of the Versailles Treaty; the demand for equal rights is simply intended to disguise rearmament."[33]

Since Germany had already rearmed (the German budget for 1934-35 exceeded that of the previous year by 352,000,000 marks), the acceptance of the limitation proposal would have jeopardized France's military position. In reality, the three hundred thousand men proposed by the Reich equaled one million, five hundred thousand, since the paramilitary formations, the S.S. and the S.A., had to be included.[34] "Faced with the rearmament of Germany," wrote Pinon, "which the weakness of our governments and the ill-will of England and Italy did not stop when there was time, it is impossible to consider any reduction of armaments: any limitation would be only a continual dupery unless it were accompanied by serious guarantees of execution."[35]

While the French nation was hearing the first German challenge, the Republic itself was menaced at home. The instability of the Leftist governments, the first repercussions of

[32] *Revue des Deux Mondes*, Dec. 15, 1933, pp. 955-956.
[33] *Le Temps*, BJ, March 2, 1934; also cf. Pinon, *Revue des Deux Mondes*, Jan. 1, 1934, p. 237.
[34] See D'Ormesson, *Le Temps*, Jan. 13, 1934; *ibid.*, March 10, 1934; Jean Fabry, *ibid.*, Nov. 16, 1933; Jacques Bardoux, *ibid.*, Nov. 14, 18, 1933.
[35] *Revue des Deux Mondes*, April 15, 1934, p. 955.

the economic depression in France, and the Stavisky scandal, in which numerous politicians were involved, caused a wave of popular discontent that was cleverly used by the press of the Extreme Right. Their antiparliamentary campaign in January, 1934, led to the famous street riots of February 6 and 7 against the second Daladier government. *L'Action Française,* the Croix de Feu, and other Extremist organizations played an important role in this abortive coup d'état. The most far-reaching consequence was the creation of the Front Commun, an alliance between the Socialist and Communist parties against the Fascist menace. It was to be transformed in 1935 into the Rassemblement Populaire by the adhesion of the Radical-Socialists to this Leftist coalition.

The immediate result, however, was the formation of a conservative government of National Union under M. Doumergue, who was sympathetic to the fast-growing leagues. The new minister of foreign affairs was M. Louis Barthou, a contemporary and disciple of Poincaré, who put into practice the traditional foreign policy of the Right.[36]

His opposition to French disarmament without sufficient guarantees of security was received with relief by the press of the Right, which congratulated the foreign minister on bringing the same *redressement* to the international situation that the prime minister, M. Doumergue, was expected to bring to the domestic situation. "It is enough to remark how the German press once more accuses France of 'sabotaging disarmament' to realize that the general *redressement* of French policy has been understood at Berlin in all its significance."[37] Barthou's note of March 17 to the British Cabinet,[38] and especially the French memorandum of April 17, which defended the thesis of security before disarmament and refused to enter into negotiations with the Reich for a limitation agreement,

[36] M. Barthou was assassinated with King Alexander of Yugoslavia at Marseilles on October 9, 1934, and M. Doumergue resigned on November 8. Flandin formed a government on the same day, with Laval as foreign minister.

[37] *Le Temps,* BJ, March 4, 1934.

[38] *Ibid.,* March 25, 1934.

were greeted by the Rightist press as a sign that France had at last taken a firm and realistic position toward Germany.[39]

Barthou undertook, on the pretense of building a Locarno of the East, to strengthen the anti-German coalition of satisfied powers. Conversations were started with the Soviet Government, now desirous of collaborating in the defense of the *status quo;* they led to the entry of the U.S.S.R. into the League of Nations in September, 1934, and the Franco-Soviet Pact of mutual assistance, signed on May 2, 1935. The treaties with Poland, Rumania, and Czechoslovakia were invigorated by the diplomacy of the foreign minister, who also worked for *rapprochement* with Italy.[40]   His traditional and realistic policy of strengthening France's bonds with Poland and the Little Entente, even his efforts to bring Russia into the system of mutual defense against Germany, were well received[41] and seemed to fortify the wavering loyalty of some Rightists toward the League.

The Extreme Right even reproached M. Barthou for not going far enough in his quest for security and for reinforcing the power of the League rather than frankly adopting the more efficient system of alliances. Thus St. Brice, after congratulating the foreign minister on his *redressement* of French foreign policy, criticized him for not preferring "solidly armed, frank alliances" to an Eastern pact that would include Germany, and link revisionists and antirevisionists together, "instead of forming a defensive alliance grouping France, Poland, the

[39] Pinon, *Revue des Deux Mondes,* May 1, 1934, pp. 236-238; St. Brice, *Revue Universelle,* May 1, June 5, July 1, 1934; Recouly, *Revue de France,* July 1, 1934; *Le Temps,* throughout April and May.

[40] A nonaggression pact with the Soviets had already been signed on November 29, 1932, under Herriot's premiership. It came up for approval by the Chamber in May, 1933, and the resolution expressing satisfaction at the conclusion of the pact, "which strengthened the organization of peace," was accepted by a vote of 551, with M. Tardieu in the opposition and 48 abstentions. This period of reconciliation was far removed from the time of hostility when Clemenceau wanted to encircle Russia with a barbed wire. It is significant to note that most Rightists accepted the pact of nonaggression of 1933 and the pact of mutual assistance of 1935, but that they rejected the latter in February, 1936, when it came up for ratification. Cf. Alexander Werth, *The Destiny of France* (London, 1937), p. 140. See below, pp. 67 ff.   [41] *Le Temps,* April 24, 28, June 25, 1934.

Baltic States, the Little Entente, and even the Soviets against *les revanches.*"[42]

Like the other Extremists of the Right, however, St. Brice was not anxious to see Soviet Russia in the defensive alliance: "When one is lucky enough to have two dangerous fellows [Germany and Russia] who cannot get along, the best attitude is not to intervene in their affairs, because that would be the best means of reconciling them over your own prostrate body." He gave as his chief argument: "We shall never admit that the co-operation of France, Italy, Belgium, Poland, and the Little Entente is not sufficient to hold Germany in check."[43] But the chief reason for the opposition of the *Extrémistes* to the Franco-Russian Pact was that "it is not with M. Litvinoff that we are dealing, it is with the Third International that we are coming to terms . . . it is Red propaganda that we are encouraging."[44]

The *Modérés*, however, generally accepted the entry of the U.S.S.R. into the League of Nations (September 18, 1934), although the dangers involved in a *rapprochement* with the Soviets were admitted. Realizing the risks, M. Pinon nevertheless affirmed in the *Revue des Deux Mondes*: "It is not France who has chosen this policy, it has been imposed upon her as a measure of precaution, not of predilection. It is the menace of rearmed Germany."[45] Nor did these "risks" appear as alarming as they later would; the bourgeoisie was beginning to modify its view of Soviet Russia.

While the memory of the grave menace that the Bolshevist propaganda caused to weigh over the entire world will always be present in all minds, . . . one must nevertheless admit that a profound evolution has been accomplished in the foreign policy and even in the domestic policy of the Soviet Union. . . . The directors of the Kremlin have finally understood that the universal proletarian revolution is far off and that, by wishing to make the existence of the new Russia depend upon the success of com-

---

[42] *Revue Universelle*, Aug. 1, 1934, pp. 361-363.
[43] *Ibid.*, p. 106.   [44] Le Grix, *Revue Hebdomadaire*, p. 369.
[45] July 1, 1934, p. 235; cf. *Le Temps*, Sept. 19, 1934.

munism in the whole world, they were leading their great country to an irremediable catastrophe.[46]

The Right's hostile attitude toward the advent of Hitler and the proposal of a four power pact, their firm reaction to Germany's withdrawal from the League of Nations and the Disarmament Conference, and their approval of Louis Barthou's vigorous foreign policy during 1934, indicate that with only a few exceptions the Rightists were still continuing their anti-German policy, characterized essentially by the will to maintain the territorial *status quo* of the peace treaties.   Their firmness was further illustrated by their angry reaction to the Führer's first open violation of the Versailles Treaty in March, 1935, when military conscription was re-established in Germany.

[46] *Le Temps,* Sept. 17, 1934.

CHAPTER III

ANSWERS TO A CHALLENGE:
THE STRESA FRONT AND THE SOVIET PACT

FRANCE'S INTERNATIONAL position at the end of 1934 was favorable. Great Britain, Poland, the Soviet Union, Italy, the Little Entente, and the League of Nations were her potential allies. Barthou's skillful handling of foreign affairs had counteracted Germany's abrupt withdrawal from the League by strengthening France's weakened defense system in the East. The entry of the Soviet Union into the League of Nations in September, 1934, was a signal victory for French diplomacy, soon followed by another: M. Laval, who succeeded Barthou after the latter's assassination on October 9, 1934,[1] continued the negotiations with the U.S.S.R., and a pact of mutual assistance was signed in Paris on May 2.

The foreign policy of Laval differed somewhat from that of his predecessor at the Quai d'Orsay; the emphasis was less on French security and the maintenance of the *status quo* than on finding a *modus vivendi* acceptable to all nations, including Germany, whom he endeavored to bring into a regional peace system. M. Laval was not averse to the idea of giving Herr Hitler and Signor Mussolini certain concessions in exchange for their effective participation in the system of international co-operation.

His passive attitude toward the Saar plebiscite implied that Germany was expected to appreciate France's good deed: a bone of contention was to become a *trait d'union* between the

[1] M. Doumergue had been replaced as premier by M. Flandin on November 8, 1934, after the defection of the Radical-Socialists from his cabinet of National Union. The new cabinet marked an evolution away from the Right. M. Flandin was considered by the Left more democratic than his predecessor, whose authoritarian aims and sympathy for the leagues were highly objectionable to the anti-Fascists. Laval was to keep the direction of the foreign affairs of France until January 23, 1936.

two countries. But more than Germanophile he was Italophile. In January, 1935, he concluded the Rome Agreement that was to buy Italy's friendship; that country was to be ceded a strip of French Equatorial Africa bordering upon Libya and a small triangle of French Somaliland adjacent to Eritrea. In exchange, Signor Mussolini agreed among other things to consult and collaborate with France in the event of any threat to Austrian independence.

The climax of this effort to obtain a general settlement in Europe by minor concessions was reached with the Franco-British conversations in London at the beginning of February, 1935. The final declaration of February 3 stated that France and Great Britain would agree to reconsider Part V of the Versailles Treaty concerning the limitation of German armaments. The agreement consisted essentially in the recognition of the *fait accompli* of German rearmament in return for the strengthening of collective security in the West and the establishment of an Eastern Locarno. France would thus give up the theoretical and legal superiority of her army in exchange for a German guarantee of the territorial *status quo* of the peace treaties. This arrangement appeared to be a good bargain to the French, since Germany had already rearmed illegally to an alarming degree,[2] and since Great Britain now seemed to be accepting new responsibilities on the Continent.

When the Franco-British proposals were turned down on March 2 by the German Government, which agreed to guarantee the security of Western Europe but not that of Eastern Europe, the Rightist press without exception condemned this discrimination. "She [Germany] has been offered that equality of rights within the system of organized security which she has always been demanding. . . . How does she answer such a proposition? By preparing to keep what helps her and reject what hinders her; by trying to dislocate the

[2] Colonel Fabry told the Chamber on March 15 that Germany had 600,000 men under arms against 240,000 for France (*Le Temps*, May 17, 1935), and the *rapporteur* of the bill (*loi des deux ans*), M. Archimbaud, gave similar figures. See also Flandin, *JO. S., March* 20, 1935, p. 319.

system of security that forms a whole. . . ."[3] M. Recouly was even more specific: "Peace in the West, at least for the moment, bellicose intentions in the East, it is thus that the present policy of Germany could be described. . . . One is astonished to see Hitler make such a confession, display all his ambitions with such frankness."[4]

On March 16, 1935, Herr Hitler denounced Part V of the Treaty of Versailles concerning the limitation of German armaments, and re-established conscription in Germany. This challenge was of relatively little importance in a military sense, for Germany's secret rearming was well known. M. Flandin told the Senate on March 20: "As a matter of fact, Gentlemen, we may be sure that the twelve army corps and the thirty-six divisions whose legality Germany has proclaimed by the law of March 16, 1935, were not born suddenly in one night. They had existed for a long time."[5] By comparison with the next German *fait accompli,* the remilitarization of the Rhineland, which was to give a deathblow to France's postwar system of security,[6] this coup did not appreciably change the balance of forces in Europe; thanks to the demilitarized Rhineland, the French Government was still in a position to take measures against any future German aggression in Central or Eastern Europe.

Since the principle of equality for the German Army had already been accepted at London, it would have been difficult for the French Government to gain the support of Great Britain in forcing Germany to renounce her action. More- over, the results of the Rome Agreement and of the London conversations had been encouraging for France and had indi- cated the road for her government to follow: a united front of Western powers should be built up, which, in addition to the Eastern bloc, would present a coalition strong enough to

[3] *Le Temps,* BJ and RP, Feb. 17, 1935.
[4] *Revue de France,* April 15, 1935, pp. 727-728.
[5] *JO. S.,* p. 319.   [6] See below, pp. 86 ff.

restrain Germany and might even force her to accept a general European settlement.

Nevertheless, the German *fait accompli* of March 16 was a diplomatic blow of the first order, since it not only created a dangerous precedent of treaty violation, but also deprived France of an excellent bargaining position which consisted in making Germany accept a system of effective collective security in exchange for France's renunciation of the theoretical superiority of her army. The coup only made more obvious the refusal of the Reich to guarantee the security of Eastern Europe. Its easy acceptance by the Right would therefore have been synonymous with granting Germany a free hand in that part of Europe. Such, however, was not the case.

The temper of the Right had already manifested itself during the Chamber debate of March 15 on the re-establishment of a two years' military service in France[7]—which was the pretext used by the German Government for its decision of March 16. The Right believed that this measure was necessitated by the coming of the "lean years" (when there would be a shortage of recruits caused by the low birthrate during the World War) and that the increased term of service was justified more than ever by Germany's intensive rearmament and recent refusal to accept a general European setlement. The patriotic mood of the Right was reflected by Charles Maurras in *L'Action Française;* his statements are especially striking if compared with his future "neo-pacifism."[8] "One of our most imperious duties," he wrote on February 25, "is to insist on what a German victory would mean. . . . Each Frenchman, with his possessions, his liberties, and his skin, would be its certain victim." He spoke of the "ferocious plans that she [Germany] would execute coldly in case of a defeat of France, England, and Italy," and concluded: "We repeat that there is no financial, civic, or military sacrifice that is not one thousand

[7] One-year military service had been established on April 3, 1928. It made possible an annual incorporation into the army of about 250,000 men. But from 1935 to 1939 the annual quota would have fallen to 118,000 men.

[8] See below, pp. 91-92, 171.

times preferable to the frightful fate in store for us should German fury master us."

Thus, immediately before the German coup, the Right showed their traditional patriotism by advocating an unpopular measure, the *loi de deux ans,* for the sake of France's security,[9] while the pacifist Left, with the exception of a majority of the Radical-Socialists, opposed the bill vigorously on the grounds that it was an unnecessary measure, incompatible with a policy of reconciliation. M. Léon Blum even spoke of the "Napoleonic plans for a strategic offensive" of the French General Staff, contrasting his own program of disarmament and mutual assistance with the "militarist" policy of the Right;[10] and the Communist party's *L'Humanité* loudly criticized the measure using the slogan: *Les deux ans, c'est la guerre*—the very party that was soon to contradict itself by adopting an ultrapatriotic attitude.

Similarly, after the coup of March 16, the reaction of the press of the Left was colored by their traditional pacifism. While many of the Right were to accuse the Leftists of "bellicism" in 1936, at the time of the remilitarization of the Rhineland, Wladimir d'Ormesson could in 1935 charge them with pacifism, appeasement, and, although the phrase did not then exist, with "fifth column" activities:

The truth is that Chancellor Hitler was right when he thought that he would have as allies to make things easier for him all the laborites, Socialists, Communists, blind ideologists, who still believe that by satisfying all the demands of Hitler's Germany she will be appeased. . . . We are witnessing today this monstrous alliance, that of the die-hard pacifists and the most extravagant Prussian militarism. Ten million human lives and Western civilization will pay for it.[11]

[9] *JO.Ch.,* March 15, 1935; Colonel Fabry, pp. 1027 f.; P. Reynaud, pp. 1040 f.; Louis Marin, p. 1050; Franklin-Bouillon, pp. 1051 f.

[10] Cf. *Le Temps,* March 17, 1935. The Confédération Générale du Travail took a similar attitude. See *Le Temps,* March 20, 1935, speech of Léon Jouhaux at the Comité national of the C. G. T.; also *Le Populaire,* March 19, 1935, special edition: "Contre les deux ans."

[11] *Le Temps,* RP, March 20, 1935.

In the Rightist press, on the contrary, even the papers that were to show the greatest indulgence toward Germany at the time of the Rhineland crisis displayed great firmness. Typical was the attitude of *L'Action Française* (March 18): "One opportunity—the last—is perhaps still being offered to the former allies to prevent disaster," wrote Delebecque. "Shall we let it slip by? . . . If national feeling is not entirely dead among those who have charge of our destinies, the moment has come to prove it"; and Daudet insisted that *"L'Allemagne éternelle"* wanted "a war of revenge" and described her "Teutonic appetite for combat." "This is not March," he declared, "but June, 1914." On March 22 he wrote:

When the representatives of France, England, and Italy meet— if they meet—immediate military co-operation on land, at sea, and in the air must not be just thought of—that stage is passed—but must be made effective. . . . To imagine that a nation in such a state of warlike fury . . . will not soon turn to acts when we try to calm her with words is pure folly.

Similarly Léon Bailby stated in *Le Jour* (March 23): "What is certain is that after Germany's provocation it is the duty of the pacific powers to take immediate measures without which the Reich will continue its course of reconquests tomorrow. . . ."

Hence the greater part of the Rightist press was considering the policy to be adopted toward Germany with respect to the future, and in terms of Franco-Italo-English collaboration with the supplementary help of Russia, rather than in terms of immediate unilateral action. It was not surprising, therefore, that "the obstinately conciliatory attitude of England"[12] should arouse the anger of many when it became evident that the British Government was not going to participate in any action against Germany, and was not even going to call off the much publicized trip of Sir John Simon to Berlin.[13] Stéphane

[12] *Ibid.*, March 20, 1935.
[13] *Ibid.*, March 20, 21, 1935. On the invitation of the German Government Sir John Simon was to go to Berlin on March 8 for a direct Anglo-German exchange of views. The publication on March 4 of a British Government statement con-

Lauzanne wrote in *Le Matin* (March 22) that, because of England, France had had to yield successively on the questions of war guilt, of reparations, of guarantees, and of clandestine German armament: "And in spite of all that she has no certainty of peace. Perhaps she would have had it for a long time if she had resisted the faithless stranger and if she had once for all said 'no' to all the irresponsible advisors." Contrasting Italy's attitude to that of Great Britain, M. Pinon plainly stated the position of the Right in the *Revue des Deux Mondes* (April 1): "The time has come to oblige England, in a friendly way, to face her responsibilities; if she does not accept them it will be up to the Continental powers to organize security and peace by a system of equilibrium based upon alliances."

The Rightist press approved the appeal made to the League of Nations by the French Government on March 20, but only as an opportunity to give Germany an official scolding. The great hope of the Right lay not in the doubtful action of the League, but in the construction of an anti-German coalition firmly opposing any further violation of the treaties by the Third Reich. The general feeling was that the German coup, however "revolting," was also somewhat "reassuring," "because after all it is not possible that the attitude of the leaders of the Third Reich will not arouse a radical reaction everywhere in Europe. In this case it is scarcely probable that Germany will rush headlong against all Europe."[14] There could be neither a Franco-German war, nor a Russo-German war, but only a war between Germany and Europe: "All the peoples of our continent must convince themselves of this reality today. . . . Germany will be with Europe or against her. Today she is at the crossroads."

The basis of this defensive European coalition was supposed to be the close union of France with Italy and, if possible, with Great Britain, which would give effective strength to collective security. But the growing hopes manifested by the

---

demning German rearmament gave Herr Hitler a diplomatic cold, and the visit was put off until the twenty-fifth of March. Cf. S. I. A., pp. 130, 132, 147.

[14] *Le Temps*, March 31, 1935.

Rightist press in regard to the Stresa Conference, which was to be held between the three Western powers in April, were less concerned with present sanctions against Germany than with future ones in case of a new violation of the treaties. "What France wants is to have such violations condemned and not remain without sanctions in the future."[15] Since Great Britain did not seem willing to abandon her traditional role of arbitrator in Europe, a defensive coalition might be organized even without her. "This is the great aim of Stresa: an agreement between France, Italy, and the Little Entente, with the benevolent tolerance of London," suggested Pertinax in *L'Echo de Paris* on April 12, adding, "It would be imprudent to hope for more." Incidentally, even the Left seemed to have more hope in Italy than in Great Britain for the defense of collective security. M. Léon Blum wrote in *Le Populaire* (April 12): "As far as one can see clear in the designs of Mussolini, his state of mind does not differ essentially from that of the Soviet Government. . . ," and hopefully added: "Any day the racist dictator and the Fascist dictator may find themselves face to face on the Danube."

Although the Stresa Conference (April 11-14) amounted in practice to "nothing more substantial than the publication of a communiqué,"[16] the Rightist press was enthusiastic. Even the usually prosaic "Bulletin du Jour" of *Le Temps* optimistically stated: "It must be emphasized: the striking confirmation of Anglo-Franco-Italian solidarity, despite the divergence of views, the opposition of doctrines and interests that were disclosed at the beginning [of the Conference] has the value and import of a capital act. . . . We emerge from uncertainty and contradictions to act from now on in full light. The absolute solidarity of the three governments is thus confirmed in circumstances that make it impossible to compromise or disturb it."[17] The results attained at Stresa were reviewed with satisfaction: the reaffirmation of the British and Italian guarantees

---

[15] *Ibid.*, April 14, 1935.
[16] S. I. A., 1935, p. 159.   [17] April 15, 1935.

of the Locarno Treaty, the projected negotiations for a Western air pact, the insistence upon the necessity of Austrian independence, the international conference to be held in Rome at the end of May to establish a pact of mutual assistance in Central Europe, and, finally, the continuation of the negotiations for a Franco-Russian pact with the approval of England and Italy. Only a few at the Right criticized the Stresa Conference as insufficient.[18] The rest of the press was full of praise for the establishment of the "Stresa Front," which appeared to these papers as a realistic undertaking after all the Geneva dreams of collective security. "This is the first time," exulted *L'Ami du Peuple,* on April 15, "that a diplomatic conference, instead of getting lost in the clouds, grasps realities and prepares serious measures"; and *Le Petit Parisien* spoke of the "impression of calm power"[19] that was given by the decisions of Stresa. On April 24, *Le Temps* summarized the general attitude of the Right toward the Stresa Front; it stated that the agreement of England, France, and Italy insured peace in Eastern as well as Western Europe, and maintained that "the permanent co-operation of France and Italy constitutes the new element that has entirely modified the international situation and has brought the first ray of light enabling the peoples to regain confidence." The lasting character of Franco-Italian collaboration, based on the community of interests of both countries, was apparently not doubted, and while English help was of course appreciated, it was considered secondary to the eventual military collaboration of the two Latin countries, especially for the defense of Central Europe.

The creation of the Stresa Front was followed by the condemnation of the German *fait accompli* by the Council of the League of Nations, a move that was greeted politely but unenthusiastically by the Right.[20] More important than this condemnation by the League, and as significant as the Stresa

[18] *L'Echo de Paris,* April 15, 1935; see also *Revue de France,* May 15, 1935, *Candide,* April 18, 1935.

[19] *Le Temps,* RP, April 16, 1935; also *Revue des Deux Mondes,* May 1, 1935, p. 236. [20] *Le Temps,* RP, April 17, 1935.

Conference itself, was the signing of the Franco-Soviet Pact in Paris by M. Laval and the Russian ambassador, M. Potemkin, on May 2. This date found public opinion sharply divided upon the desirability of the pact: while the Left and a majority of the Right favored it, the agreement was bitterly opposed by a minority, mainly composed of *Extrémistes*. One of the most consistent of these opponents was the royalist historian Jacques Bainville. He argued that, since a Russian agreement was not looked upon with favor by London and Rome, it was dangerous to play "a two-faced diplomacy"; that Soviet Russia was a doubtful and dangerous ally; and, most important of all, that France had no interest in fighting Germany to keep her from expanding in the East.[21] Léon Bailby of *Le Jour* also scored Moscow's "satanic plan" of leading France into a war with Germany in order to precipitate the Communist revolution in Europe, and emphasized that an alliance with the U.S.S.R. meant a grave risk of war with Germany. These were all objections that were to be expressed a year later by most of the Rightist papers, but now only a minority voiced criticism, and seemed in favor of giving Germany a free hand in Eastern Europe at the expense of Soviet Russia.[22] The failure of their anti-Soviet propaganda, aimed at convincing the *Modérés* of the danger of the pact, was admitted by Jacques Bainville when he stated in *Candide* (May 9): "The most serious event of these last years has just taken place. The Russian alliance has been renewed with the Soviets. It is accompanied by enormous risks against which only an independent élite has warned the public. The public was not moved. It did not even pay attention. As for the Chamber and Senate, they say 'amen.'"

The majority of the Right accepted the Franco-Soviet Pact, if not with enthusiasm, at least as a measure necessary to face

[21] *L'Action Française*, Feb. 10, 12, 13, March 9, 27, 1935; also *Candide*, Feb. 21, April 18, 1935; *Je Suis Partout*, April 21; *Revue Hebdomadaire*, Feb. 23, March 30, April 6.

[22] According to M. Le Grix, the pro-Fascist royalist editor of the *Revue Hebdomadaire*, German expansion in the East would be the diversion which would save France (March 30, p. 627).

the most pressing danger in Europe: the threat of Pan-Germanism. This was the attitude not only of Pertinax and Emile Buré,[23] who went so far as to demand a military agreement with Russia, and who consistently maintained this position; but also of those *Modérés* who less than a year later were to oppose the pact as presenting more dangers than advantages.[24] They of course showed no great enthusiasm for the pact and frequently pointed out the potential menace arising from the identity of the Soviet Government and the Third International. But their criticism was mild and not to be compared to their future opposition; the government was asked to take precautions, rather than condemned for signing the pact. Moreover, the agreement was not at this time considered as necessarily leading to a military alliance. "It is a question of a pact of security and not of a military alliance," declared *Le Temps* on April 21, which further stated that the pact supplemented the Covenant and only made the obligations of the latter stronger. It was made clear in the press that the pact was only important as a complementary guarantee, secondary to that given by the Western powers, and that its usefulness was mainly negative, since it would prevent any possible Russo-German collaboration in the future. Russian help, although essential in a negative way, was not considered necessary for the defense of the *status quo* as long as the Stresa Front existed. "The Europe of Stresa is capable of defending herself against an aggression by Germany or an attempt to destroy the Europe of 1919, but the mass of the U.S.S.R. must not go on the opposite side, where the German military power would be. The Stresa Front balances the Teutonic pressure, but on condition that Russia does not go to the other camp. The treaty just signed sees to that."[25]

Apparently in May, 1935, the majority of the Right was still true to its traditional anti-German policy, and, whatever its

[23] *Le Temps*, RP, March 28, 1935; *ibid.*, March 30, April 28, 1935; also Pinon, *Revue des Deux Mondes*, May 15, 1935, p. 480.

[24] Cf. *Le Temps*, RP, March 24, April 15, 22, May 2, 1935.

[25] Pinon, *Revue des Deux Mondes*, May 15, 1935, p. 479; cf. also *Le Temps*, RP, March 28, 1935.

antipathy to bolshevism, anxious to keep all possible guarantees against Pan-Germanism. The fear of a social revolution, which the Third Reich was already using in its propaganda among the French Conservatives, had not yet overshadowed their fear of German aggression. M. Pinon's reaction was typical. He wrote of the danger involved in Hitler's refusal to accept an Eastern pact and pointed out the Führer's clever use of the theme of "Bolshevist danger" in furthering his aims of conquest. This stratagem he called "the battle horse on which Germany is advancing toward a position of military preponderance in Central Europe. . . ."[26] Since Pan-Germanism presented the main danger to France, the advantages of the Franco-Soviet Pact outweighed its disadvantages. "On the one hand, Germany's threats oblige us not to neglect any support, however mediocre it may be," wrote Raymond Recouly of the *Revue de France,* who a year later emphasized only the dangers of the pact, "and on the other hand, certain of our natural allies, especially the nations of the Little Entente, are showing the keenest desire to see us sign an agreement with the Soviets. These are the two principal reasons that have impelled our government to begin negotiations with the leaders at Moscow."[27]

The last scruples of the majority of the Right were swept away by M. Laval's trip to Moscow and the famous declaration of Stalin on May 15 that put an end to the antipatriotic and antimilitarist policy of the French Communist party. *Le Temps* (May 15) underlined the importance of the visit, and was pleased by the warm welcome given to M. Laval at Moscow: it emphasized the return of Soviet Russia to old diplomatic traditions as "one of the signs of the evolution that has been taking place" in that country. The communiqué in which Stalin declared that he "fully understood and approved the policy of national defense carried on by France in order to maintain her armed force at the level of security" was received with satisfaction by the Right.[28] Even Stéphane

---

[26] *Revue des Deux Mondes,* April 15, 1935, p. 951.
[27] May 15, 1935, pp. 363-364.   [28] *Le Temps,* May 18, 1935; cf. *ibid.,* R?.

Lauzanne, who had been a critic of the pact, wrote in *Le Matin* (May 18) that "M. Pierre Laval returns from Moscow weighted down with commitments about whose seasonableness and value much should be said. But he is bringing back one that is not far off and problematic: it is the one in which the U.S.S.R., recognizing the necessities of national defense and the obligation for France 'to maintain her armed force at the level of security,' takes a definite position against the antimilitarist campaign carried on by the Front Commun." Although the declaration of Stalin marked the beginning of the about-face of the French Communist party, which was to become more patriotic than the old-fashioned patriots, to the surprise and terror of the latter, it was then generally considered a victory by the Right.[29] "That sentence of the communiqué whose insertion was asked for by M. Laval was readily accorded by M. Stalin," commented René Pinon, "has had the effect of a stone in a frog pond on the French Communists and Socialists. . . . That a Communist government should approve a capitalist country's having a strong army and using it in case of a European war, that is beyond their understanding and leaves them nonplused."

His conclusion well represented the mixed feelings of the Right: "For the moment it is only a question of safeguarding the security and unity of the U.S.S.R., and therefore Soviet Russia appears in the Europe of today as an element of order, of stability and of peace with which it is useful to collaborate provided that, on the other hand, all precautions are taken to eliminate from among ourselves the still virulent toxins secreted by bolshevism."[30]

In short, as Mr. Alexander Werth remarked, "the signing of the Franco-Soviet Pact was generally approved in France; the Left regarded it as a contribution to the system of collective

[29] Pierre Dominique, who later attacked the Franco-Soviet Pact, wrote in *La République:* "So M. Stalin understands what M. Cachin did not understand very well, what M. Blum did not understand at all. . . . The communiqué has thrown the camp of the French Marxists into consternation" (*Le Temps,* RP, May 15, 1935).

[30] *Revue des Deux Mondes,* June 1, 1935, p. 712.

security, and the Right—or most of it—as a contribution to France's national security."[31]   It was only the following year, when the pact came up for ratification by the Chamber in February, 1936, that the majority of the Nationalists vigorously attacked it and from then on stubbornly refused this essential element of French security. Mr. Werth was not exaggerating when he added that "the subsequent hostility of the Right to the pact and their desperate efforts to prevent its ratification are one of the most remarkable recent developments in France."[32]

With the conference of Stresa and the signing of the Franco-Soviet Pact, it seemed as though France had succeeded in establishing almost unanimous opposition to Pan-Germanism throughout Europe. The German *fait accompli* of March 16 had apparently led to a strengthening of the *status quo* along the realistic lines that had always been advocated by the Nationalists. In the eyes of the approving Right, the anti-German coalition was now stronger than ever. A few months later, however, the whole system of "realistic" collective security was to crumble with the outbreak of the Italo-Ethiopian War.

[31] *The Destiny of France*, p. 140.   [32] *Ibid.*

PART II

FROM TRADITIONAL NATIONALISM TO
NEO-PACIFISM
(1935-1936)

CHAPTER IV

PRO-ITALIAN POLICY: "SANCTIONS MEAN WAR!"

THE ITALIAN invasion of Ethiopia had been expected since the beginning of 1935, but it was not until September and October that the crisis reached a climax. On September 11 Sir Samuel Hoare's speech at Geneva emphasized England's firm stand against an Italian aggression, and France found herself obliged to choose between Great Britain and Italy. On October 3 the latter actually invaded Ethiopia, and was declared an aggressor by the League Council on October 7. Four days later committees were established for the recommendation and application of economic sanctions, which were accepted by most members of the League by the end of the month. In the meantime part of the Home Fleet had joined the British Mediterranean Fleet, and British diplomacy was actively engaged in aligning the other governments, especially that of France, behind a policy of effective sanctions.

The pressure brought by Britain finally forced M. Laval's hand in support of the League. On October 26 he gave the British cabinet a written pledge of military assistance, but coupled it with the condition that Britain should not take the initiative in any measure against Italy not in conformity with decisions taken by the League of Nations in full agreement with France.

Laval did everything to delay and discourage punitive action by the League. He acted as mediator in the Italo-British conflict, and saw his efforts crowned with success on December 8 by the signing of the ill-starred Hoare-Laval agreement which granted Italy substantial territorial gains and economic advantages in Ethiopia. This accord, repugnant to the spirit and the letter of the League, was exposed in the French press on December 9, and killed by public opinion. In France, however, indignation was not so universal as in Great Britain;

the attacks came almost exclusively from the Left. Laval's reluctance to apply sanctions and his effort to ride both the British and the Italian horse were considered supremely wise by the majority of the Right, as was shown by the reaction of the press during September and October and of the Chamber during the important debates of December 27 and 28 on his foreign policy.[1]

The application of sanctions against Italy was of necessity bound to the problem of collective and therefore of French security on the Continent. By following the British Government in a determined and effective action against the law-breaker, France had the unique chance of setting a precedent against German aggression in the future and, more immediately, of securing the long-awaited British commitments in Central and Eastern Europe in return for her collaboration. Moreover, it was essential to prove to her allies in the East that she was still firmly resolved to pursue her traditional policy of defending the territorial *status quo* of the peace treaties. A policy of compromise with Italy over Ethiopia might well be interpreted by some of them as the first step towards the appeasement of Germany at their expense, and this might encourage them to follow the example of Poland in seeking their own security through a unilateral agreement with the Reich. The policy of the Right towards the League of Nations and towards Italy in 1935 cannot therefore be divorced from their policy towards Germany. Events have shown that by opposing effective sanctions they inevitably weakened their traditional anti-German stand, which was based on the maintenance of the Continental *status quo*.

In order to understand the attitude of the Right toward the sanctions and their real motives in opposing them, it is necessary to think of this problem of collective security not from a moral or legal point of view, as did the Left, but in the realistic and amoral terms of the Right.

[1] The Laval government escaped defeat by a narrow majority of twenty votes. The whole Right, with only seven exceptions, voted for him, thus accepting his foreign policy. The right wing of the Radical-Socialists (37 of 132 deputies) also voted for the government.

Their opposition to the League's action was the logical outcome of their contemptuous attitude toward its "unrealistic" principles and methods. While the Extreme Right was opposed to the League's very existence, the *Modérés* accepted it as a camouflaged coalition against Pan-Germanism, a conception which could only lead them to refuse to alienate a powerful ally on the Continent for the dubious advantage of supporting a lofty but unrealizable principle. "The French were apt to think of the League of Nations as an essentially European organization, and, more than that, as an organization which was designed to operate against one, and only one, European power. In fact, the essential function of the League, in French eyes, was to mobilize the rest of Europe in support of France in the event of France being attacked by Germany."[2] Typical of this realistic attitude of the Right toward the sanctions was the conclusion of St. Brice in *Le Journal* (October 3, 1935): "However important might be the results one could expect from a precedent under entirely different circumstances, it is far more useful to foresee the European complications that can grow out of the Ethiopian conflict."[3]

Three policies were put forward by the Rightist leaders regarding the Italo-Ethiopian War. A small minority urged France to follow Great Britain all the way in applying Article 16 of the Covenant, and to take full advantage of the situation in order to obtain the long-desired British commitments in Central and Eastern Europe. In the press this pro-League policy was advocated mainly by Pertinax in *L'Echo de Paris* (where his views clashed with those of the antisanctionist De Kerillis) and by Emile Buré, owner and editor of *L'Ordre*. In the name of traditional nationalism, Buré now defended the League of Nations, which he had long suspiciously regarded as unrealistic:

If it is true that England has finally decided to apply the Geneva Covenant, to make the formula "All for One" her own,

[2] S. I. A., 1935, II, 38.
[3] This "realism" was further exemplified by M. Paul Thellier, one of the speakers for the Right during the important Chamber debate of December 27 on the foreign policy of the Laval government (*JO. Ch.*, Dec. 27, 1935, p. 2822).

then France must from now on turn toward the League of Nations, which has so long worked against her interests. Yesterday when her [France's] troops occupied the left bank of the Rhine, when Germany had not rearmed, our country had the means of assuring her own security; today, she is obliged to seek it at Geneva.

Pertinax emphasized that popular emotion had obliged the British Government to abandon its passive attitude toward the enforcement of collective security, and that England no longer "retreated, as formerly, from heavy responsibilities in Europe."[4] In the Chamber the leaders of the few prosanctionist Rightists were Paul Reynaud and Ernest Pezet, a Démocrate Populaire and a member of the Chamber Committee on Foreign Affairs. Reynaud took a definite stand in favor of the automatic operation of sanctions, stressing its necessity in the future against possible German aggressions.[5] M. Pezet held a similar view: ". . . if we refuse to fulfill our duty, the others will refuse also; by preaching defeatism and conscientious objection, one justifies them in advance for all circumstances, even in case of an aggression against France. . . ."[6]

This Rightist minority, which defended the system of collective, and therefore French, security, found itself allied to the majority of the Left, which after a period of hesitation, and despite its traditional pacifism, finally came out in favor of the policy of sanctions, whatever the risks might be.[7]

[4] "L'Occasion manquée," *L'Europe nouvelle*, Feb. 8, 1936, p. 119; the only other exceptions to the pro-Italian attitude in the Rightist press were the Catholic daily *L'Aube*, whose editor Georges Bidault defended the principle of indivisible peace, and the Catholic weeklies *Sept* and *Politique*, with a relatively small circulation, which condemned the Italian aggression on Christian principles. These periodicals did not, however, represent the general attitude of Catholic opinion. According to M. Vignaux's excellent study of the foreign policy of the French Catholics, "the Catholic masses, who followed the Parisian or provincial Rightist press, allowed themselves to be easily won over by the antisanction campaign. With the main exceptions mentioned above, only a few political leaders of the *Démocrates populaires*, a few theologians, and some intellectuals, like Jacques Maritain and François Mauriac, were openly hostile to Italian aggression ("Les Catholiques français et la politique étrangère," *Politique Etrangère*, Oct., 1938, p. 450).

[5] *JO. Ch.*, Dec. 27, 1935, p. 2813.   [6] *Ibid.*, p. 2846.

[7] Sir Samuel Hoare's declaration on September 11 that Great Britain stood for collective resistance to all acts of unprovoked aggression seems to have decided many

Most Rightist leaders were strongly opposed to the application of effective sanctions against Italy. An important distinction must be made, however, between the attitude of the pro-Fascist Extreme Right, which openly appeared as the champion of Italy and the adversary of the League and even of Great Britain, and the policy followed by most of the *Modérés,* who accepted the sanctions in principle as long as they were not powerful enough to force Italy to a desperate stand. The hope of the latter, apparently, was to maintain the friendships of both Italy and Great Britain for France. Although the policy of each group led to the same practical result—the failure of effective sanctions—the distinction corresponds to two definite currents in Rightist opinion; it should be emphasized in order to establish the different motives that led each group to jeopardize future French security.

The chief organs of the press of the Extreme Right were the dailies *L'Action Française, Le Jour,* and *Le Matin;* the weeklies *Candide, Gringoire,* and *Je Suis Partout;* and the periodicals *Revue Hebdomadaire* and *Revue Universelle.*[8] During the months of September and October they carried on a virulent anti-British campaign and made full use of the indignation aroused by the signing of the Anglo-German naval agreement in June, which had effectively punctured the Stresa Front. They consistently opposed the principle of sanctions, violently criticized the League of Nations and Great Britain, and openly supported the Italian point of view even after the League Council agreed upon economic sanctions on October 19. The famous article of Henri Béraud, "Must we reduce England to slavery?" published in *Gringoire* on October 11, was only the most immoderate of many examples.

The Extreme Right viewed the sanctions against Italy in terms of their amoral conception of international life as a

---

of the Left to follow a prosanctionist policy. They supported economic sanctions and even, after hostilities had broken out in Ethiopia, the possibility of military sanctions. On October 8 the pacifist Socialist, M. Léon Blum, for the first time accepted the possibility of war if it were necessary to enforce collective security. See *Le Populaire,* Oct. 8, 1935.

[8] To those may be added the daily *La Liberté* and the periodical *Choc.*

perpetual game of power politics.[9] "Why should not Italy have the same rights in Ethiopia as England in Irak or India?" asked Stéphane Lauzanne in *Le Matin* (September 16). "The League of Nations, they often repeat to us, is justice. But there is no justice without equality. What one can do, the other must also be able to do. And there is no reason to unleash war in Europe because Italy chooses to treat blacks as England chose to treat whites." The colonial ambitions of Italy were perfectly in line with their own nationalistic and imperialistic doctrines; Great Britain's colonial interests in keeping Italy out of Ethiopia should not be allowed to interfere with France's interest in keeping Italy's friendship.

The largest section of the Right, however, hesitated directly to oppose Great Britain by refusing the principle of sanctions, although they, like the *Extrémistes,* had no illusions as to Britain's motives in demanding punitive action against Italy. "England," wrote the *Modéré* René Pinon, "is indulging herself . . . in one of her favorite sports, a crusade of aggressive philanthropy which benefits British interests."[10] Yet the same René Pinon admitted the necessity of the limited application of financial and economic sanctions if Great Britain were to be kept on the side of France in her struggle to defend the *status quo* on the Continent. "If they [the sanctions] did not take effect with moderation against Italy apropos Ethiopia, how could they take full effect on the day when the independence of a European state is threatened?"[11]

[9] This hard-boiled "realism" was not, however, the monopoly of the Extreme Right; although a "Centrist," M. Fabre-Luce boldly declared: "It was the good fortune of the conservative powers that there still existed in Africa a country that had not been colonized by them or their friends, and whose conquest would not necessarily arouse any opposition other than that of the natives. But instead of rejoicing . . . they made a colonial expedition, similar to twenty others . . . into the greatest scandal of modern times. . . . These imbeciles [the Sanctionists] did not hesitate to sacrifice the only alliance that could have saved Central Europe from Nazi domination" (*Le Secret de la république,* Paris, 1938, pp. 36 ff.; see also Jean Montigny, *France, libère-toi!* Paris, 1939, pp. 66 ff.; Wladimir d'Ormesson, *France,* London, 1939, pp. 149 ff.; Paul Lombard, *Le Chemin de Munich,* Paris, 1938, pp. 6 ff.).

[10] *Revue des Deux Mondes,* Oct. 1, 1935, p. 714.

[11] *Ibid.,* Nov. 1, 1935, p. 237.

This position was not based on an abstract belief in the necessity of creating a precedent, and even less on a question of international morality, but it was considered imperative to accept "moderate" sanctions if Great Britain was not to be antagonized. A Franco-British entente "can only be carried out through the League of Nations," wrote D'Ormesson in *Le Figaro* (October 1), "and the real bond between London and Paris passes through Geneva."[12] The desire to maintain the friendship of England was the essential difference between the policies of the *Modérés,* the majority of the Right, and the pro-Fascist *Extrémistes,* who did not hesitate to risk the alienation not only of Great Britain but of France's Eastern allies as well.

Some of the arguments advanced by Rightist leaders to justify their opposition to effective sanctions must be dismissed as obviously having little to do with the actual determination of their policy. At the head of these were the invocations of "Latin solidarity"[13] and the lamentations over a "fratricidal war." "Must we shed the blood of our Italian brothers?" burst forth M. de Kerillis in *L'Echo de Paris* (October 2). "Just at the thought, a poignant despair, a horrible disgust, or rather an irresistible revulsion invades our hearts!" Since the Latin sister had only of late decided to abandon her campaign for revision of the peace treaties and her flirtations with Germany, the "poignant despair" cannot be taken too seriously on these grounds alone.

The "pacifist" argument based on the repugnance of the French people for war was often put forward. Typical of the neo-pacifist campaign in the Rightist press was this excerpt from an editorial in *Le Temps* on October 6, 1935:

France, truly pacifist in the full sense of the word, intends to maintain her neutrality. Her will not to allow herself to be dragged into a bloody adventure is absolute, and the Popular Front must

[12] Cf. D'Ormesson, *France,* p. 160.
[13] This was merely an emotional introduction to the more realistic argument of the necessity of maintaining the Stresa Front.

have noticed—a little late—that any "war party" in France strikes unfailingly against the repudiation and hostility of the masses.[14]

Even M. Laval assumed the voice of another Briand when he told the Chamber of "my misgivings, my recurring fear of an incident of which history offers so many examples and which could drag our country into a war which I have done everything to avoid."[15]

In the light of future events it is undeniable that the temper of the French public, especially of the bourgeois and peasants, was decidedly opposed to war with Italy in 1935; not only had the Italians always been looked upon in a friendly (if perhaps slightly condescending) manner, but the Stresa Front had just been greeted with enthusiasm by the Right. Nevertheless, this sudden preaching of the doctrine of peace by the nationalist leaders, who had always criticized the traditional pacifism of the Extreme Left, was a very interesting phenomenon. Although fear of war or distaste for it may have been genuine in the social groups represented by the Rightist leaders, their appeals to pacifism as such were in contradiction with their traditional doctrines, and they could hardly be credited with a sincere belief that bloodshed should be avoided at all costs.

This neo-pacifism can be justified still less on the ground that defeat was probable or possible. Even when the spectre of an Italo-German coalition was evoked, the military inferiority of the defenders of the *status quo* was seldom alleged. It seems unlikely, moreover, that effective economic sanctions

[14] M. Ernest Pezet pointed out the danger of the neo-pacifism of the Right. "When our public opinion says: 'No war, unless our frontiers are directly menaced, unless we are directly interested,' how will public opinion, how will the governments of our friends and allies translate it? This is how. They say to themselves: 'If we are attacked some day or menaced with aggression, and if the situation is such that the immediate security of France is not directly threatened, France will discuss instead of acting.' And they begin to wonder.

"But then the treaties of guarantee and assistance that reciprocally bind us to the countries of the Little Entente, for example, to mention only a few, run the risk of being of no value to them and consequently to us" (*JO. Ch.,* Dec. 27, 1935, p. 2846). See also S. I. A., 1935, pp. 34-35.

[15] *JO. Ch.,* Dec. 27, 1935, p. 2800.

against Italy would actually have brought about war. To the contention of the Right that "sanctions mean war" must be opposed the belief of the Left that Italy would not have dared to face half the world. "The Italo-Ethiopian conflict cannot possibly lead to war," M. Blum told the Chamber; "there is no danger of the possibility of war, if all the states are loyally and firmly resolved to fulfill their obligations to the League of Nations." He went on to condemn Laval's policy of compromise. According to him, "the unpardonable fault of Laval" was that "he had given Mussolini reason to hope that his threat would find France compliant, consequently Europe divided. He thereby created the risk of war which he is now using to justify his policy."[16]

A more plausible basis for the opposition to sanctions of the majority of the Right was given in the realistic and strongly emphasized argument that the military support of the Italian armies was much more important to France in the future than the reinforcement of the League's authority, since a precedent established against Italy would not necessarily bring about effective collective security. "To many, if not to all Frenchmen of the Right," wrote Mr. Brogan, "the sacrifice of the new-won friendship of Italy on what they genuinely thought a frivolous or hypocritical pretext, was absurd. To the numerous Fascist sympathizers it was a crime."[17]

This fits in well with their distrustful attitude toward the League, its principles and methods. One has to admit that if Italian help actually were necessary to maintain the *status quo* in Europe, the Right were only continuing their traditional anti-German policy in opposing the sanctions. The problem in which the Right saw no legal or moral issue, therefore, rests exclusively on a pragmatic basis; the question is reduced to whether the defensive power of the League of Nations minus Italy would have been sufficient to defend the European *status quo,* even against an Italo-German coalition. "Did M. Laval really believe," questioned Mr. Toynbee, "that the armed sup-

[16] *Ibid.,* pp. 2804-2805.
[17] Brogan, *France Under the Republic,* p. 694.

port of Italy would be worth more to France as a help in meeting a possible attack from Germany than the combined strength of all these other powers?"[18]

It seems clear that the Extreme Rightists, who actually encouraged the alienation of Great Britain and France's Eastern allies, willingly jeopardized a better system of guarantees for a poorer one; their attitude cannot be explained by the realistic argument that they supported Italy in order to strengthen the position of the anti-German *status quo* powers.[19] The *Modérés,* on the contrary, who apparently kept on hoping that both the guarantees against Germany given by the League and those furnished by the recent *rapproachement* with Italy could be maintained, may be given the benefit of the doubt, although they risked sacrificing the support of Great Britain, the Little Entente, and Russia in order to keep the problematic good will of Italy.

The main cause of the attitude of the Right toward Italy appeared to be the role—for the first time of primary importance—played by ideological factors in the determination of foreign policy. The ideological struggle between the anti-Fascist Left and anti-Communist or even pro-Fascist Right transcended the realm of domestic politics in 1935, and extended into the sphere of foreign policy. It was the contention of the Left that the Right were more interested in saving the Fascist regime than in protecting the European *status quo,* and of the Right that the Left were more interested in destroying fascism than in establishing collective security throughout the world. The bitterness and persistence of these counter-accusations indicated that ideological fears and prejudices played an essential part in the Right's opposition to effective sanctions against Italy.

The charge that the Left wanted war with Italy because of their hatred of fascism was the continual theme of the anti-

[18] S. I. A., 1935, p. 34.

[19] Many of them wanted the Italian alliance in order to constitute a powerful Western bloc capable of stopping German expansion in Central Europe while orientating Germany toward a Russian adventure that would destroy communism and possibly satisfy Germany's appetite.

sanctionist campaign in the Rightist press. The Popular Front was called the *"parti de la guerre,"* and the prosanctionists were labeled *"pacifistes belliqueux."* The coalition against fascism was usually presented as a three-headed monster. "The war party," wrote Pierre Gaxotte in *Candide* (September 25), "has three parts: Free Masonry, the Socialist International, the Communist International. . . . It is an offensive against fascism, that is to say, against Italy and Germany. . . . Marxism has chosen France for its shield." The Communist International was generally considered the chief element in this anti-Fascist coalition: "World communism, which directs the Popular Front in France, dares to play this insane game that consists in demanding a big war in order to stop a little one, and in demanding this war out of obedience to peace. . . ."[20]

The success of the campaign against the "bellicists" was admitted by M. Blum when he told the Chamber that the Rightist press had disguised the situation to such a point that "a great number of very good and sincere people believe that as far as we are concerned the problem of peace and war, the problem of our security, depends upon the Franco-Italian problem."[21]

The more patriotic *Modérés,* however, anxious to keep the good will of Britain, often condemned the openly pro-Fascist attitude of the *Extrémistes;* "especially for reasons of domestic politics, they are ready to espouse the rancors and hatreds of Italy against England, thus showing themselves more Italian than the Italians themselves."[22]   They were accused of putting

[20] Le Grix in *Revue Hebdomadaire,* Sept. 14, 1935. As eminent a critic as M. Thibaudet reiterated the accusation of bellicism against the Left apropos the *Manifesto of the Intellectuals of the Right* who had been called to oppose the sanctions for the sake of "Western civilization." "The antisanctionist manifesto corresponds to very legitimate French anxieties, extremely widespread throughout the country, and not only among the Right; the French people are afraid of being dragged into the 'next war' for causes that are not more theirs than that of Russia was in 1914" (*Nouvelle Revue Française,* Jan. 1, 1936).

[21] He denounced the accusation of bellicism made against the Socialists: "As for us, we are no longer mocked as Utopians, we are denounced as warmongers. We have not changed. We are still the same men. Yesterday we were the 'bleating pacifists,' today we are the 'sanctionists' and the bellicists'" (*JO. Ch.,* Dec. 27, 1935, p. 2804).   [22] Recouly, *Revue de France,* Nov. 1, 1935, pp. 1602 f.

their love for dictatorship above the interests of France, and the dangers of their neo-pacifism were underlined. "A nation that declared that it would not make war in any case whatsoever would be certain to undergo war; it would renounce any authority in the society of nations. . . . This kind of patriotic pacifism . . . would be in reality abdication."[23] Thus the attitude of the *Modérés* cannot be assimilated to that of the champions of international fascism; the development of the foreign policy of the Right will show that these two currents continued during the successive international crises until the outbreak of war.

There was, however, a considerable element of truth in M. Ramon Fernandez' generalization:

The friends of Italy do not say what they mean, . . . that Fascist Italy represents in their eyes an antidemocratic force in internal affairs. The friends of England and of peace do not say what they mean . . . namely, that the English action is a guarantee against fascism.

This war, whose moral and legal significance could not be exaggerated, and which tangibly presents an important problem of civilization, has only created among us *des réflexes de politique intérieure*.[24]

This accusation was of course more applicable to the *Extrémistes* than to the *Modérés*. The pro-Fascist sympathies of the former were evident throughout the crisis,[25] and it has

[23] Pinon, *Revue des Deux Mondes*, Jan. 15, 1936, p. 474; also see *ibid.*, Dec. 1, 1935. The editorial of *Le Temps*, "L'Esprit de mesure," Sept. 14, 1935, also differentiated between the attitude of the *Modérés* and that of the *Extrémistes*, and tried to justify Laval's policy of conciliation as both realistic and patriotic, since it was an attempt to keep the Stresa Front alive against Germany and was in no way caused by pro-Fascist leanings. Laval himself was at pains to allude to Franco-German *rapprochement* during the debate of December 28, and to specify that he did not conceive of it as a separate agreement between the two countries, but only as a fitting link within the collective organization of European security. *JO. Ch.*, p. 2866.

[24] *Nouvelle Revue Française*, Nov. 1, 1935, p. 755. A year later M. Fernandez, like M. Drieu la Rochelle, another contributor to this periodical, had been converted to fascism and to a policy of direct *rapprochement* with Germany.

[25] Mr. Toynbee emphasized the fact that "the French Right were led to support Signor Mussolini with a more than double enthusiasm because they saw in him not merely a future ally against Germany but also a present patron of their

been remarked that outbursts of activities by the Fascist leagues coincided with the crucial stages of the international situation.[26]   To them, the success of Italy would present great advantages: it would ward off a blow to Mussolini's prestige and perhaps prevent the possible overthrow of the Fascist regime in Italy; at the same time the electoral chances of the Popular Front would be weakened by the defeat of their "bellicist" policy of sanctions, and fascism would be strengthened at home and abroad. M. Le Grix admitted the real motive of many *Extrémistes* in defending the Italian aggression when he wrote in the *Revue Hebdomadaire* (October 12, 1935):

> Mussolini beaten, it is not England who would be victorious, but Moscow. Muscovite barbarianism sweeping over France first, and next, without doubt, all over Europe, would find only Hitler in its path.
>
> . . . but if Mussolini holds firm, on the contrary, as all civilized men must hope and passionately wish, if he establishes himself in Ethiopia, and if he thereby definitely strengthens his regime in Italy, what happy consequences may we, too, not expect from the contagion of the spirit of this new civilization that he is trying to construct, a civilization that is not tyrannical and inhuman . . . but, for the first time, truly "social"?[27]

The Italo-Ethiopian War was the first crisis in which ideological passions made numerous Rightists take sides with international fascism, that is, with Italy and Germany. This orientation can be perceived both in the accusations of the political opponents of the Extreme Right and in their own admissions. It was not surprising that the Communist deputy M. Gabriel Péri should accuse them of desiring the appeasement of Germany, and should tell the Chamber of his fear

---

domestic ambition to transform France from a parliamentary into a Fascist state" (S. I. A., 1935, p. 36).

[26] "This homage of the French Fascists to Signor Mussolini in 1935 . . . was evidently a factor of considerable effect in determining the directives of French foreign policy under M. Laval's regime" (*ibid.*, p. 38).

[27] Cf. the accusation of treason made against the antisanctionist Right by M. Georges Bernanos in *Scandale de la vérité* (Paris, 1939), p. 74; *Les grands cimetières sous la lune* (Paris, 1938), pp. 302-303.

that the anti-League policy of the Right would encourage an "anti-Soviet enterprise in Eastern Europe,"[28] but the Radical-Socialist M. Delbos also accused them of desiring appeasement of Germany at the expense of Soviet Russia, and of hoping "to kill two birds with one stone by turning aside the German peril and exterminating bolshevism." Even M. Pezet, a member of the Right, warned the Chamber of the dangerous pro-German attitude of many of the neo-pacifist friends of Italy.[29] These accusations received confirmation from the statements of some leaders of the Extreme Right. M. Taittinger, deputy and leader of the Jeunesses patriotes, bluntly admitted: "Germany will perhaps ask for a free hand in such and such parts of the world. We do not demand that this nation of sixty-five million inhabitants be deprived of all means of expansion. As long as this expansion is not made at our expense, we cannot regard it with an unfavorable eye."[30]

The sanctions against Italy may be seen as a *cas de conscience* for the Right, hesitating between their ideological bias—anti-Communist and pro-Fascist—and their desire to maintain the *status quo* of the treaties against future German aggression. In terms of foreign policy, anti-Marxism became from then on synonymous with opposition to the Franco-Russian pact, while pro-fascism was already translating itself as "appeasement" and direct *rapprochement* with Germany as well as with Italy.[31]

The Right's opposition to sanctions against Italy was inevitable; they realized that the loss of this potential ally would oblige them to choose between two policies repugnant to most of them: appeasement of Germany, or a pro-Soviet and anti-Fascist stand. Resistance to Pan-Germanism was possible only as long as Italy and not Soviet Russia could be considered

---

[28] "It is not surprising," he also stated, "that in France those who want to give liberty of action to Italian fascism are the very ones who admit that we must give a free hand to Hitlerism" (*JO. Ch.*, Dec. 27, 1935, p. 2824).

[29] *JO. Ch.*, Dec. 27, 1935, p. 2324.

[30] *Ibid.*, p. 2820, quoted by M. Jean Zay from the weekly *Choc*.

[31] See below, pp. 70 ff., 89 ff.

France's main ally on the Continent; the Franco-Soviet Pact could be accepted only as a complementary guarantee of the *status quo,* not as its essential element.   Until the Italo-Ethiopian War the Right could still be anti-Communist and pro-Fascist and at the same time anti-German; but from the moment Italy was thrown into the arms of the Reich an anti-Communist and pro-Fascist stand was no longer compatible with resistance to Pan-Germanism.

CHAPTER V

OPPOSITION TO THE FRANCO-SOVIET PACT: FEBRUARY, 1936

It was on February 11, 1936, soon after the ousting of the Laval cabinet, that the Franco-Soviet Pact of mutual assistance came before the Chamber. The head of the government was now M. Albert Sarraut, with M. Pierre-Etienne Flandin as Foreign Minister. This cabinet, which was composed in part of Radical-Socialists and had the support of the Socialist party, was opposed by the "Right" and regarded with suspicion by the "Center"; they feared that this transitional government of moderate Leftist shade was preparing the success of the Popular Front at the coming general election of April.

In foreign policy, however, there was no break with the past. M. Flandin had assured his party colleagues of the Alliance Démocratique, who on the whole were not enamored of the Sarraut cabinet, that he would support Laval's policy "except in some details."[1] Outwardly Flandin still defended the League of Nations and the Franco-Soviet Pact in February, 1936, but by the end of 1937 he was to become the principal leader of the appeasers or future *Munichois*.[2]

When Laval signed the Franco-Soviet Pact in May, 1935, it was opposed only by the press of the *Extrémistes*,[3] but now,

[1] M. Laval had cleverly delayed the discussions of the oil embargo against Italy until he could launch his scheme for a compromise peace (December 7), and they were not resumed until January 20. M. Flandin further retarded them until the oil embargo was definitely abandoned, following the remilitarization of the Rhineland.

[2] Yet on February 25 Flandin defended the ratification of the Russian pact, to the applause of the Left, and vigorously opposed the idea of letting Germany expand in Eastern Europe (*JO. Ch.*, p. 586).

[3] See above, pp. 46 ff. M. Fabre-Luce defended the thesis in his book *Le Secret de la république* that the entrance of the U.S.S.R. into the League in 1934 had already led many conservatives to side with Germany since "the dilemma fascism-democracy, very favorable to our cause, was replaced by the dilemma fascism-communism" (p. 40). This interpretation appears to be a *post-facto* generalization not confirmed by the attitude of the Right in 1934 and 1935.

less than a year later, a majority of the *Modérés* had joined
in criticism of this offspring of Barthou's foreign policy, and
only a small minority defended the ratification of the pact;
in the Chamber, most deputies of the "Right" and "Center"
voted against it.[4] In the press, the same few newspaper editors
that were in favor of effective sanctions against Italy defended
the Russian pact.[5] The others were either openly hostile or
accepted it reluctantly and conditionally.

The opposition of the Extreme Right was to be expected,
but the change in the attitude of the *Modérés* was surprising.
The pact presented the same character in 1936 as in 1935, and
was even more necessary for the defense of the European
status quo, as Germany was now stronger than in the preceding year and Italy had been alienated by the sanctions.
Astonishment at this new attitude of the Right was expressed
to the Chamber by the *rapporteur* of the bill, M. Henri
Torrès. He declared that the country had shown no apprehension when the pact was signed, although that action then
seemed definitive, since the further step of submitting it to the
Chamber for ratification was not obligatory, and since it was
not known that this would be done. He was amazed to see
the present reaction, for Barthou had never been criticized as
wanting to sign a treaty which public opinion did not accept.[6]

It is essential to notice that this new criticism of the Franco-
Soviet agreement was directed not so much against the actual
as against the potential dangers it might present. Laval had
stated to the Chamber on December 28, 1935, that the pact of
mutual assistance with Russia could not be considered a military alliance, and the Right had been even more completely
reassured when he had added that it would be subordinated to
the treaty of Locarno and that he was not able "to accept an
automatic application of the pact without a previous examina-
tion by the Council of the League of Nations."[7]

[4] Cf. *Le Temps,* Feb. 29, 1936; 164 voted against the pact; 45 abstained;
353 voted for it; 22 were absent.
[5] Principally: Pertinax, Buré, Georges Bidault. *Le Petit Parisien* and *Le Petit
Journal* were also defending the necessity of the Franco-Russian Pact early in 1936.
[6] *JO. Ch.,* Feb. 11, 1936, p. 354.   [7] *Ibid.,* Dec. 28, 1935, p. 2866.

The opposition of the majority of the Right to the pact two months later seems to have been essentially caused by the fear that it might become a full-fledged military alliance in the hands of a Popular Front government friendly to Moscow and inimical to the Fascist states. "The agreement in the hands of a moderate government did not menace or irritate anyone," wrote Jean Martet in *Le Journal* (February 11). "In the hands of a Popular Front government, clinging to the Soviets, it would change its character and would be aimed directly against Germany. And yet it would be too bad if tomorrow France should find herself dragged into the uproar, merely for the sake of *les beaux yeux de M. Staline et de M. Litvinov.*"[8] Even M. d'Ormesson, who still supported the Russian pact with reservations, wrote in *Le Figaro* (February 11): "The character of the Franco-Soviet Pact will be determined by those who are charged with administering it. It can be inoffensive and even advantageous. It can lead to the worst perils."[9]

The Chamber re-echoed the same fear of a close alliance with the U.S.S.R. M. Montigny, the most outspoken opponent of the Franco-Russian Pact at the Center, emphasized the danger it might involve: for the last two years the Soviet Government had been trying, "both through diplomatic action

[8] The fear that the agreement would become a dangerous instrument in the hands of a Leftist government was clearly illustrated by the evolution of the attitudes of the specialists on foreign affairs of the *Revue des Deux Mondes* and the *Revue de France,* who may be considered as expressing the foreign policy of an important section of moderate Rightist opinion. Until the fall of the Laval government they had little or no objection to the Franco-Soviet Pact, but they began to doubt its desirability as soon as the Leftist government of Sarraut was in power. See *Revue des Deux Mondes,* Jan. 15, Feb. 15, 1936; *Revue de France,* Jan. 15, Feb. 15, 1936.

[9] In his *France,* M. d'Ormesson stated that the pact would have been "inoffensive" had it not been for the electoral triumph of the Communists in the general elections of April-May, 1936. From then on "it was feared that the new political majority would defer to the clamorous demands of the Communist party, and that French foreign policy would play into the hands of the Soviets. Europe would thus be confronted with a definite alliance . . ." (p. 184). As a consequence, he added: "A part of Europe became insensibly pro-Hitler in exact proportion as . . . in the eyes of superficial observers . . . France seemed to be drifting into communism" (p. 186).

and through its hold on France's domestic politics," to obtain a military agreement with France, and he warned the Chamber that such an agreement might be negotiated tomorrow "if a certain majority should seat itself on the benches of this Chamber." He further explained his main objection to the pact:

To ratify the treaty of mutual assistance means signing a blank check for the government of today, and, above all, for that of tomorrow.

On this blank check these governments will be free to write all the military engagements that they may think useful to our country, and we cannot limit in advance their scope, duration, and importance.[10]

It is obvious that the attitude of the Right toward Soviet Russia represented the other side of their attitude toward Nazi Germany, not because their anti-bolshevism necessarily meant pro-fascism, but because their traditional policy of keeping Germany within her existing frontiers was jeopardized by their refusal to accept a powerful ally. Since in 1936 the fast-disintegrating Stresa Front could no longer be held up as a guarantee against Pan-Germanism, the Russian alliance would have been the logical answer to Germany's open ambitions and strong rearmament, and the Franco-Soviet Pact should have been welcomed by the heirs of the foreign policy of Delcassé and Poincaré. The refusal by the majority of the Right to accept the pact, therefore, revealed a break in the traditional policy of the French nationalists which may be interpreted as the prelude to the appeasement of Germany at the expense of Eastern Europe.

At the beginning of 1936, only a small minority of the Right defended their traditional foreign policy without regard to ideological issues. For these Traditional Nationalists, Germany was the chief enemy; they advocated a policy of integral resistance to Pan-Germanism and, as a consequence, the neces-

---

[10] *JO. Ch.*, Feb. 13, 1936, p. 393. All the objections against the pact with the Soviets and the arguments in favor of direct agreement with the Reich can be found in his book *France, libère-toi!* (Paris, 1939).

sity of the Russian agreement. Their chief representatives were MM. Paul Reynaud, Georges Mandel, and Ernest Pezet in the Chamber; Pertinax, Buré, Georges Bidaut, and, later, De Kerillis in the press. As Pertinax remarked in *L'Europe Nouvelle* on February 29, 1936:

> In short, it is a question of establishing for the next few years (let us not try to look beyond) an order of priority between the German danger and the Bolshevist danger. We, for our part, are convinced that doubt is not admissible about their order of priority.

This conviction, however, was not shared by the great majority of the Rightists, who opposed any understanding with Russia; among them a distinction must be made according to their respective attitudes toward Pan-Germanism, a distinction that is essential to understand the Right's foreign policy from 1936 to the second World War.

The more radical adversaries of the pact openly accepted the inevitability of the *Drang nach Osten* and considered it inadvisable or impossible to oppose it. They advocated the abandonment of France's commitments in Eastern Europe and the defense of only a limited area against the menace of Pan-Germanism. This policy may be labeled one of *Resigned Nationalism*.[11] At the beginning of 1936 its principal advocates were the Extreme Rightists,[12] but it was also upheld by a small section of the "Center."

In the Chamber the leader of the "Centrist" group advo-

[11] The term "appeasement" could be used to characterize this group, but it implies the negative policy of temporarily avoiding the German menace by diverting it first toward others more immediately threatened. The policy of direct understanding with the Reich that they advocated was also motivated by the positive desire to see Soviet Russia destroyed by Germany and, in many cases, by the apparent belief that France's future security would not be threatened by German expansion eastward. On the other hand, the term "isolationism" would not take into account the seemingly sincere determination of some of the leaders to oppose German expansion in Central as well as Western Europe, although they were resigned to German expansion in the East.

[12] The chief exception among the *Extrémistes* was the former premier, André Tardieu, who advocated a policy of firmness toward Germany in *La Liberté* and *Gringoire,* although his position was often in contradiction with the editorial policy of these papers.

cating Resigned Nationalism was Jean Montigny, the lieuten-
ant of M. Caillaux; it was represented in the press by *La
République,* a militantly anti-Communist sheet presenting the
views of the right wing of the Radical-Socialists. This group
expanded both toward the Right, when M. Flandin became
its leader at the end of 1937, and toward the Left when some
Radical-Socialists and Neo-Socialists, like M. Déat, became
open advocates of direct *rapprochement* with Germany. Apparently its adherence to the policy of Resigned Nationalism
originated in the old dream of Franco-German understanding
entertained during the twenties and early thirties by many
"men of good will," especially of the Left and Center.[13] Although the majority of the French people were still hoping
for such an entente, the Left and the Traditional Nationalists
of the Right insisted that it could only follow Germany's
acceptance of collective security. A policy of direct conversations with the Third Reich, on the contrary, would necessarily
involve "concessions," most probably at the expense of the
countries of Eastern Europe and, ultimately, of France.[14]

The bulk of the advocates of a policy of Resigned Nationalism in 1936 were, however, the Extreme Rightists. They
usually put forward a policy of only partial abandonment of
the *status quo* to the detriment of Russia and possibly Czechoslovakia, but not of Austria or Poland. Paradoxically enough,
while facilitating Germany's expansion in the East, they refused to accept the idea of Franco-German *rapprochement.*
One of the most distinguished exponents of this policy was
the royalist historian Jacques Bainville, who had for years
been advising France to stay outside the inevitable struggle
between Germanism and Slavism. Like others of the Extreme
Right, he considered the defense of the East of Europe far
less important than that of the Center.[15] The obvious design

[13] Cf. Jules Romains, *Le Couple France-Allemagne* (Paris, 1935), as a good
example of intellectual sentimentality concerning Franco-German relationship.

[14] Thus Pertinax declared that the counterpart of direct *rapprochement* "is a
German policy of a free hand in Danubian and Eastern Europe," and ultimately
the domination of France (*L'Echo de Paris,* Feb. 29, 1936).

[15] *L'Action Française,* Dec. 17, 1935; Jan. 2, 1936.

of this section of the Resigned Nationalists was to let the
mortal enemies of France and of the French bourgeoisie, Nazi
Germany and Soviet Russia, fight each other for the benefit
of the onlooker. Thus M. Le Grix, the pro-Fascist and royalist
editor of the *Revue Hebdomadaire,* calmly declared on April
6, 1935, that the two essential conditions for preserving Western civilization were to avoid war and eliminate Pan-Germanism and bolshevism by "leaving them grappling with each
other." He hoped that Germany would beat Russia, in which
case "it is very possible that she will consider herself satisfied;
at least Western Europe would have a respite to get organized."[16]

Although cordially inviting Germany to an adventure in
Russia, only a few *Extrémistes,* however, like Taittinger and
Doriot, accepted the idea of collaboration with the Reich; most
of them illogically pretended to scorn *rapprochement* with the
hated Germans.[17] Yet, despite their rather desperate efforts
to dissociate a policy of abandonment of Eastern Europe from
a pro-German attitude, their position was scarcely defensible,
and their acceptance of the *Drang nach Osten* must be approxi-
mated to the more radical policy of complete retrenchment
behind the Maginot Line and of Franco-German *rapprochement* that was advocated by the other Resigned Nationalists.[18]

The majority of the Right, on the other hand, chiefly con-
sisting of the *Modérés,* were opposed to letting the Reich
expand in any direction, either toward the East or the Center
of Europe. Yet they refused a military alliance with the
Soviets on the ground that France would be strong enough

[16] *Revue Hebdomadaire,* April 6, 1935, pp. 118 ff.

[17] Cf. Charles Maurras, *L'Action Française,* Feb. 27, 1936; Le Grix, *Revue
Hebdomadaire,* March 30, 1935, p. 634.

[18] The most important newspapers of the Extreme Right advocating Resigned
Nationalism in 1936 were the dailies *Le Matin, L'Action Française, Le Jour*
(the last two defended a curious anti-German policy while giving the Reich a free
hand in the East); the weeklies *Je Suis Partout, Choc, Candide, Gringoire* (although
there were often contradictions in the articles of their contributors), the *Revue
Hebdomadaire* and to a lesser extent the *Revue Universelle.* To these must be
added the papers of the Fascist leader Jacques Doriot: *La Liberté* and *L'Emancipation
Nationale.* For the policy followed by Colonel de la Rocque and Doriot, see below,
pp. 130-131.

against Germany with her preşent allies and the addition of Italy, who was expected to side with her in the future. This group may be called the Conditional Nationalists since they advocated a policy of conditional resistance to German expansion based on the rejection of Soviet Russia and the reintegration of Italy in France's system of alliances. From 1936 until the war, they consistently opposed both Pan-Germanism and the Russian alliance. Their slogan, *"Ni pour Berlin ni pour Moscou,"* well translated their double fear of German hegemony and social revolution. . M. de Kerillis, who in the beginning of 1936 was still one of the leaders of this group, clearly expressed their dilemma: "At the same time that it [the Franco-Soviet Pact] offers us a guarantee against the German danger, it threatens us with the Soviet menace, and between the danger coming from Hitler and the danger coming from Stalin we do not wish to make a choice."[19]

This division of the Right into three schools of thought concerning their attitude toward Pan-Germanism was already apparent early in 1936, and became increasingly so during the following years. It is significant to note that the bulk of those urging the radical policy of Resigned Nationalism were the *Extrémistes,* while the majority of the *Modérés* advocated the compromise policy of Conditional Nationalism. By 1936 only a small minority of the Rightist leaders, who had not allowed their class interests to influence their foreign policy, still advocated the Traditional Nationalism of the Right.

The arguments advanced by the Resigned and Conditional Nationalists against the ratification of the Franco-Soviet Pact were essentially based on realism and ideology. The neo-pacifist arguments used by the first group must be discounted, although they appeared in the foreground of the campaign against the Soviet pact just as they had in the campaign against the Italian sanctions; whatever the real distaste for

[19] *L'Echo de Paris,* Feb. 10, 1936. M. de Kerillis, who defended the Franco-Soviet Pact in 1935 and opposed it early in 1936, changed his attitude again shortly afterwards. Although he sided with Franco in the Spanish Civil War, he became one of the chief advocates of integral resistance to Germany.

war on the part of the public, this neo-pacifism, which was in absolute contradiction with the traditional doctrines of the nationalist Right,[20] can in no way be likened to the sentimental and doctrinal abhorrence for war of the internationalists of the Left.[21] It seems evident from the personality of those advocating the new pacifism that it was only a means to an end: direct understanding with Germany at the expense of Eastern Europe.[22]   Thus M. Taittinger spoke to the Chamber as M. Blum would have done a year before: "We must not go on for months and years looking at another nation and always considering her as the hereditary enemy." This statement, revolutionary on the lips of an ultranationalist, called forth the retort from a Socialist deputy, M. Moutet: "When we used to say that, we were called the agents of Germany."[23]   M. Taittinger explained that his attitude toward Germany had changed, and trustingly added that he saw a favorable sign for *rapprochement* in the warm welcome given the French athletes at Garmisch during the Olympic Games, a remark which elicited an acid interruption from the respected

[20] While the advocacy of Franco-German *rapprochement* by the Alsatian deputies at the Chamber could possible be explained by the understandable desire not to make a battlefield of Alsace, as well as by a conflict of loyalties among the Autonomists, the *volte-face* of the nationalist deputy M. Oberkirch, a leading member of the Fédération Républicaine, cannot be similarly accounted for.   At the convention of his party in April, 1935, he had presented a report on foreign policy in which he stressed the German danger to the security of France and Europe (*Le Temps,* April 14); yet on February 18, 1936, he opposed the ratification of the Franco-Soviet Pact on the ground that it would close the door to direct conversations with the Reich (*JO. Ch.,* p. 467).

[21] The contrast between Leftist pacifism and Rightist neo-pacifism was clearly expressed by Charles Maurras' disciple, J. P. Maxence, in his *L'Histoire de dix ans,* pp. 305 ff. See below, p. 224.

[22] The neo-pacifist campaign in the press in favor of direct *rapprochement* between France and Germany culminated in the interview given by Hitler to Bertrand de Jouvenel, published by *Paris-Soir* on February 29.   The reaction to the Führer's proposals was generally cool, still it was hesitant rather than unfriendly.   The "Bulletin du Jour" of *Le Temps* even stated on March 3: "There is no reason to doubt Hitler's sincerity. . . . We in France have perhaps contented ourselves too easily with replying to Hitler's advances either by silence or by generalities that could not lead to anything definite."   It is interesting to note that both *L'Action Française* and *Le Jour,* which were among the most outspoken adversaries of the Soviet pact, warned their readers against Hitler's proposals for *rapprochement.*

[23] *JO. Ch.,* Feb. 18, 1936, p. 458.

guardian of the traditional anti-German policy, M. Franklin-Bouillon. But the latter, significantly enough, took no part in the debate.

The realistic arguments used by the opponents of a Franco-Russian alliance in the Chamber debate of February as well as in the press were essentially based on the contention that the pact presented more risks than advantages for France.[24] Benefits flowing from a covenant were minimized by the Right on military and geographic grounds. Even if Russia's army were excellent (and doubts were expressed by some in this respect), how would it be in a position to reach the German Army, since there was no common frontier, and since their mutual neighbors, Poland and Rumania, would refuse to let the Soviet troops pass over their territories?[25] The pact would be a bad bargain for France, for if Russia were attacked, as Xavier Vallat, a Right-wing leader of the Fédération Républicaine, told the Chamber: "France brings her powerful and immediate military help, whereas, if we are the victim of an attack, the U.S.S.R. will bring us only fragmentary, late, and I have the right to say it, almost platonic help."[26] The obvious answer to this argument is that even incomplete and tardy support on the part of the Russian Army would seem preferable to no assistance at all. M. Paul Bastid, President of the Commission des affaires étrangères, had this thought in mind when he told the Chamber: "Mutual assistance is by definition reciprocal. One cannot know in advance who will be its first beneficiary. But has not mutual assistance been part of French policy for many years? . . . Is it good sense, or fitting the dignity of a great people, to seek accords in which all the advantages would be for it, and all the risks for others? Frankly, isn't it even a little puerile?"[27]

[24] A financial argument was also advanced by some, without too much conviction: the pact should not be ratified until the Soviet Government had recognized the debts of Czarist Russia to French investors. Cf. Fernand-Laurent, De Lasteyrie, *JO. Ch.*, Feb. 11, 1936, p. 346.

[25] *JO. Ch.*, Fernand-Laurent, Feb. 11, 1936, p. 359; Vallat, Feb. 18, 1936, p. 453; Héraud, p. 456; Taittinger, p. 457; Henriot, p. 460.

[26] *Ibid.*, Feb. 18, 1936, p. 454.   [27] *Ibid.*, Feb. 25, 1936, p. 578.

The contention that the risks of the pact would be greater than the advantages was an implicit admission that the Right believed a German aggression against Russia much more probable than an attack upon France; otherwise, Russian aid would scarcely have been scorned. This belief was even admitted expressly by Montigny when he told the Chamber that "the greatest risks of war certainly appear in the East of Europe, and it does not seem very sensible to me that France should spill the first blood in a new clash between Slavism and Germanism."[28] Similarly Charles Maurras argued in *L'Action Française* of February 27 that France should let Germany and Russia fight each other, and intervene only at the last moment with her forces intact. This grand strategy would of course have nicely settled the dilemma of the Right, at least temporarily, by destroying both communism and the German menace to French security.

The opponents of the pact also affirmed that the French Army was built for the defensive and not for the offensive, and therefore could not intervene in Eastern Europe to defend her allies;[29] the corollary was that France should give up her pacts of mutual assistance with these allies. Pierre Gaxotte openly made a statement to this effect in *Candide* on February 13:

When it is a question of assuming obligations of assistance or protection, it is always of the French army that all think.

We are beginning to wonder if the task is not beyond our strength and if we are able to guarantee all the frontiers of Europe and Asia. The French public feels confusedly that these ever-increasing pacts are dragging them into redoubtable complications.

It could hardly be said, however, in February, 1936, that France's army was incapable of a successful offensive on behalf of her allies of Eastern Europe. Later this weakness was to be the main contention of the Resigned Nationalists, but it could not be convincingly put forward at this time. As long as Germany did not remilitarize and fortify the Rhineland,

[28] *Ibid.*, Feb. 13, 1936, p. 394.   [29] *Ibid.*, Feb. 18, 1936, p. 457.

the French Army was in an excellent position for a quick blow against the industrial heart of Germany. A demilitarized Rhineland was therefore indispensable to an effective defense of the European *status quo*,[30] yet not only was a section of the Right to oppose a firm stand against Germany after the Rhineland coup of March 7, but they actually admitted the probability of the remilitarization in February while emphasizing France's inability to oppose it.

Thus Xavier Vallat told the Chamber that the ratification of the pact would give Germany the impression that she was encircled, and tempt her to remilitarize the Rhineland and take over Austria.[31] "The pact with the Soviets," affirmed Charles Maurras in *L'Action Française* (February 17), "will offer Berlin a pretext for an immediate offensive to which we could give no strong answer," and he added that "France would find herself in the tragic dilemma between the acceptance of the *fait accompli* and the immense risk of defeat." Delebecque, writing in the same paper (February 13), declared that "the time for a preventive war . . . has decidedly passed" and that, faced with the remilitarization of the Rhineland, the French Government would not act. "Can one imagine our government taking the position of an aggressor? Everything forbids it to do so: its principles, the diplomatic situation, and also, alas! the state of our military forces." By thus prophesying the reoccupation of the Rhineland and accepting it in advance, the Extreme Right played directly into the hands of the Reich; they encouraged it to undertake the momentous and dangerous move which, if successful, would make future German aggressions possible with a minimum of risk.

It was further argued by the Right that the Franco-Soviet agreement was not necessary for French security, since France, with the help of her present allies, was strong enough to oppose German aggression effectively in Central or Eastern Europe. Maurras, although it obviously contradicted his fear of defeat expressed above, approvingly quoted this thesis as expressed in

---

[30] See below, p. 86.   [31] *JO. Ch.,* Feb. 18, 1936, p. 455.

Le Journal des Débats: "The new apostles have invented the story that France could not escape from the dilemma, either the Muscovite alliance or Germany's friendship. . . . If we make the effort to be strong, we shall be able, with our friends of Central Europe, to maintain between Russia and Germany the only position that is favorable to peace."[32] Here again the possibility of holding Germany in check without Russian help could be admitted only if France had been in a position to invade Germany easily through the demilitarized zone of the Rhineland. The ready abandonment shortly afterwards of this essential element of French superiority by the Right in general, and M. Maurras in particular, must disprove their contention that France did not need Soviet Russia to stop Pan-Germanism.[33]

Finally the critics of the pact also contended that Moscow would not only try to transform the agreement into a full-fledged military alliance, but would attempt to drag France into a war with Germany, while keeping out of the struggle in order to impose bolshevism on an exhausted Europe. It is impossible to determine the sincerity of the apparently profound mistrust of the Russian Government; however, the French Right would unquestionably have accepted the help of a potential ally, admittedly more threatened than France herself by a common enemy, had that country had a conservative bourgeois government. The fear of Soviet *Realpolitik* opposing France to Germany in order to turn the German menace from East to West was obviously multiplied by the bourgeois dread of the Third International. The realistic argument that the Soviet Government should not be trusted as an ally cannot therefore be separated from the ideological elements which played an essential part in formulating this mistrust.

The electoral chances of the Popular Front, especially those of the Communist party, in the coming general elections of April would, the Right believed, be increased by the ratifi-

---

[32] *L'Action Française*, Feb. 27, 1936.   [33] See below, pp. 89 ff.

cation of the pact. The importance of this electoral factor was recognized by M. de Kerillis: "The Communists, in as much as they are active elements of the Popular Front, are trying to gain power, and we cannot combat them while at the same time proclaiming our friendship for M. Stalin."[34] It is hard to believe, however, that the fear of another move toward the Left was sufficient in itself to make the Right jeopardize France's postwar system of security unless the results of the 1936 elections were regarded as affecting their vital class interests, or unless they actually believed that the Franco-Soviet Pact in the hands of a Popular Front government would lead not only to a military alliance but to war and revolution. De Kerillis went on describing the *cas de conscience* of sincere patriots who refused to ratify the agreement:

At the Right, nationalist deputies have been declaring: "What a tragedy to have to vote against a possible ally even if that ally is monstrous, at the moment when the German menace is becoming real!"

But we do not hesitate to say here that our friends have done well to vote in a body against the pact, considering the conditions in which it was presented and the risks that it involves at present.

The growing fear of a social upheaval following the success of the Popular Front apparently led many to look for protection in an authoritarian or even totalitarian regime and oppose any threat to the dictators. Typical of this attitude was Raymond Cartier's article in *L'Echo de Paris* (January 9): "Mr. Roosevelt's denunciations of the dictatorships have aroused a thrill of joy and hope among the Leftists of all countries. More than ever we are being excited to a crusade against fascism, to a holy war for democracy. More than ever we reply: No!" Dictatorship, he wrote, had everywhere resulted from the failure of democratic regimes. "What would be the outcome, supposing it were successful, of a crusade against the dictatorships? Probably the overthrow of those that exist at present and their replacement by others. Fascism, Hitlerism and all their off-

---

[34] *L'Echo de Paris*, Feb. 10, 1936. Cf. D'Ormesson, *France*, p. 184.

springs have only one logical successor, bolshevism." The
ideological war that had opposed Right and Left over the sanctions against Italy was gaining momentum. Domestic and
foreign policy could no longer be dissociated: the Franco-
Soviet Pact now presented a double and concomitant threat,
to the future of the counterrevolution in Europe and to the
electoral success of the Right, in whose eyes the triumph of
the Popular Front meant an alliance with the U.S.S.R. and the
hated "crusade against fascism."

The critics of the agreement with the U.S.S.R. made it
clear that their chief objection was the identity of the Soviet
Government with the Third International, which gave orders
to the French Communist party. The pact with the Soviets
would be a pact with bolshevism at home and abroad, with all
the dangerous consequences for the domestic and foreign policy
of France.[35] France would become "the brilliant second for
bolshevism";[36] the fear of seeing her enlisted as the "soldier
of Moscow" in a crusade against the Fascist states was voiced
from the Extreme Right to the Center. The idea was expressed
that the Russian Government, threatened by Germany and
Japan, had negotiated the Franco-Soviet Pact and created the
Popular Front in France, through its control of the French
Communist party, in order to direct France's foreign policy and
to plunge her into a war with the Fascist states; this would
serve the double purpose of protecting the U.S.S.R. from the
German menace and of bringing about the revolution in a
Europe exhausted by war.[37]

This scheme of the Russian Government was described to

[35] M. Philippe Henriot developed before the Chamber what he called the chief
argument against the pact: that the Russian Government was intent upon achieving
world revolution without regard to the methods used to reach that goal (*JO. Ch.*,
Feb. 18, 1936, pp. 461-462). A similar denunciation was made by the former
Communist deputy, Jacques Doriot (*ibid.*, p. 488).

[36] Pierre Gaxotte, *Candide,* March 5, 1936.

[37] A typical expression of this attitude was given by *Le Matin* (*L'Action
Française,* RP, Feb. 18, 1936): "It is then understood that, if the Franco-Soviet
Pact should unfortunately come into force and if France had to give aid to
Russia, the Communists would only see therein a stroke of good luck which would
enable them to crush the French Government. All the rest—indivisible peace,
mutual assistance, war on war—is only stuff and nonsense."

the Chamber by the future Fascist leader Jacques Doriot. Germany, he declared, had become "a barrier against bolshevism" which the Soviets found necessary to destroy with French help "in order to realize their great plan of world revolution. . . . There is not a single serious man living who will henceforth not be convinced that, if war breaks out, it will hasten the social evolution."[38] Russia, according to him, was following a double policy in order to accomplish her revolutionary goal; she was letting the French bourgeois, like M. Herriot, believe that she had given up her design of world revolution, and at the same time, through the French Communist leaders, she was declaring to the workers that the pact was a means of attaining it. M. Fernand Laurent expressed the same thesis to the Chamber; he refuted the classical argument that the kings of France had not hesitated to ally themselves with the Turks even when the Crescent was menacing the Cross, by remarking that "a king of France would never have tolerated the Crescent's engaging in Moslem propaganda in France." According to him, the aim of the Soviet Government was the extension of bolshevism; only its tactics had changed, and now consisted in dominating the future government of France through the alliance of the Communists with the Socialists and Radicals, while pretending to defend collective security.[39]

The attitude of the Left was in contrast with the Right's conception of the revolutionary aims of the Russian Government. The pacifist Socialists and even the bourgeois Radical-

[38] *JO. Ch.*, Feb. 20, 1936, pp. 490 ff.

[39] *Ibid.*, Feb. 21, 1936, p. 495. The idea of a plot organized by the Soviet Government to bring about war and world revolution had been a favorite one with the Extreme Right and to a lesser degree with the *Modérés* ever since the middle of 1935, especially after the Seventh Congress of the Communist International in July. MM. Le Grix, Gaxotte, Bainville, and others had also seen the hand of Moscow in the sanctions directed against Italy and had explained that Stalin wanted France to fight Germany in order to turn the danger of invasion away from Russia. Even D'Ormesson, who was not yet opposed to the Franco-Soviet Pact, wrote in *Le Temps* on August 31, 1935, that the U.S.S.R. had obliged the French Communist party to create the Popular Front in order to control the foreign policy of France. See also a similar statement by De Kerillis in *L'Echo de Paris*, Feb. 10. Cf. *L'Action Française*, Feb. 18, 1936.

Socialists defended the pact as a necessary and not dangerous weapon against Pan-Germanism. M. Herriot told the Chamber that the Soviets, by coming to Geneva in September, 1934, had shown the change in their policy, which was formerly revolutionary as well as pro-German, to a conservative and pro-French stand. According to him, France was obliged to make a defensive agreement with Russia in order to assume her responsibilities toward the Little Entente and Poland.[40]

Pro-Fascist bias and fear of communism—its electoral successes, or its triumph in a violent revolution following war—may be considered the basis of the anti-Soviet attitude of the Right. The idea of an anti-Fascist plot, organized by Moscow to start a European conflagration, had first appeared during the Italo-Ethiopian conflict and had blossomed during the campaign against the ratification of the Franco-Soviet Pact; it will be found again at the time of the remilitarization of the Rhineland and will reach its climax during the Spanish Civil War; in 1938 it will be the basis of the pro-Munich arguments.

The "Communist danger" was undoubtedly used as a weapon by German propagandists. Some leaders of opinion may well have stressed it under the influence of foreign gold, or for the purpose of saving fascism in Italy and Germany, and increasing the chances of counter-revolution in France. The slogan of the "Red menace" was certainly destined to frighten the peasants and *petits bourgeois* into voting for the Front National against the Front Populaire. Still, it could not have been used successfully for years in the press and in Parliament had it not corresponded to a real fear on the part of the French bourgeois. The existence of this fear may be more readily understood if one remembers the formation of the Popular Front, the electoral successes of the Extreme Left, and especially of the Communist party, in the local elections of 1935,[41] and finally the abrupt reversal of the foreign and

[40] *JO. Ch.*, Feb. 21, p. 495. M. Flandin took a similar stand and urged the Chamber to ratify the pact; it is interesting to compare this with his later policy of retrenchment behind the Maginot Line.

[41] Cf. *Le Temps*, May 13-14, June 3, 1935; *ibid.*, RP, May 14, 15, June 3, 1935; *Candide*, May 9, 16, 1935; *Revue Universelle*, June 15, 1935; *Revue des Deux*

domestic policy of the latter. The Communists' sudden defense of the republican institutions did not convince the skeptical bourgeois, and their passionate espousal of *cocardier* patriotism apparently frightened many of them into the defense of fascism at home and abroad.

Their dilemma was clearly presented by M. Taittinger in *Candide* (November 28, 1935):

> By a policy of total alliance with the U.S.S.R. we would be immediately dragged into a conflict with Germany. The result of this conflict would, no matter what the outcome, be terrible for us. Germany defeated, our country will be gangrened by bolshevism within a short time. Germany victorious, France will be definitely crossed off the map of the world.

Thus it was admitted that the Right's neo-pacifist and anti-Soviet campaign was motivated as much by fear of victory as by fear of defeat, since an effective military agreement with the U.S.S.R. would undoubtedly have given the defenders of the *status quo* overwhelming superiority over the potential aggressors. Coupled with the Right's easy acceptance of the remilitarization of the Rhineland in the following month, the opposition of the nationalist leaders to the Franco-Soviet Pact in February, 1936, was a dangerous and momentous step toward the abandonment of their traditional foreign policy.

Mondes, July 1, 15, Nov. 1, 1935; *Revue de France,* Nov. 1, 1935; *Revue Hebdomadaire,* June 1, Aug. 31, 1935.

CHAPTER VI

REMILITARIZATION OF THE RHINELAND: "ABOVE ALL, NO WAR!"

As a number of Rightist leaders had predicted, the ratification of the Franco-Soviet Pact gave the German Government a pretext for reoccupying the demilitarized zone of the Rhineland, and on March 7 German troops entered it in violation of the Versailles Treaty and the Locarno Agreement.

When the headlines of the Parisian papers spread the news, *"Les troupes allemandes entrent en Rhénanie,"* people queried: *"Alors, c'est la guerre?"* and they wondered what England was going to do about Hitler's latest coup. But the British Government was not inclined to take any action; British public opinion considered the occupation of the Rhineland as nothing more than a march into what was, after all, German territory, and it was believed that the safety of France's soil had long been assured by the Maginot fortifications. "This helps to explain why Great Britain was so little disturbed by the remilitarization of the Rhineland. Since the new situation spelled no immediate danger for France, Britain could see no reason for alarm about a change which at the worst made it possible for Germany to act more freely in respect to Central Europe, a region in which Great Britain still considered herself not vitally interested."[1] Furthermore, France's legal position under the Locarno Treaty was not entirely flawless; *à la rigueur,* the treaty could be interpreted in the sense that France was not allowed to proceed against Germany unless the latter should enter the Rhineland with the intent of waging war against her. Only in that case was France assured of British help and the support of the League; otherwise, her sole recourse was to apply to Geneva for economic and financial sanctions.

England's attitude must have played an essential part in

[1] Wolfers, *Britain and France Between Two Wars,* pp. 96-97.

the decision of the Sarraut cabinet, which refused to take radical measures; apparently only M. Mandel advocated general mobilization, and in spite of the rather energetic speeches of Premier Sarraut on March 8 and 10, it was decided merely to reinforce the frontier garrison and appeal to the League of Nations. The golden opportunity of reaffirming France's shaky superiority was irretrievably lost.

The remilitarization of the left bank of the Rhine was a far greater blow than the coup of March, 1935, to the maintenance of the territorial *status quo* established by the peace treaties, which was the keystone of France's foreign policy. The re-establishment of conscription was important only as Hitler's first illegal move against the Versailles Treaty, for it did not appreciably change the ratio of strength between France and Germany. The fortification of the Rhineland, on the other hand, would signify the quasi-impossibility for France effectively to help her allies in Central and Eastern Europe in case of aggression. Until then it was easy for the French to send their armies into the richest industrial area of Germany; if this threat to its industrial life did not succeed in keeping the Third Reich from following a policy of force in Danubian and Eastern Europe, the war would at least be waged on German soil. For Germany, the remilitarization of the Rhineland was therefore the necessary first step toward a forced revision of the territorial clauses of the peace treaties. For France, it was not only a threat to her own security, but it was an even greater menace to the security of her allies in Central and Eastern Europe; it meant the beginning of the end for her postwar policy of balancing German power by an effective system of collective security.

The disastrous consequences for France of a successful remilitarization of the Rhineland were fully understood and underlined by some political writers. Fabre-Luce, who later asserted that it was on March 7, 1936, that Germany took Central Europe, was pointing out these consequences in *L'Europe Nouvelle* as early as January 25.

This move would really be a way of asking France about her attitude in case of war in Eastern Europe. The absence of any military reaction would be considered a sufficient reply. From that moment on, Germany—until further orders—would no longer pay any attention to us. She would prepare her war in the East, confident of being eventually able to hold us on the Rhine she had fortified, and doubtless even confident that this modification of the conditions of war would lead French opinion to declare itself against any intervention.[2]

Only the day before the German coup Pertinax had told the readers of *L'Echo de Paris* that "the important thing to know is whether Germany will be left free to fortify the Rhine so that she can direct her main forces toward the East where she will build *Mittel Europa* at her ease."[3]

Yet, strangely enough, the essential importance of the German coup seems to have completely escaped the editors of the Rightist press throughout the whole crisis. Instead of emphasizing that its success would mean the end of France's traditional policy of maintaining the European *status quo,* and the jeopardy of her position as a first-rate power, the Rightist papers took pains to show that the German action, although of course inexcusable, presented little danger to the nation. It was not an affair to be settled between France and Germany alone, they declared, but between Germany and Europe; it was a question for the League of Nations to consider and decide.[4] It is significant that even anti-League Stéphane Lauzanne advocated League action—and at the same time sarcastically implied that the Geneva institution was of course incapable

---

[2] He emphasized that such a move on the part of Germany would mean an irrevocable turning point in France's foreign policy, an argument which he and many others later used to justify Munich: "The greatest of absurdities would be to intervene in the war in the East, of which the remilitarization of the Rhineland would certainly be the preface, after having accepted this handicap. . . . We are now at the maximum of our moral, diplomatic, and military force. If we do not utilize it, let us abdicate frankly" (p. 76). Cf. his *Le Secret de la république,* pp. 47 ff.

[3] See also *L'Echo de Paris,* March 14, 15; *Revue des Deux Mondes,* March 1, 1936, pp. 237 ff.

[4] Cf. D'Ormesson, *Le Figaro,* March 9, 1936; also *Le Temps,* BJ, March 9, 1936; *Le Matin,* March 8, 1936.

of stopping Germany: ". . . the days to come . . . will decide the fate of the League of Nations rather than the fate of Europe. It is not Europe that is in danger of death, but the League."

According to the Right's conception of international politics, the only practical and efficient way of opposing the new *fait accompli* would have been direct action by France alone, in case effective action by the Locarno powers were impossible or even unlikely. Yet the entire Rightist press pointed out that France could not move without help from the other Locarno powers, although such help seemed highly doubtful from the beginning, especially if France did not force their hands by mobilizing her army.[5] It was clear that Italy would not participate in sanctions against Germany. The coup of March 7 was a godsend to her, since it put the Ethiopian Affair in the background, and gave first place to Germany as a treaty breaker. The Right knew that action by Great Britain was also more than doubtful. Bailby, for example, after insisting on March 9 that British help was a necessary condition for France to start reprisals against Germany, gave, the very next day, the reasons why England would certainly not join France in such action.

Only a small section of the Parisian press of the Right took a consistently firm tone toward Germany—essentially the same minority that supported the Italian sanctions and the ratification of the Russian Pact.[6] The other papers were either lukewarm in their opposition to the German coup, or frankly against sanctions of any sort.

[5] Thus on the ninth D'Ormesson wrote in *Le Figaro:* "The debate is not between France and Germany. It is between France, Belgium, England, and Italy on the one side, and Germany on the other." Similarly, Recouly declared in the *Revue de France* of March 15 that the conduct of the French Government was clearly indicated: "It is dictated both by our rights and by our interests. We are not obliged to act except in perfect accord with the League of Nations and the co-signatories of Locarno. Our entire policy since the war has been based on these two points. Good or bad, this is certainly not the moment to change it."

[6] Pertinax wrote on March 20 in *L'Echo de Paris:* "We must admit it: in order to obtain more, we should have mobilized either the day after the seventh of March, or when the destiny of the London Conference was wavering."

A remarkable mildness marked the first reaction of the great majority of the Rightist press toward the German *fait accompli*. The "Bulletin du Jour" of *Le Temps* (March 8) made this rather too diplomatic statement—illustrative of the general self-possession of the press: "Undoubtedly one must never refuse to discuss or bar the way to all negotiations. One must admit, however, that the fact of accompanying a demand for negotiations with the brutal violation of a treaty still in force is not exactly the kind of thing to facilitate conversations and strengthen confidence in a new pact."

Those most outspoken in their opposition to action against Germany were the Extreme Right, although traditionally they were the most jealous guardians of France's security and prestige. In their papers not only the editorials but the headlines and headings as well played a part in their pacifist campaign. The case of *Le Matin* was characteristic: the layout of the front page on March 8 suggested that Hitler had reoccupied the Rhineland in the interest of France, and should be cordially thanked. Below the main headline announcing "THE DENUNCIATION OF LOCARNO BY THE REICH" stood out in capital letters across several columns:

IN HIS ELOQUENT AND IMPASSIONED SPEECH ADOLF HITLER SHOWED
THE COMMUNIST PERIL

"I have," he said, "warned France. . . . I tremble for Europe."

FRANCO-GERMAN CONVERSATIONS ARE STILL POSSIBLE

THE COMMUNIST PERIL

The parts of Hitler's speech quoted on the first page were the allusions to his good will toward France and his fear of a possible Bolshevist revolution in France and all over Europe. Thus the impression was given that while Hitler had used an original and not entirely commendable method in denouncing the Locarno Treaty, he had done it out of friendship for France and fear of communism, their common enemy.[7]

[7] In contradiction to the headlines and editorial policy of *Le Matin* was the article of Philippe Barrès, who was reporting the situation from Berlin. He warned of the necessity of taking a strong stand against Germany, but his report

L'Action Française, organ of integral nationalism, showed no greater concern for France's basic interests; the arrangement of the headlines suggested that the dissolution of the Leagues of *L'Action Française* was as important as the reoccupation of the Rhineland. The subtitle and the *manchette* drew attention to the danger to peace caused by the action—not of Germany—but of the parties of the Left, under the command of Moscow.

THE REICH DENOUNCES LOCARNO AND VERSAILLES

THE SARRAUT GOVERNMENT HAS PRONOUNCED THE DISSOLUTION OF THE LEAGUES OF THE ACTION FRANÇAISE

THEY HAVE TRIED TO LEAD US TO WAR

It is a question of intervening against friendly Italy in an affair that is none of our business. It is a question of satisfying the vengeance of the Masonic Lodges against the fascism they abhor, of serving the interests of England and obeying the Soviets who need this war in order to unleash the universal revolution. . . .

An important aspect of the neo-pacifist campaign is that it appears to have been directed toward influencing the government, which was suspected of wanting sanctions, either military or economic, against Germany. The Prime Minister, Albert Sarraut, was criticized for the rather firm tone of his broadcast to the nation on March 8,[8] and for his declaration to the Chamber on March 10. He was warned against rash or bold talk and was often accused of playing Moscow's game.[9] The editorials by Léon Bailby of *Le Jour* illustrate

---

was relegated to the middle pages. Soon he was to withdraw from collaboration with the paper.

[8] Cf. S. I. A., 1936, p. 51.

[9] The *Extrémiste* François le Grix wrote in *L'Ami du Peuple* (March 9) that he was alarmed by Premier Sarraut's proclamation that he would negotiate only when Hitler's soldiers had left the Rhineland and that he would ask the aid of the Locarno signatories. He affirmed that economic sanctions would lead to war. A week later he wrote in the *Revue Hebdomadaire* (March 14) that Sarraut had no right to risk the destiny of France for a warped idea, and he warned his readers of being led to butchery by such dangerous words as *l'Union sacrée*. The three weeklies of the Extreme Right, *Candide, Gringoire,* and *Je Suis Partout,* also criticized Sarraut's declarations and opposed not only war but sanctions. The Soviets were accused of wishing to impose their ideology upon the world and of doing everything possible to "envenom" the situation.

this campaign. "The present government," he declared on March 9, "lives under the protection of the Russian revolutionaries. And the latter dream of a war against Germany in which we French would bear all the expense." On the tenth he wrote in an almost threatening tone that "the government, when it speaks, will do well to weigh its words"; and added that economic sanctions would lead to military ones and thus to war, and that France would find herself alone if she should ask the League to apply sanctions. Even M. de Kerillis, in an article in *L'Echo de Paris* of March 9 entitled "The Popular Front Is Leading Us to War," cast responsibility for the "present *impasse*" on the ratification of the Franco-Soviet Pact. Particularly striking was the reaction of *L'Action Française;* a transparent attempt was made to blend neo-pacifism with patriotism for the benefit of those readers who might have objected to an about-face in the policy of the paper.[10] Hitler was still the villain, but he was in grave danger of being supplanted by Stalin. "What shall we do?" wrote Maurras on March 8. "We do not have to march against Hitler with the Soviets. We do not have to march with Hitler against the Soviets. Between these two Kamtchatkas of stupid folly lies the sphere, the immense sphere of the interests of Western Europe and their protection." The significant statement, of course, was not: "We do not have to march *with* Hitler," but: "We do not have to march *against* him." On the same day José le Boucher doubted that France was in a position to act against the strong Germany of 1936 since she had not acted against the weak Germany of 1935.

On the tenth Maurras declared that a stable and foreseeing national government would not have become embarrassed by the situation and would have sent French troops into the Rhineland. But he hastened to add that this action was unfortunately impossible in the present circumstances and that

[10] Similarly Pierre Gaxotte, one of the leading neo-pacifists of the Extreme Right (cf. *Candide,* March 19), patriotically declared on March 26, when all danger of war was over, that "Flandin should have chased the soldiers of Hitler from the Rhineland without any discussion; there they are and there they will stay." He thus cleverly and safely sounded the chord of patriotism as well as that of pacifism.

"there is only one public counsel to give the government of the Republic: First of all, no war! . . ." On the twelfth Maurras continued his defeatist campaign and the next day accused the Left of wanting to provoke a holy war when France was no longer in a position to fight Germany and should concentrate on her own defense:

As for provoking a holy war, let us leave that task to the parties of the Left! It was time in 1922, '23, '24, it was still time in 1930 and even in 1935 to take certain aggressive measures of defense. But these times have changed completely. Defense! Defense! Defense! And for this defense, armaments! But to insure this rearmament, let us closely watch Moscow!

On the same day an article by Marcel Pujo criticized the government for its bellicism under the title "No confidence in *Sarraut-la-Guerre!*" On the fourteenth, under the heading "The Russians Want War," Maurras warned his readers that war would bring a Communist revolution to the world, that Moscow wanted it for this reason, and that while "Sarraut, Boncour, and Flandin are not especially eager for war . . . they believe, like the idiots they are, that it is worth running the risk of war to make the Great Powers give way."

The neo-pacifist campaign to discourage the government from taking any effective measures against the German action did not stop short at editorials. On March 14, *L'Action Française, Le Jour,* and *Le Figaro* organized a public meeting in Paris at "Magic City" for the young *mobilisables;* the Russian plot against peace was denounced, as well as the Popular Front's newly bellicose attitude toward Germany.[11] The declaration of Colonel de la Rocque to the press, broadcast on March 9, was as usual rather hazy. In sibylline phrases the Colonel opposed an entente with either Germany or Soviet Russia, and advocated a "sacred egoism exclusive of foreign pressures"; he went on to speak of the desirability of "creating between Paris and Berlin the state of equilibrium indispensable to the equilibrium and harmony of Europe."[12] In his declara-

[11] *L'Action Française,* March 15, 1936.
[12] *Le Temps,* March 10, 1936.

tion of March 17, he was more specific in his support of a neo-pacifist policy; he denounced Moscow and the bellicism of the government and of the Left, who "are brandishing a sword they don't know how to handle." After stating that he had a horror of anti-Semitism, he added that he nevertheless kept a watchful eye on some prominent Jews, and concluded by warning the government not to forget "the old plan of the Komintern, inseparable from the government of Moscow, which wishes to establish the world revolution upon the occasion of a bloody European conflict."

Although the press of the *Modérés* did not go as far in its neo-pacifism as that of the *Extrémistes,* they frequently followed the example of the latter. The *Revue des Deux Mondes* clearly showed their attitude:

Only the Soviets and the Internationalists have suddenly discovered bellicose feelings, and leaders with little self-control have uttered some useless words. We have this unexpected and curious spectacle: the pacifists, the humanitarians, the revolutionaries, even the Radicals, were lightly accepting the idea of sanctions and even the idea of mobilization for France. The *Nationaux* parties are those who have shown most perspicacity, *sangfroid,* and wisdom.[18]

The *Modérés* not only opposed war, but often condemned economic or financial sanctions against Germany, declaring that they would bring war, or cause more harm than good. "Even supposing that they could be decided upon, would they not cause more damage to European economy than the German dictatorship?" wrote A. L. Jeune in *Paris-Midi* (March 9); and in *Le Figaro* Lucien Romier showed on March 14 the risk of war that would result from the application of sanctions, as well as the danger of uniting Italy and Germany in common resistance. He advised strengthening defense rather than the application of sanctions.

[18] "Interim," *Revue de la Quinzaine,* April 1, 1936, p. 713. This avowal of the neo-pacifist reaction of the Right as a whole was confirmed by the criticism of Pierre Dominique, who accused the Right of opposing sanctions in order to win the coming election as they had those of 1871 or 1885 with the cry of "Down with war!" (*L'Europe Nouvelle,* March 14, 1936).

Thus the press of the Right answered the most momentous move against the security of France and her allies by a campaign of neo-pacifism that directly played into the Führer's hands. Special emphasis must be given to the arguments advanced as justification in order to understand the strange position of the Nationalists.

After all danger of war was over, it was admitted at the Right that mobilization of the French Army would have been the only means of obliging Germany to recall her troops from the Rhineland. The *Revue des Deux Mondes* acknowledged: "In order to stop Germany short, they [France and England] disposed in theory of one means, and of only one. Let's call things by their names. The former allies could make Germany yield only by using force."[14] The article emphasized, however, that "they were neither *morally* nor *militarily* capable" of following such a course.[15]

This argument, repeated frequently, that France was not militarily capable of taking action against Germany was sweeping in its implications and clearly conveyed a defeatist attitude. No political writer, however, specifically declared the French Army to be actually inferior to the German;[16] and whether or not offensive weapons were lacking, the ability of the French Army to have ejected the German troops from the Rhineland is generally accepted today.

[14] "Interim," April 1, 1936, pp. 712-713.

[15] "Part or all of the French Army should have been mobilized," wrote René Pinon in the same periodical on June 1, p. 716, "for it is useless to negotiate in serious cases if the possibility of recourse to the *ultimo ratio* is not silhouetted in the background of the negotiations. Otherwise the diplomatic game is lost in advance." But unfortunately, he added, France did not have "an offensive army capable of dislodging Germany. One must have an army suited to one's policy, or a policy suited to one's army." The same argument and almost the same words were used in the *Revue de France* by Raymond Recouly, who stated that the French Army was a purely defensive one, and that while France was safe from aggression, she was incapable of a quick offensive (April 1, pp. 537 ff.).

[16] Rather, it was stated that effective action against the Third Reich would have required a slow, involved, and costly mobilization, which might have been the first step toward war. "It is possible," wrote M. Recouly, "that Germany, who militarily is not yet ready, would not have risked our ultimatum. . . . But another opinion is possible. In reality it was a game of poker" (*Revue de France*, April 1, 1936, p. 537).

There is little doubt that even mobilization would have obliged the German General Staff to withdraw its troops; this fact would seem to prove that, contrary to the claims of the Right, England's aid was not a necessary condition of French action unless one should contend that such action would have alienated her from France. That Great Britain would have been far more likely to side with France had the latter taken the initiative was indicated by M. Paul Reynaud during the Chamber debate of January 26, 1937. Having first stated that the government did not care to start operations against Germany in spite of the fact that the General Staff had recommended mobilization (a revelation which M. Flandin, interestingly enough, did not attempt to refute),[17] Reynaud declared that English aid would have been forthcoming had France taken a firm stand. All the members of Parliament he knew agreed that "it is true that at the time we [the English] had no desire to march; it was essentially your [France's] affair, that of your security. But if you had marched, we would naturally have followed."[18]

The Right's insistence upon the "military unpreparedness" of France may therefore be interpreted as a skillful way of getting out of an unpleasant and unwanted responsibility. Similarly, the resentment expressed by many against Great Britain for taking the part of an arbitrator between Germany and France, instead of siding with France as a guarantor of the Locarno Treaty,[19] may be considered in many cases a *post-facto* justification for inaction, rather than a sincere regret for having been unable, because of England's default, to dislodge the Germans from the Rhineland.[20] In some instances, of course, the disappointment at Britain's failure to act against

[17] In an article written for the *Christian Science Monitor,* published on March 27, 1939, Flandin declared that France actually announced to Great Britain her intention of intervening militarily and was dissuaded by pressure brought by the latter.

[18] *JO. Ch.,* p. 170.

[19] Cf. *Le Temps,* RP, March 19, 26, 1936.

[20] Pierre Dominique even asserted in *L'Europe Nouvelle* (March 28) the "joy of the Rightists when it seemed possible in Paris that England would refuse us her automatic assistance in case of aggression."

Germany appears to have been genuine; and it is quite possible that a strong stand by the British Government from the
beginning would have changed the attitude of many from
irresolution to firmness, both among members of the government and among the leaders of opinion.[21]

The charge that the country was not "morally" ready to
risk war seems far more valid than the argument of France's
military unpreparedness. "Our country," one reads in the
Revue de France, "which no one had taken care to warn of the
imminence of this danger, was far from the degree of tempera-
ture wanted for an act of such consequences."[22]   While the
statement that France had not been warned did not corre-
spond to the facts, the apparent apathy with which the public
received the news of the remilitarization of the Rhineland
seems to justify the argument that France was not morally
prepared to fight.[23]   The Right loudly bemoaned this passive-
ness, this "moral unpreparedness," which, they firmly declared,
made any action against Germany impossible. Yet the responsibility for this inertia in the face of a serious menace may be
largely attributed to the neo-pacifist campaign of the Rightist
press, which had been gathering momentum since the Italo-
Ethiopian Affair. The leaders of the Right indirectly admitted
their responsibility for the public's lack of patriotic reaction
by accusing the "bellicose" Left of trying to lead France into
war, and contrasting this "warmongering" with the "wisdom"
of the Right.[24] Not only did they attempt to disguise the dangerous consequences that would result from the remilitarization of the Rhineland, but in the face of the German coup

[21] In his *France,* p. 170, M. d'Ormesson affirmed that the government did not
act because of Great Britain's opposition and of her moral isolation; war would not
have been justifiable in the eyes of the world since Germany had not violated any
frontier. This was also M. Flandin's contention (*JO. Ch.,* Jan. 26, 1937, pp. 169 f.).

[22] Raymond Recouly, April 1, 1936, p. 537.

[23] Dominique described the reaction of public opinion to the Rhineland coup in
the following words: "If she has been surprised, France has not shown any anger.
As a matter of fact, during these last few days, the observer has noticed only
slight resentment in the streets and countryside of France. Fear was sometimes
expressed, but in mild terms. Are the French then resigned to everything? . . .
Even the newspapers have not tried to arouse public opinion. Must I see wisdom
in all that, or weariness?"   [24] See above, pp. 58 ff., 90 ff.

they preached pacifism with the apparent purpose of discouraging action by the government. Their success was conceded by M. Flandin during the Chamber debate on January 26, 1937. After stating that his government had not acted in March, 1936, because it wanted to maintain those guarantees of security which France had obtained by the Locarno Treaty, he added: "If you will be good enough, moreover, to remember that the French Government of that time was little supported in an action of resistance by a certain section of public opinion, I will have said enough to explain the attitude of the government of which I was a member."[25]

Considering the neo-pacifist attitude of the Right toward Italian sanctions in the latter half of 1935 and toward the Russian pact in February, 1936, their reaction to the German move of March 7 may be regarded as another step toward the acceptance of German expansion in Eastern Europe. This time, however, the step was decisive. It is not impossible to believe that the acceptance of the *fait accompli* was deemed by a section of the Right to be the best way of obliging France to change her foreign policy from the integral defense of European security to the defense of only a limited sphere. Their attitude toward Great Britain and their avowed preference of the Stresa Front to the League system of collective security, with its corollary of the Franco-Russian Pact, may be interpreted as a desire on their part to achieve the protection of Western Europe at the expense of the East.[26]

After March, 1936—the turning point in her postwar foreign policy—France changed from the foremost power in Europe to a mere satellite of England. The future dominion

---

[25] *JO. Ch.*, p. 170.

[26] This hope, although seldom admitted openly, had often been indirectly expressed by their spokesmen. The relative unimportance of defending the East and the necessity for concentrating on the security of the West and Center of Europe was still emphasized, sometimes to the extent of urging the abandonment of France's allies in the East. Cf. St. Brice, *Revue Universelle*, March 15, 1936; see also the anti-Czech article in *Je Suis Partout*, March 14, 1936. This idea was best expressed by Jean Montigny in his *France, libère-toi!* (pp. 134 ff.), in which he gave all the arguments used by the Resigned Nationalists, from 1936 on, to justify a policy of retrenchment behind the Maginot Line.

status of France in foreign policy may well have been fore-
seen and accepted at this time by those who urged following
the British lead; they knew that Great Britain was not inclined
to protect Eastern Europe from German ambitions and that
the remilitarization of the Rhineland would be the strongest
argument against a firm policy in Europe disapproved by
Downing Street.

Moreover, their seemingly illogical attitude toward the
League before, during, and after the crisis of March also points
to the desire of a section of the Right to give Germany free
play in Eastern Europe. The *Extrémistes* had consistently
opposed the League's principles and methods and had vigorously attacked it during the Italo-Ethiopian War; yet, strangely
enough, they urged League action against Germany during the
Rhineland crisis. This sudden loyalty to collective security
disappeared, however, as soon as the danger of effective action
by France and her allies was over, and was replaced by un-
usually bitter criticism of the League and its failure to achieve
any tangible results.[27] This contradictory attitude may well
be interpreted for a minority—the so-called Resigned Nationalists—as a rather Machiavellian method of bringing about the
reversal of France's foreign policy by the failure of the League
system of collective security, a system which, it may be argued,
even by 1936 could be enforced only through Franco-Russian
collaboration.

Obviously the Right were anxious to replace Geneva by
Stresa, that is, the U.S.S.R. by Italy as France's main Continental ally. This desire to reconstruct the Stresa Front was
indicated by the insistence of the Rightist press that the sanctions against Italy be withdrawn, since this withdrawal was
the first condition for an Italian entente. "There is not one
hour to lose in normalizing our position toward Italy," wrote
José le Boucher in *L'Action Française* on March 18. "It is
up to us to make Mussolini come out of his silence. . . . We

[27] The fight against the League was led by Stéphane Lauzanne of *Le Matin*,
March 18, 20, 26, 1936. See also *Le Temps*, March 24; *Le Figaro*, April 12, 1936.

still have the means to do it. The sanctions still have an exchange value. Perhaps not for very long."[28]

Rapprochement with the Latin sister had been urged by the antisanctionists in the latter part of 1935 as the only effective guarantee against Germany. This contention did not then appear to be valid. Still less could it be accepted in 1936; a sincere and realistic desire to increase the security of France could scarcely be reconciled with the Right's refusal to sanction the Russian guarantee and with their opposition to a firm stand against the German occupation of the Rhineland. Their negative attitude toward these two essential conditions of European stability coupled with their advocacy of the return to the Stresa Front may be interpreted at best as taking a grave risk with French security by making it contingent upon an unlikely alliance with Italy. To avoid a policy of integral resistance, in which the Soviets would have played a major part, the majority of the Right preferred either the abdication of France in Europe or a policy of conditional resistance precariously founded on wishful thinking.

Neo-pacifism in March, 1936, was based less on "realism" than on fear of the consequences of war—of even a victorious war.[29] A French success against Germany might have dealt a deathblow to the Nazi regime and encouraged a proletarian uprising there, just as a League success against Italy in 1935 might have destroyed fascism in Italy and replaced it by a Socialist regime. It would at least have tremendously increased the prestige and strength of the Popular Front in France, and especially that of the Communist party. Furthermore, it was believed that Nazi Germany presented the most effective barrier against communism, and that there was danger of the bolshevization of Europe following a major war.

[28] Cf. *Revue des Deux Mondes,* April 15, 1936, p. 956; May 1, pp. 230 f.; Recouly, *Revue de France,* April 1, 1936; also D'Ormesson (*France,* pp. 173, 188 f.).

[29] Real pacifism, or sentimental and humanitarian abhorrence of war must be eliminated as a factor in the new attitude of the Right toward Germany, although the realization that "war does not pay" and that France could not afford to lose her precious blood must have played a part in their determination to avoid war

Only the conflicting fears of social revolution and of Pan-Germanism explain the attitude of the majority of the Right toward Germany since 1935, when many began to believe that communism was as great a menace as German hegemony and had to be dealt with even to the detriment of the security of France. In the press we find the same passionate opposition of the Right to the Left over the Rhineland question as over the Italian sanctions and the ratification of the Franco-Russian Pact. The role played by the ideological struggle in an international affair concerning above all the security of France was thereby clearly revealed. The importance of this ideological war between liberalism, fascism, and communism, waged both on the international scale and by the Right and the Left on the home front, was brought out by Pierre Dominique in *L'Europe Nouvelle*. He accused both Rightists and Leftists of seeing the foreign policy of France only through the "party prism":

Certain conservatives have gone as far as to say that in case of war they would not march against Hitler's Germany. Of course they meant: "For the Russia of the Soviets." But several neglected the *sous-entendu*: the truth is that Chancellor Hitler seemed to them only a German Mussolini, and that they were hunting desperately—without finding him—for a French Mussolini. . . .[30]

The reluctance of most Nationalist papers to take a firm stand after the coup of March 7 may be partly explained by the desire to increase the Right's electoral chances in the coming elections in April. An antiwar platform was believed to be able to win over to the *Front National* many wavering votes. "The thought of the coming elections dominates all political preoccupations," wrote Pierre Gaxotte in *Candide* on March

[30] *L'Europe Nouvelle*, March 28, 1936, p. 323. "But aside from the few Frenchmen who are not prisoners of the parties or at least of the party spirit," continued Dominique, "most of our compatriots can only envisage the entente with England, Italy or Germany, or the Franco-Soviet Accord, through the party prism." He added that apropos of this reaction, "M. Herriot wrote that for the first time he understood the spirit and policies of the *émigrés*. M. Herriot is right. We still have our *émigrés*. They are for a party against the nation; for an idea, against France. They are already giving information to foreign powers, they will be traitors tomorrow. And the worst of it is that they are legion" (*ibid.*).

19. "Faced with bellicose antifascism, French patriotism is increasing its chances tenfold." It is difficult to believe, however, that the perspective of another Leftist victory was a sufficient motive to make them jeopardize French security; both their pathological fear of revolution and the desire of an important minority to establish an authoritarian or totalitarian regime in France must have played an essential part in their neo-pacifist attitude.

Although the Resigned Nationalists did not dare to defend the idea of *rapprochement* immediately after the German remilitarization of the Rhineland,[31] the importance of this group was stressed by the pro-Fascist political essayist Georges Suarez in *Le Temps* on March 17:

Today an important part of Conservative [Extreme Right] and Moderate opinion has rallied itself to the thesis of Franco-German *rapprochement* which it repudiated at the time of Briand and which it now opposes to the Geneva spirit, and inversely Leftist opinion defends the spirit of Geneva against the armed pacifism of Hitler and of some Rightist groups in France. The Franco-German *rapprochement*, which under Briand was the keystone of the League, has become under Hitler the keystone of militarist, traditional, and anti-Genevan pacifism.

The defenders of direct conversations with Germany appeared as the vanguard of the neo-pacifist majority of the Right, while the others, although opposing mobilization in March, 1936, still seemed to be hesitating between the dangers of Pan-Germanism and of communism, between France's national interests and their own class interests.

This majority of Conditional Nationalists pretended that

[31] Maurras indignantly denied the accusation brought by the Socialist paper *Le Populaire* that "the heart of the Right is obviously not with France. . . . It is with Hitler just as it was with Mussolini." He justified his neo-pacifism on the grounds of the danger presented by the crusading spirit of the Left, which wanted a "religious war," "a war of Revolution and Counter-Revolution." Yet after condemning those Rightists who were "lured by a Germanic alliance," he affirmed that the "immediate peril . . . lies where the mad crusade for the Covenant is preached . . . where the confusion within the Government is exploited for a revolutionary war whose first effect would be to revolutionize our own country" (*L'Action Française*, March 12, 1936).

their anti-Soviet policy was compatible with an anti-German attitude. Outwardly they refused to choose between *rapprochement* with Germany and the Soviet alliance. *"Ni pour Berlin, ni pour Moscou!"* was their slogan. Their policy of rejecting the immediate guarantee of Russia for the future aid of Italy was frequently presented as "realistic" in the press and in Parliament, but it was actually founded on fear: the fear of revolution—and on hope: the hope of regaining Italian friendship. The greater part of the Right was obviously and uncomfortably squeezed between their desire to maintain the security of France and the dread of serving the interests of the Third International; and their spokesmen found it increasingly awkward to reconcile their traditional nationalism with their anti-Communist stand.

A good example of the hesitation within the Right was the case of M. de Kerillis, whose patriotism and integrity cannot be doubted. For ten days after the German coup of March 7 he seemed to ignore the danger of Pan-Germanism. Not until March 18 did he suddenly awake to the realization that many Nationalists were heading toward the acceptance of German domination in Europe. On that date, warning the Right in an article in *L'Echo de Paris,* he showed the conflicting forces to which he, like many others, had been exposed. Under the title *"Nationaux, Attention!"* he began first to criticize the Left which "suddenly, under the influence of the Soviets, the German refugees and the anti-Fascist Freemasons, have dug up the war hatchet and become aggressive bellicists and furious warmongers. Confronted with this complete about-face, worthy of a chalatan, it was fitting that the *Nationaux* should maintain their *sang-froid,* and even put on the brakes. They did it. Without their determined resistance we would perhaps today be on the path of the most terrible of all wars." But while stressing the dangers coming from the "warmongering" of the Left, he violently opposed the idea of *rapprochement* with Germany as defended by a section of the Right: "I am speechless when I hear Franco-German *rapprochement* still being spoken of. For God's sake, dear friends, not at this time! You have the right to choose any opinion you wish in foreign policy. But not when Hitler derides and menaces. Ah, no!"

The next day he showed more clearly his shift, confirmed by his later attitude, from neo-pacifism back to traditional nationalism, from emphasis on class interest to emphasis on national interest:

Indeed, the attitude of certain elements of the *Nationaux* parties is distressing. . . . I do not understand anything about it. I only understand that they are speaking of *rapprochement* with Germany at the very moment when the latter is tearing up a treaty, is deriding and menacing us, and is manoeuvering to isolate us in Europe and then crush us. . . . *Rapprochement* with Hitler? Ah! you'll see. Today it is the Rhineland coup. Tomorrow, it will be Austria, and the day after tomorrow, Czechoslovakia. . . .

But your resentment and your anger [at the ratification of the Franco-Soviet Pact] must not make you lose sight of the immense drama which is unfolding itself. I beg of you, think that at this moment France is risking her independence and her destiny. . . .[32]

If M. de Kerillis, who later proved his sincere patriotism by being the only Rightist to vote against the Munich Pact, had to wait ten days after the German coup to see the dangers involved in neo-pacifism, and even then declared that the *Nationaux* had been right in "putting the brakes" on the bellicism of the Left, it is not surprising that many should have been blinded by their fears and prejudices into preaching peace at all costs.

Another indication of the conflicting fears that troubled the Right was given by the attitude of the Senate when called upon to ratify the Franco-Soviet Pact on the twelfth of March, only a few days after the German coup. Their vote may be considered as a barometer of the hesitations of the Right between the German menace and the threat of social revolution. Since a majority for the ratification of the pact was already assured, and in view of the repercussion of the German viola-

[32] Although M. de Kerillis sided with Franco a few months later, he soon became one of the leaders of the Traditional Nationalists.

tion of the Versailles and Locarno treaties upon France's
security, one would have expected the Senators of the Right
to vote unanimously in favor of the pact as a patriotic manifestation of "Sacred Union" in the face of national danger.
A section of the Right did take this attitude under the eloquent leadership of Alexandre Millerand: "The action of
Chancellor Hitler does not change the character or dangers
of the pact, but it is enough to convince us that the clearest
and most urgent of our duties is to give the example of this
patriotic union. . . ."[33]   The Union Républicaine, concluded
M. Millerand, would either vote in favor of the pact, or would
abstain from voting.   This manifestation of patriotism, however, was ill received by the Extreme Right, and *L'Action
Française* angrily stated: "The greatest political mistake was
committed the night before last by the Senate. . . . The mistake of the Chamber was folly.   The mistake of the Senate,
and especially of M. Millerand, was a crime."

As many as thirty-four Senators of the Right abstained and
forty-eight voted against the ratification of the pact.   This
vote takes on added importance in view of the international
tension caused by the violation of the Rhineland status only a
few days before; it may be interpreted as showing the proportion of those who, in spite of the coup of March 7, still thought
that Pan-Germanism was not the paramount threat, and who
followed their ideological preferences and fears to the detriment of France's security.

The arguments used in the debate seem to justify this interpretation.   One of those most advanced was the hoary one
that the Russian Government was the head of the Third International, and was therefore interfering with France's political life through its control of the French Communist party.[34]
The German *fait accompli,* while characterized as an inexcusable action,[35] was used as an illustration of the dangers

[33] *JO. S.,* p. 267.
[34] *Ibid.,* March 13, 1936: cf. Armbruster, p. 262; Monsservin, p. 268; Dumesnil,
p. 268.
[35] *Ibid.* Cf. De la Grandière, p. 263; Comte Louis de Blois, p. 267.

that the pact would bring to France. The method followed by some orators of the Right was to express indignation against the "insolent defiance" of Germany, but to add that the dangers of the Russian pact were as great as ever. After patriotically stating that the Senate "wished to manifest the profound union of Frenchmen before the German menace," M. Henri Lémery nevertheless added that he still opposed the pact as "a treaty whose sole positive effect will be to make the Franco-German duel the preface to the inevitable struggle between Slavism and Germanism." He concluded: "Since, finally, I do not want the infeudation of France to the designs of Red imperialism, and since I resent as an insult the meddling of a foreigner in our foreign affairs (exclamations at the 'Left,' applause at the 'Right'), I declare, Gentlemen, that I shall abstain."[36]

The neo-pacifism expressed or implied by many of the speakers of the Right was most frankly put forward by Senator Desjardins, who, moreover, made no attempt to hide his preference for Franco-German *rapprochement*: "If Germany happened to attack Russia, we would be the ones who have to fight. Consequently, as a rural man representing rural people who have suffered from war—and how much!—I come to declare to you that we will not fight for the Russians (applause at the 'Right'). Every time that France concludes a new pact, cannon and machine guns come nearer to her border. You have entered a blind alley and the Soviet pact will wall you in. . . ."[37]

Ideological rather than realistic factors appear to have been preponderant in determining the new pacifism of the Right in March, 1936. It may be that the French people were not psychologically prepared for a showdown with the Reich; nevertheless, the fact that their Nationalist leaders had been preaching neo-pacifism for months and did not even attempt to out-

[36] *JO. S.*, p. 254; MM. Armbruster and de Blois also made allusions to giving Germany a free hand in Eastern Europe (pp. 262, 267).
[37] *Ibid.*, pp. 266 f.

line the gravity of the remilitarization of the Rhineland to the public, not to speak of recommending a firm stand, is difficult to justify on the grounds of ignorance, sincere abhorrence for war, fear of defeat, or "realistic" interpretation of France's best interests. Only the growing importance of ideological factors, of class fears and prejudices in the determination of foreign policy furnishes a plausible explanation for the dangerous policy evolved by the majority of the Right since the beginning of the Italo-Ethiopian War. The acceptance of the *Drang nach Osten* by some and the dangerous compromise of others who refused to take the necessary risks involved in an effective anti-German policy could only lead to abdication or to half-hearted and inefficacious resistance, and, ultimately, to defeat.

PART III

FROM NEO-PACIFISM TO APPEASEMENT
(1936-1938)

CHAPTER VII

SPAIN AND THE INTERNATIONAL CIVIL WAR

THE RIGHT, now baptized the Front National, tried to capitalize on their anti-Marxism and neo-pacifism during the general elections of April and May. Their electoral campaign stressed the two great dangers that would threaten the country should a Popular Front government be elected: social revolution and war.[1] In spite of these forebodings, however, the success of the Rassemblement populaire[2] was received without surprise or undue alarm by the press of the Right.[3] The demagogues, it was declared with sadistic pleasure, would now have to show what they could do.[4] De Kerillis wrote in *L'Echo de Paris* on May 5: "The *Nationaux* would be wrong, from my point of view, to take the responsibility of agitation. The country has voted 'Popular Front.' It wanted the experience and must of necessity undergo it. In fact, this is the only way to make it suffer regret quickly. Their opposition must be firm and constant, but essentially legal."[5]

[1] Cf. *L'Echo de Paris*, March 23, 1936; *Le Temps*, May 3, 1936. The issue of foreign policy was so important that the neo-pacifists of the Right even attacked the Traditional Nationalists (attacks on Reynaud, "the little traitor," and on Mandel and Buré by *L'Action Française*, April 23, May 1, 2, 1936). In domestic politics the parties of the "Right" and "Center" advocated order and authority (a stronger executive) and reform of the suffrage, while the Left put the emphasis on the Fascist menace and on the economic program of the Rassemblement populaire (40-hour week, paid vacations, wheat office, reform of the Bank of France, nationalization of munition factories). This program is described in Alexander Werth's *Which Way France?* (New York, 1937), pp. 233-237.

[2] The elections were held on April 26 and May 3. The Front National lost 178,419 votes and 37 seats in the Chamber; the Front Populaire gained 434,248 votes and 40 seats. The Communist party was responsible for these gains; their votes jumped from 796,630 in 1932 to 1,453,923 in 1936, an increase of almost 100 per cent. The Socialist vote was stationary, and the Radical-Socialists lost almost one fourth of their following in the preceding elections. The electoral coalition of these three parties worked to the advantage of the Socialists, who gained 20 seats in the Chamber, and of the Communists, who saw their representatives pass from 12 to 72; the Radical-Socialists, on the other hand, lost 48 seats. See Appendix, composition of the Chamber in 1936, p. 237.

[3] *Le Temps*, RP, May 5, 1936.   [4] *Ibid.*, May 6, 1936.

[5] Only the sheets of the Extreme Right predicted a *"crise de régime"* (*Le Jour*,

Most Rightists, although worried by the electoral successes of the Extreme Left and especially of the Communists, seem to have been reassured concerning the danger of social revolution by the presence of the bourgeois Radical-Socialists in the Popular Front. They knew that this party actually held the balance of power between the conservative Right and the Marxists, and that it would put the brakes on too radical experiments.[6] In fact, the Popular Front program was reminiscent of a Socialist program of which Herriot said that it reminded him of a restaurant he had once seen which bore the sign: *"Restaurant ouvrier, cuisine bourgeoise."*

The Right advocated strict application of the rules of parliamentary democracy; such a procedure was, of course, all to their advantage as it protected them against the possibility that the new Leftist government might yield to the temptation of exercising dicatorial powers. Thus *Le Temps'* editorial stated on May 18: "France is going to have the government she has chosen. This legal government must be confronted by an opposition which must be not only legal, but scrupulously legalistic. This opposition must enforce constitutional observance to the most rigorous extreme; it must be the more deliberately parliamentary since certain elements of the Popular Front are not."

While the advent of the Popular Front to power did not unduly frighten the Right (the triumph of the Communists was their main source of worry), their alarm was noticeably

---

May 3, 1936) and proposed opposing the will of the *"pays réel"* to the "revolutionary assembly" (*L'Action Française,* May 4, 1936). In *L'Action Française* of April 29, Maurras even wrote that fascism might be the only solution to maintain order if the Communists attempted to gain control of the government, either violently or gradually. See also Pinon, *Revue des Deux Mondes,* May 15, 1936, pp. 474-475.

[6] See Recouly, *Revue de France,* July 15, 1936, p. 375. At the Radical-Socialist Congress at Biarritz in October, 1935, M. Daladier made it plain that his party had nothing in common with Marxism; he emphasized that it defended democratic individualism, in economic as well as in political life, and declared that he was opposed to a planned economy which could only lead to the class dictatorship of a giant bureaucracy. Thus the realization of social progress was to be placed under the aegis of the Declaration of the Rights of Man, with due respect to private property and individual liberty.

increased by the sit-down strikes of May and June, which appeared to a large part of the bourgeoisie as "the great maneuvers for the revolution." The Communist party and the Confédération Générale du Travail were accused of organizing the strikes in order to keep the revolutionary troops in condition while bringing pressure on the future government to adopt as radical a program as possible "by means of a display of force as significant as a warning."[7] On the ninth of June, speaking of the "revolutionary situation,"[8] *Le Temps* declared: "It appears with blinding certitude that the formation of the Popular Front, which was presented as an electoral formation with democratic tendencies, has only served as a screen for an offensive in the grand manner intended to establish the dictatorship of the proletariat in France." René Pinon similarly stated that the strikes were organized by the Communists in order to prove to the government that it was subordinated to organized labor and the Third International;[9] and two weeks later he spoke of the "revolutionary strikes" as a "dress rehearsal for the *grand soir*," and of the "threat of social revolution which is becoming more definite after a first and decisive success."[10]

The debates in the Chamber on June 23 and July 31 reflected the mistrust of the Communists and the growing fear of social revolution. Anti-Marxism manifested itself in foreign policy by the increasing opposition of the Right to the League system of collective security[11] and its corollary, the Franco-Soviet Pact, as well as by the advocacy of *rapprochement* with Italy and even with Germany.[12] After prescribing the Right's cure-all, the return to the Stresa Front, M. Louis Rollin significantly stated:

[7] *Le Temps*, May 30, June 5, 1936.   [8] Cf. also *ibid.*, RP, June 4, 1936.
[9] *Revue des Deux Mondes*, June 1, 1936, p. 955.
[10] *Ibid.*, June 15, 1936, p. 232.
[11] In the debate of June, only Ernest Pezet at the Right defended the policy of collective security of the Blum government. Most speakers advocated the end of sanctions against Italy and the return to the Stresa Front.
[12] Cf. *JO. Ch.*, June 23, 1936: Jean Montigny, pp. 1534-1536; Louis Rollins, pp. 1556 ff.; Alfred Wallach, p. 1547; J. P. Mourer, p. 1562; Michel Walter, p. 1562; Wiedemann-Goiran, p. 1552.

What worries us, Mr. Minister of Foreign Affairs, in regard to settling the German problem, is the position adopted by an important section of your majority, the Communist party. This party wants collective security as it has affirmed many times. We want it too. . . . But we do not agree when the Communist party tries to make our foreign policy subservient to questions of doctrine, class and party, which would separate us from certain nations [Italy and Britain] in order to link us more closely with others [the Soviet Union].

He then alluded to the "international crusade" against fascism and urged the government to follow an "objective policy" similar to that of England.[13]

Not only did Resigned Nationalists, like Montigny, continue to warn the Chamber of the danger coming from the Third International, but even De Kerillis, while expressing his apprehension of German ambitions and advocating the creation of a motorized, offensive army, made the startling statement: "We will accept the Franco-Soviet Pact when there are no longer seventy-two Russian deputies on the benches of the French Chamber."[14]   Paul Reynaud also declared that the pact did not bring France all the advantages that it should because of the identity of the Third International and the Russian Government, which exposed France to the accusation of being the "brilliant second" of the Soviets, and because of Moscow's intrusion in the domestic and political life of France. He added, referring to the sit-down strikes, that the government was following the dangerous policy of appealing to the "plebiscite of the masses" rather than accepting the normal functions of the parliamentary system and that, unless it did so, the Franco-Soviet Pact would justly be criticized both abroad and in France.[15]

The Spanish Civil War, which broke out in July, 1936, added still further to the anxiety aroused in Rightist circles by the success of the Popular Front and by the wave of sit-

[13] JO. Ch., p. 1558.
[14] Ibid., p. 1544.   [15] Ibid., July 31, 1936, p. 2307

down strikes. It was not surprising that the French Right
should have sided with General Franco as the champion of
the forces of "Order" against the forces of "Revolution" represented by the Spanish Government. In their eyes the civil war
was "a formidable struggle between the two Spains: that of
the People's Revolution, in power since the elections of last
February, and that of the Counter-Revolution, which groups
all the forces hostile to the regime, from the Moderate Republicans to the former Carlists. . . ."[16]

It is significant that the Spanish Loyalists were not represented by the press of the Right as a republican government
fighting a Fascist rebellion, but as a coalition of anti-Fascist
forces dominated by the Communists. "In this paradoxical
alliance between the bourgeois parties on the one hand and the
Socialists and the Communists on the other [the Spanish
Popular Front]," wrote Raymond Recouly, "it is, as always,
the most radical elements that pull and direct the team. In
order not to break this alliance, the moderates are constantly
obliged to yield to the revolutionaries. . . ."[17] "This government," he wrote later, ". . . has not hesitated, in order to resist
its powerful adversaries, to put itself entirely and definitely
into the hands of the Communists, who have everywhere, at
Madrid, at Barcelona, at Malaga, applied their theories and
their system immediately. The government has thus abdi-
cated to the extremists the little authority and credit that it
still had. Under these conditions," he concluded, "to aid the
government of Madrid is to furnish arms to communism, to
permit it to establish itself firmly in Spain."[18] Therefore, by
identifying the Spanish Government with its extreme Leftist

[16] *Le Temps*, BJ, July 24, 1936.

[17] *Revue de France*, Aug. 15, 1936, p. 723.

[18] *Ibid.*, p. 727. Pinon expressed this same conception of the Spanish Government, which was generally entertained by the Right, in the *Revue des Deux
Mondes* on Aug. 1 (p. 716): "If it is the government that prevails, it will be in
the hands of the Communists and the workers whom it has imprudently armed,
and Spain will become a Soviet country, prey to the most bloody repression. That
would make a very dangerous neighbor for France." See also St. Brice, *Revue
Universelle*, Aug. 15, 1936, p. 482; Le Grix, *Revue Hebdomadaire*, Aug. 8, 1936,
pp. 249-251.

component—a minority at that—the Right found the justification for their pro-Franco attitude.[19]

Of course, the events of July, 1936, in Spain—the anti-Catholic and anticapitalist excesses—also played an important part in bringing the Catholic bourgeoisie of France to sympathize with the rebels against the "revolutionaries." As M. Paul Vignaux wrote in his study of the foreign policy of the French Catholics: "Even in France the 'horrors of Barcelona' have determined the pro-Franco position of the mass of believers. Paul Claudel has expressed this attitude in a poem. Even in the summer of 1936 as ardent a democrat as M. Gay explained the impossibility for Christians to give their support to a republic that did not disavow the worst anti-ecclesiastical outrages." M. Vignaux went on to declare that the vital factor in determining the attitude of the Catholics was the assimilation of the Spanish Rebellion to an anti-Communist crusade, a conception that was cleverly encouraged by the propaganda of the Fascist states. According to him, only a relatively small minority of the Catholics—some intellectuals like Jacques Maritain, François Mauriac, and Georges Bernanos, and the organs of liberal Catholicism such as *L'Aube*—refused to be regimented into the *"parti de la Croisade"* and defended mediation between the Rebels and the Spanish Government.[20] The great majority, however, followed the lead of the *Grande Presse* in siding with General Franco and defending the policy of nonintervention which best served the interests of the *Nationaux*.[21]

[19] Pierre Dominique, although himself a champion of nonintervention in Spain, wrote in *L'Europe Nouvelle* (Aug. 8, 1936, p. 799): "The French Conservateurs [Extreme Right] have made their choice. From hate of Marxism and revolutionary syndicalism, they declare that they are the friends, the sympathizers of the generals Franco, Mola, Queipo de Llano; and not only the Conservateurs, but most of the *Modérés*. The big *journaux d'information*, which they control, and which have the art of knowing how to present things, present them in a light favorable to the insurgents."

[20] "Les Catholiques français et la politique étrangère," *Politique Etrangère,* Sept. 5, 1938, p. 453; see also Jacques Maritain, *Foreign Affairs,* Jan., 1942.

[21] "Neutrality is, in the present circumstances, nothing but a blockade of the Spanish Government. To blockade governmental Spain is to help the Rebels,

The ardent compaign for neutrality in the Rightist press was increased by the Communists' advocacy of intervention on behalf of the Loyalists (a policy which was also urged by a section of the Socialist party and the C. G. T.), and by the indecisive attitude of the Blum government during July and August. The papers of the Right spoke of the "duty of neutrality"[22] and declared that the best interests of France were served by nonintervention, since otherwise she would find only herself on the side of Soviet Russia in an international civil war between the "Nations of Order" and the "Proletarian Countries."[23] This campaign was doubtless aimed at influencing the decision of the government toward intervention in Spain, but it was continued even after the cabinet, by officially stating France's neutral position, had partly reassured the Right.[24] It was then directed almost exclusively against the Third International: the Communists' demand for intervention on behalf of the Loyalists, as well as the military help given Madrid by the Soviets, was naturally interpreted by the Right as a proof of the bellicose intentions of the Russian Government and the Third International.[25] The argument that Moscow was obviously trying to bring France into a war with the Fascist countries was frequently used in the press of the Extreme Right. Typical was Pierre Gaxotte's declaration in *Candide* on July 30 that "French intervention in the Spanish Civil War would be the beginning of the European conflagration wanted by Moscow. . . . The Soviets, as a matter of fact, are condemned to perish, choked in the Nippo-German vise,

---

since they are assured of the efficacious help of those who undertake the Fascist crusade" (*L'Humanité*, Aug. 18, 1936).

[22] *Le Temps*, July 26, 1936; *L'Action Française*, Aug. 2, 1936; *Le Figaro*, Aug. 2, 1936.

[23] *Le Journal*, Aug. 2, 1936; *Le Temps*, RP, Aug. 4, 1936; *L'Action Française*, Aug. 2, 1936.

[24] Yvon Delbos, *JO. Ch.*, July 31, 1936, p. 2328. The policy of nonintervention was proposed by France on August 2; however, the speech of Léon Blum at Luna Park on September 6, stating the neutrality of France in Spain, did not convince the Extreme Right of his sincerity; see *Revue Universelle*, Oct. 1, 1936, pp. 101-112; *Revue Hebdomadaire*, Sept. 12, 1936, p. 247.

[25] *Le Temps*, Aug. 12, 17, 1936; *Revue de France*, Dec. 15, 1936, pp. 730-731.

if they do not very shortly provoke an Occidental war which will free their frontiers and plunge Europe into bloody chaos. . . ." The same accusation was also made in the press of the *Modérés*. It was explained that the "Komintern's authority over the French Communist party had been recently reinforced," in order to prepare for "the gigantic struggle of the proletarian states against the dictatorial states, which the events in Spain may cause to burst forth any day."[26]

Thus, in the eyes of the Right, Spain was the battlefield between two ideologies represented by two groups of nations. This struggle, however, was not between fascism and democracy, but between anti-Communist and pro-Communist forces.[27] There can be little doubt that the sympathy of the French bourgeoisie had been gained by the crusade against communism organized by Germany.[28] "M. Hitler has presented himself as the champion of order against disorder," Paul Reynauld told the Chamber. "This propaganda, Gentlemen, has succeeded. It has succeeded among others, and to a large degree, among ourselves."[29] M. Recouly explained the reasons for this anti-Bolshevist stand in the *Revue de France:*

In all the countries where communism is not to be feared, notably among the Anglo-Saxon peoples, no one wants to hear this crusade mentioned, for it seems useless and even dangerous.

It is quite otherwise in the nations where Communist propaganda is redoubtable, above all in France. The fear of revolutionary troubles—not at all imaginary—the perspective of a general strike under cover of which the attack would be made against the Republic, all that seems to many of our compatriots as near possi-

[26] Pinon, *Revue des Deux Mondes*, Sept. 1, 1936, p. 232.

[27] *Revue des Deux Mondes*, Sept. 1, 1936, p. 238; see also *Revue de France*, Dec. 15, 1936, pp. 729-730; *Revue Universelle*, Oct. 1, 1936; p. 103; *Revue Hebdomadaire*, Aug. 1, 1936, p. 118; Dec. 5, 1936, p. 123.

[28] *Revue des Deux Mondes*, Nov. 1, 1936, p. 238; Nov. 15, 1936, pp. 471-480; Dec. 1, 1936, p. 717; *Revue Universelle*, July 1, 1936, p. 93; Sept. 15, 1936, p. 744; Oct. 1, 1936, pp. 103-104; Dec. 15, 1936, p. 668; *Revue Hebdomadaire*, Aug. 1, 1936, p. 118; Sept. 12, 1936, p. 247; also cf. Jacques Bardoux, *J'accuse Moscou* (Paris, 1936), pp. 33-36; W. d'Ormesson, *Le Communisme, c'est la guerre* (Paris, 1936).

[29] *JO. Ch.*, Dec. 5, 1936, p. 3323.

bilities. This very serious risk seems to them to dominate all others.

Thus they begin to feel anger, a growing fury against Russia, as the first and principal cause of this evil.[30]

But the reaction of the Right to the Spanish war was not purely negative or based solely on fear of socialism. The outcome of the struggle, they believed, would indirectly determine the future regime of France and, therefore, the ultimate triumph or defeat of fascism in Europe. As M. Le Grix explained to his readers in the *Revue Hebdomadaire,* a victory of the Soviets in Spain would mean communism in Paris, but the triumph of Franco might mean "the hour of French regeneration."[31]

It must be emphasized, however, that the danger of a new "religious war" was pointed out not only by the Rightist leaders but also by many at the Left, who apparently either put their love for peace above their ideological preferences, or were already drawn by their anti-Marxism to the side of fascism, or adhered to the belief that France had been made incapable of action by internal division. Marcel Déat, still a prominent member of the Popular Front, wrote in *L'Europe Nouvelle:* "If France appeared as the champion of another totalitarian system, there would be danger of war immediately. Europe is overanxious to organize herself into two camps. When Sovietism meets Hitlerism, there is a metaphysical shock which foreshadows the physical shock. . . . If France seems to be the ally of fascism, half the people at least will not march. If France becomes the soldier of Stalin, the other half will not want to have anything to do with it."[32] M. Yvon Delbos, the foreign minister of the Blum Government, spoke of his efforts to stop the division of Europe into two opposing blocs of nations and of "the long horror of religious wars." He declared that "we do not want to see them reborn (loud applause), whether for or against democracy, for or against

[30] Dec. 15, 1936, p. 731.   [31] Aug. 8, 1936, pp. 249-250.
[32] *L'Europe Nouvelle,* July 25, 1936, p. 755; see also Gaston Bergery, *JO. Ch.,* July 31, 1936, pp. 2315 ff.

fascism, for or against communism."[33]   Again in the debate of December 4, 1936, this Popular Front minister spoke of the "spirit of propaganda and crusade, whose growing virulence tends to divide Europe into two enemy camps," of "religious war," and of the "generalized civil war" which might result from the Spanish tragedy.[34] Thus the attitude of the Right toward the Rebels cannot be a subject of astonishment, since many Leftists and the Popular Front government itself accepted a position of neutrality.

The Right, of course, played upon this apprehension of a "generalized civil war" to defend their policy of nonintervention in Spain, which well suited their own class and ideological interests. Their fear of war, although based on different grounds, seems, however, to have been as genuine as that of the pacifist Left. It even threatened to make them forget the second element of the situation: the struggle for the domination of Europe; and this was undoubtedly the aim of Germany's timely and successfully organized anti-Communist crusade.

The postwar balance of forces in Europe had been radically disturbed by the entente between Germany and Italy, which began with the Austro-German Pact of July 11, 1936, unopposed by Italy,[35] and the Italo-German collaboration in Spain; it was made official by the formation of the Rome-Berlin Axis on October 25, 1936. Thus another blow had been given to the system of collective security, which had until then been implemented by the overwhelming military superiority of the victors over the defeated nations. Now, in the second half of 1936, the Italo-German *rapprochement* threatened to

[33] *JO. Ch.*, July 31, 1936, p. 2328.   [34] *Ibid.*, p. 3327.

[35] Italy belonged to the have-not countries; Fascist dynamism and Italian imperialism could not be satisfied with the preservation of the *status quo*. By the nature of her claims, most of them could be satisfied only at the expense of France. Only the fear of an Austro-German union had made her willing temporarily to relinquish her claims in order to gain France's support against Germany. After the pact of July 11, a step toward the *Anschluss* which was accepted by Italy, it was evident that she had already chosen between a pro-French and a pro-German policy.

create a powerful revisionist bloc in Central Europe, while at the same time the Spanish Civil War tended to bring about a realignment of powers on an ideological basis.

The former coalition of *status quo* powers, which in the first half of 1935 included both Italy and the U.S.S.R., was split in two by the question of intervention in the Spanish Civil War, to the obvious advantage of the revisionist group. France had had the choice of intervening in Spain on the side of Soviet Russia or of following England's lead in taking a neutral position. By choosing this latter course, the French Government had not only determined upon a policy of neutrality in Spain, but had also renounced for some time to come the most effective method of insuring the security of Central and Eastern Europe: it had become psychologically impossible for the noninterventionist Popular Front government to reinforce the Franco-Soviet Pact by a military agreement without appearing to enter the international civil war on the side of Soviet Russia. This step would have caused the dangerous opposition of the British Government and a clamorous uproar by the French conservatives. The noninterventionist stand in Spain may consequently be interpreted as leading to a neutral position in Eastern Europe as well; at any rate, it offered the temptation of following the British in a policy of noncommitment in Central and Eastern Europe and letting Nazi Germany and Soviet Russia fight it out by themselves.

The intervention of the Fascist states on the side of the Rebels in Spain was of great immediate importance for France, for her security would be jeopardized by the creation of a third front on the Pyrenees. The ideal for the Right would of course have been what M. de Kerillis suggested—that the French Government side with General Franco, thus cutting the ground from under the feet of his German and Italian backers. Since, however, this action could not be expected from a Popular Front government (notwithstanding M. Taittinger's statement that "M. Franco has never concealed his republican sentiments"),[36] the Right chose as an alternative

[36] *JO. Ch.*, Dec. 5, 1936, p. 3356.

to assume outwardly a strictly neutral attitude.   Yet by denouncing the French Government in the press and in Parliament for the alleged sending of planes and shipments of war
materials, a section of the French Right played directly into
the hands of the totalitarian powers.   M. Brosselette, writing in
L'Europe Nouvelle, accused them of furnishing Germany and
Italy with excuses for their intervention in Spain by charg-
ing the French Government with secretly sending airplanes
to the Spanish Republicans.   "Rarely, indeed, has irrespon-
sibility been pushed to this point.   The peak, which seemed
to have been attained during the Ethiopian affair, has been
surpassed.   This time it is not against Ethiopia that a foreign
power is being aided; it is against France herself that Germany and Italy are being excited."[37]

The ideological bias of the Right led them to risk France's
security, not only in regard to Spain, but also in regard to
Central and Eastern Europe.   The failures of the League of
Nations in 1935 and 1936 and the new Italo-German collaboration had entirely discredited the old system of collective
security.   A more realistic foreign policy had to be formulated
in order to maintain the boundaries of the peace treaties.   The
last defenders of the League at the Right had by the end of
1936 abandoned any hope in its efficacy.   In the Chamber M.
Ernest Pezet, who had supported the League as late as June
23, 1936,[38] admitted on December 5 that he had given up
hope in its ability to guarantee European stability.[39]   M. Paul
Reynaud reached the conclusion in December, 1936, that
France had only one choice left: to strengthen her pact with
Russia by a military agreement, or to accept a *rapprochement*
with Germany.[40]   In the new situation created by the collaboration between Germany and Italy he still advocated a close
entente with England.   "But," he added, "the assistance that
England can give us on land during a short war is limited.

[37] Aug. 8, 1936, p. 795.   [38] See above, p. 110 n.
[39] *JO. Ch.,* pp. 3352, 3362; Flandin, *ibid.,* p. 3359.
[40] Compare with his speech of July 31, in favor of effective collective security
(*JO. Ch.,* pp. 2306-2308).

And the war may be short.   Therefore, Gentlemen, we have
the choice between two policies: either to seek a general agreement with Germany or to make our pact with Russia efficacious
from the military point of view.   I do not see any other
choice possible."[41]   Reynaud considered a Franco-German
rapprochement impossible, since France could not enter into
conversations with Germany at the expense of any other nation
whatsoever.   Nor was a military pact with Russia possible,
according to him, as long as the government depended upon
Communist support in order to achieve a majority.   "You
yourselves feel profoundly—for you know the public opinion
of our country well—," he said, "that our people, always so
jealous and even suspicious of their independence where
foreigners are concerned, will never allow a government . . .
depending for its daily life upon the vote of men who rely
upon the Third International to carry out such a policy."
He thus indicated that the elimination of the Communists from
the governmental majority would be necessary to permit a
policy of collaboration with the U.S.S.R.

The choice between Berlin and Moscow, thus frankly presented by M. Reynaud, appears now as obvious as it was then
difficult to face.   After the new alignment of Italy and Germany, the only powers that could join with France in efficacious opposition to the revisionist group were Great Britain and
Soviet Russia, if it is admitted that Poland's position was
dubious and the Little Entente incapable of effectively resisting the new Italo-German bloc.[42]   Great Britain, however, was
still not convinced of the desirability of defending Central and
Eastern Europe; in any case her military help, as Reynaud indicated, would have been insufficient.   In the last analysis, collective security in Europe could be insured only by a Franco-
Russian military agreement.

As has been shown, the Right was determined to oppose
any such reinforcement of the Franco-Soviet Pact.   Their
dilemma was illustrated by Wladimir d'Ormesson in a pam-

[41] *JO. Ch.*, Dec. 5, 1936, p. 3323.
[42] King Leopold had announced Belgium's policy of neutrality on October 14.

phlet written in 1936 and subtitled *Le Communisme, c'est la guerre*. A year before the author had stated that the "vital instinct of France is necessarily opposed to Germany," and that "the only peril that is constant and redoubtable for her is the German one."[43]   Now, however, in view of the electoral triumph of the Extreme Left in France, and their position in the Spanish Civil War, he affirmed that the Communist problem had become paramount. He explained that there was the possibility of revolution in France, that the new situation had brought about a real upheaval of "psychopolitical international factors."   According to him, "problems exclusively concerning foreign policy could no longer be separated from purely social ones. . . ."[44]   Germany "is taking full advantage of the Communist question, which since the French elections and the events in Spain have dominated European preoccupations, in order to place all the European problems upon the plane of order and disorder, of bolshevism and antibolshevism. France's thoughtlessness . . . has led her to the very edge of this deadly snare."[45]   She had been dragged by Germany into a "terrible dilemma," and would have to choose between close collaboration with the U.S.S.R. and complete abandonment of the latter.   The first alternative would mean war under the worst conditions, since the enemy would appear as the champion of order against revolution, and the second would mean abdication to Germany.   It was necessary to get out of this "intolerable alternative, a pro-Soviet war or capitulation in Europe," and to clarify the equivocal situation in which "the champions of European order [France] appear as the allies of disorder and revolution [U.S.S.R.] and in which the adversaries of European order [Germany] appear as the ramparts of social order."[46]   D'Ormesson's conclusion was that France should get rid of the Popular Front government and

[43] *Le Temps,* July 27, 1935.

[44] *Op. cit.,* pp. 23-24.   See also his *France,* pp. 184 ff., and Jacques Bardoux's pamphlets: *Les Soviets contre la France, J'accuse Moscou, Le Chaos espagnol, Staline contre l'Europe,* and his *L'Ordre nouveau: face au communisme et au racisme* (Paris, 1939), pp. 171 ff.   Also: Fabre-Luce, *Le Secret de la république,* pp. 73 ff.

[45] P. 35.   [46] Pp. 34 f.

then start a policy toward Germany that would be both "realistic" and "chivalrous"; by this he meant an understanding with a Germany that would not ask for either *le tête à tête* or *le corps à corps,* but would be contented to exercise "normal" influence in Central and Eastern Europe.[47]

The Rightist press, as well as the parliamentary debates, reflected this position of the conservative bourgeoisie, pressed between the menace of Pan-Germanism and the fear of a Russian alliance. Illustrative of the indecisive attitude of the Conditional Nationalists were the articles by René Pinon in the *Revue des Deux Mondes* from June to December, 1936. He alternately pointed to the German and the Bolshevist danger, apparently incapable of establishing an order of priority between them. According to him, the "spectre of Communism" was both an easy pretext for German rearmament and ambition, and a tragic reality. Of the anti-Communist front formed by Germany, Japan, and Italy, he wrote that it was a "legitimate aim" to oppose communism, but that it "also corresponds to a complete plan, less praiseworthy and more disturbing, of European domination."[48]

A foreign policy dependent upon the British position of noncommitment toward Central and Eastern Europe was a logical, although dangerous, alternative to the Berlin-Moscow dilemma. It would in reality have been only a disguised policy of laissez faire in the East, made respectable by the British example. Such a policy was defended in the Chamber at the end of 1936 only by Pierre-Etienne Flandin, who was most careful not to uncover its real meaning. Although pretending to oppose Germany's advance in Eastern Europe, he warned the Chamber against the "tragic dupery where we would risk giving our blood in return for a simple moral encouragement."[49] Since collective security no longer existed, he added, France alone should not keep on protecting the rest of Europe against Germany. By stating that France and Great Britain

[47] Pp. 42 ff.
[48] Dec. 1, 1936, p. 117; cf. issue of Dec. 15, 1936, pp. 153-156.
[49] JO. Ch., Dec. 5, 1936, p. 3359.

could not have two different conceptions of their obligations toward the League, Flandin hinted that France should follow the English policy of noncommitment in Central and Eastern Europe; he then emphasized the advantage of Franco-British neutrality. "Franco-British cooperation would constitute the essential guarantee of peace. In fact, it permits the reduction to much less menacing proportions of the ideological conflict between the two totalitarian blocs, of which the two great Western democracies are, when united, the incontestable arbiters."[50] He accompanied these declarations, however, with denials that he was defending a policy of retrenchment. It was only a year later that he openly became the chief advocate of this policy.[51]

Significantly, the sole foreign policy advocated by the other Rightist deputies in December, 1936, was that of the stubborn and vain hope in the possibility of reconstructing the Stresa Front.[52] This hope had apparently not been stifled by the Austro-German agreement of July 11, nor by the Italo-German collaboration in Spain, nor even by the formation of the Rome-Berlin Axis. While the Austro-German agreement had been greeted by the Right as a serious blow to collective security and to the *status quo* of the treaties,[53] yet it was not believed that Mussolini had definitely gone over to the German side; he was supposed to be following an opportunist policy, and in any case never to allow Hitler to realize the *Anschluss*.[54] Despite Italo-German collaboration in Spain and Mussolini's reference to the Rome-Berlin Axis in his speech at Milan on November 10, M. René Pinon expressed what seems to have still been the general opinion of the

[50] *Ibid.*   [51] See below, pp. 140-142.

[52] *JO. Ch.*, Dec. 5, 1936; Ybarnégaray, p. 3346; Felix Grat, p. 3362; Pezet, p. 3362; Marin, pp. 3348, 3349; Taittinger, p. 3357.

[53] "The whole political system created by the treaties that mark the end of the Great War is crumbling. The League of Nations has no longer any reality. . . . Europe, whether we wish it or not, is returning little by little to her prewar condition, to the system of alliances and ententes" (*Le Temps*, BJ, July 18, 1936).

[54] Recouly, *Revue de France*, Aug. 1, 1936, pp. 546 ff.; cf. Pinon, *Revue des Deux Mondes*, Aug. 1, 1936, p. 719; St. Brice, *Revue Universelle*, Aug. 1, 1936, p. 356.

Right when he wrote: "M. Mussolini is not at all ignorant of the future peril to him represented by the Teutonic power in Europe, and one may consider it a certainty that he has avoided and will avoid tying his hands; he wants to keep his liberty of movement for a reversion of his policies that might seem profitable."[55]

The return to Stresa was not only a pious hope, but apparently the only convenient or even conceivable exit from the Berlin-Moscow dilemma. Since neither a policy of a free hand to Germany in Eastern Europe nor a military pact with Russia was acceptable to most Rightists, and since Great Britain was unwilling and unable to join France in insuring the security of Central and Eastern Europe, it was evident that only Italy could bring the necessary help for the maintenance of the *status quo*. The fact that Italian assistance was not likely to materialize was perhaps of secondary importance in the minds of many, as long as the hope in Franco-Italian *rapprochement* could be used as an alternative to the Russian military alliance and made the Right appear as faithful defenders of their traditional foreign policy. Another advantage in advocating a return to Stresa was that the door would be kept open to a possible *rapprochement* with Germany, or at least to the conclusion of a four power pact, with Italy as useful go-between. Whatever motives might have prompted the Right to cleave to the hope-in-Stresa policy, it was a convenient excuse that was to be used until the very end.

It became apparent, however, that for many the alternative to the reconstruction of the Stresa Front would not be the Russian alliance, but a policy of retrenchment for France, since she was incapable of insuring alone the security of all against Germany. Thus M. Recouly, after remarking sadly that Italy seemed to have left Germany a free hand in Central Europe and that England would take no responsibility there, wrote in the *Revue de France*:

[55] *Revue des Deux Mondes*, Nov. 15, 1936, p. 475.

There remains our country. But could she, would she alone undertake a war to save Austrian independence? Her present condition, her prestige, her authority—they are not increasing in strength; the facts, alas, prove it—would make very difficult for her a direct intervention that would find Germany and Italy facing her in close collaboration.

And what is true about Austria is much more so about Czechoslovakia.[56]

The struggle of Germany and Soviet Russia in Spain inevitably led the Right to aloofness from Eastern European affairs. The ideological war between fascism and bolshevism had become paramount, too often relegating the question of national security into the dim background. It became more and more necessary to accept one of the alternatives: German expansion, with its mortal risks for France, or alliance with Russia, which the Communist participation in the government made unpalatable to even determined patriots like M. Reynaud.

To many, the choice between these two foreign policies was, in the final analysis, the choice between a Fascist or a Socialist regime for France. Dread of one extreme led to the other; even the timid and the opportunist were drawn to the revolution which they feared least.

The electoral success of the Communists and the revolutionary events in Spain appear to have induced an important section of the *Modérés* to rally to the side of the Counter-Revolution, by a defensive reflex rather than by profound conviction. Just as the Fascist scare following the riots of February 6, 1934, had brought about a growth of the parties of the Extreme Left, the Marxist scare of 1936 apparently brought on a real strengthening of the authoritarian parties,

[56] May 15, 1937, p. 351. Typical of this attitude of Resigned Nationalism is the following quotation from the *Bulletin Quotidien* (Sept. 2, 1936), organ of the Comité des forges et des houillères: "In the face of this conflict [between Hitler and Stalin], whose military operations are momentarily limited to Spain, it is necessary for France to remain neutral. . . . France cannot consider hurling her sons against the fortifications of the Rhineland zone in the vain hope of bringing help to the Soviet dictatorship. . . ." The conclusion was that *rapprochement* with Germany was both necessary and possible.

the heirs of the former Leagues, in spite of or because of their less spectacular achievements and less revolutionary programs.

While the Extreme Right temperamentally approached fascism,[57] the majority of the *Modérés,* with their emphasis upon economic interests rather than upon a political ideology, had little inclination toward its collectivist element, and could only accept it as the lesser of two evils. "A real bourgeois cannot be Fascist unless the Communist menace becomes so pressing that it takes from him all freedom of action and all liberty of choice."[58]   This political shift is precisely what seems to have happened in France after 1936. The growth of the quasi-Fascist parties, the successors of the leagues that had been prohibited by the Popular Front government, and the new character and new following of the Parti Social Français (the former Croix de Feu) seem to justify this thesis.

The figures showing the enormous growth of the P. S. F. from one million in April, 1936 (the membership of the Croix de Feu) to more than two million a year later cannot be accepted without reservation,[59] but they quite possibly indicate the approximate percentage of increase. The new party's change of methods would explain this rapid growth to a great extent; it seems that the P. S. F. gained in membership what it lost in violence. The evolution of the Croix de Feu toward "legalism" had started on December 6, 1935, with the famous scene of reconciliation at the Chamber when M. Ybarnégaray, the mouthpiece of Colonel de la Rocque, agreed to the dissolution of its paramilitary formations. From that time on, it

[57] Of the three essential elements of fascism—nationalism, dictatorship, and collectivism—the first two were already part of the doctrines of the Extreme Right, and the third was accepted to some extent soon after the triumph of fascism in Italy (Maxence, *Histoire de dix ans,* pp. 156 ff.). Although originally very different, aristocratic traditionalism and revolutionary totalitarianism came, especially after 1934, to follow parallel courses, and the first was led to borrow from the second its collectivist element in order to keep up with the times.

[58] Emmanual Berl, *Frère bourgeois, mourez-vous? Ding! Ding! Dong!* p. 43.

[59] *Le Temps,* Sept. 6, 1937; *L'Europe Nouvelle,* May 19, 1937, p. 315; in *Sciences Politiques* (Aug., 1937, p. 213), M. Charles Vallin affirmed that "in less than a year the P. S. F. has become the first party in France by the number of followers. It outranks by far the Communist and Socialist parties. It is in front of the Marxist bloc, the only mass party which claims allegiance to the tricolor."

apparently lost extremist elements while gaining the sympathies of many *Modérés*.[60]   In spite of its failure to "arbitrate"
the general elections, the P. S. F. continued to gain members
among the *bien pensants,* or moderate elements, of the bourgeoisie by the modification of its program and methods, and
the abandonment of its "Fascist romanticism" and "methods
of violence."[61]

The new tactics of Colonel de la Rocque appear to have
been the adoption of a program noncommittal and attractive
enough to gain the confidence of the majority of the French
electorate.   This aim was clearly admitted in the declaration
of the National Congress of the P. S. F. in December, 1936;[62]
and while the party's refusal to be classified either with the
Right or with the Left may be interpreted as an indication
of Fascist unanimism, it also showed a desire to gain the support of the majority of the people.[63]   Moreover, La Rocque's
refusal to join the Front de la Liberté, which had been created
by the Fascist leader of the Parti Populaire Français, Jacques
Doriot, in order to unite the whole Right in an anti-Marxist
crusade, illustrated the new policy of the P. S. F.: to gain the
support of the moderate elements of the Right rather than
the *Extrémistes,* who were thus thrown into Doriot's party.
In this connection, it is significant to note that only the parties
and groups of the parliamentary "Right" agreed to participate
in the Front de la Liberté, while those of the "Center" followed the P. S. F. in refusing to join.[64]

The marked resentment with which the Extreme Right

[60] Alexander Werth, *Foreign Affairs,* Oct., 1936, p. 149.

[61] Berl, *Frère bourgeois,* pp. 47-48.

[62] A manifesto in December, 1936, declared the party "firmly attached to the
republican liberties, the culminating achievement of France's glorious history which
excludes a Fascist dictatorship, Hitlerian absolutism and the inhuman enslavement
of Soviet Marxism."   Cf. Charles Vallin, *Sciences Politiques,* Aug., 1937, p. 217;
also the pamphlet of the P. S. F., *Une mystique, un programme.*

[63] François Veuillot, *La Rocque et son parti* (Paris, 1938), p. 57; also *Le Petit
Journal,* March 20, 1938.

[64] The Fédération Républicaine, the Parti Républicain National et Social of
Taittinger, and the Parti Agraire joined the Front de la Liberté; the Démocrates
Populaires and the Alliance Démocratique refused. Cf. *L'Europe Nouvelle,* May 29,
1937, p. 515; *Sciences Politiques,* April, 1938, p. 125.

greeted the new policy of Colonel de la Rocque was most interesting. Le Grix quoted a declaration of the political bureau of the P. S. F. with much disgust: "The P. S. F., a party legally constituted, intends to carry on a work of public safety within the framework of the republican institutions and not to allow the menaced democratic liberties to be impaired. . . . So," he commented, "it is a question of touching nothing that exists, of mounting guard about this nothing, this rotten nothing that is our regime. Well, France wants to change it."[65] Moreover, in July, 1937, a coalition of the pro-Doriot *Extrémistes* under the leadership of André Tardieu, who had become the great critic of the French parliamentary system, started a compaign of slander[66] against Colonel de la Rocque in order to compromise and ruin him politically—to the benefit of his competitor of the Extreme Right.[67]

Colonel de la Rocque seems to have been partly successful in his attempt to gain the support of the *bien pensants;* Mr. Alexander Werth remarked: "Conservatives, reactionaries, Croix de Feu, had come to mean practically the same thing. Did it mean that the Right had gone Fascist, or that the Croix de Feu had simply gone conservative? Actually, there was an element of truth in both."[68] Whatever the exact membership of the new authoritarian parties of La Rocque and Doriot, it seems certain that they attracted a large percentage of the old parliamentary parties of the Right and that they marked a shift away from the republican ideal that had been outwardly defended by the *Modérés.*

Significantly, M. Pierre-Etienne Flandin, who until then had been, at least to all appearances, one of the most vigorous champions of the parliamentary system at the Right,[69] stated

[65] *Revue Hebdomadaire*, Oct. 17, 1936, p. 371. See also Maxence, *Histoire de dix ans,* pp. 314 ff.

[66] This campaign was supported by *L'Action Française, Le Jour, La Liberté, Gringoire,* and *Choc.*

[67] Cf. "Casimir's Downfall," *Living Age,* Nov., 1937, p. 230; *Nation,* Feb. 5, 1938, p. 152.   [68] *Foreign Affairs,* Oct., 1936, p. 142.

[69] Cf. *Le Temps,* Nov. 18, 1935, Thirtieth Congress of L'Alliance Démocratique.

on November 7, 1937, in a political speech at Nice, that the democratic ideals and processes were losing ground everywhere in Europe: "One could almost say that even among ourselves the democratic regime is surviving much more because of the rivalry of two opposing totalitarian tendencies than by virtue of its own force. When one side cries to the crowds: 'War on fascism,' when the other side cries: 'War on communism,' it is in both cases a totalitarian rally that is being attempted."[70] In November, 1936, the Congress of the liberal Catholic party, the Parti Démocrate Populaire, which was ideologically near the Left, admitted the evolution of the Right to an antirepublican or authoritarian position. They acknowledged the "boring from within" of the "Fascist" extraparliamentary parties,[71] and proclaimed impossible from then on the traditional formula of *l'Union nationale,* which used to comprise all parties and groups from the Extreme Right to the Radical-Socialists. They proposed collaborating only with the "authentically republican" parties, which, according to them, were only the Radical-Socialists and the Socialists; thus they excluded the parties of the Right from the National Union, with the exception of their own, but included the parties of the Left with the exception of the Communists.[72]

Therefore the growth of communism and the fear of a social revolution apparently led an important section of the *Modérés* to reject, more or less consciously, parliamentary democracy while accepting the authoritarian ideology of the P. S. F. and the P. P. F. A distinction should be made, however, as to the "quasi-Fascist" character of these two parties; although their vague programs did not appear very different,[73]

[70] *Paix et liberté* (Paris, 1938), pp. 169-170.

[71] The P. S. F. and P. P. F. may be called "extraparliamentary" parties since they were born after the general elections of 1936; the P. S. F. claimed the allegiance of thirty deputies and the P. P. F. of at least one.

[72] Cf. *Le Petit Démocrate,* Nov. 22, 1936.

[73] Cf. La Rocque, *Service public* (Paris, 1934), *The Fiery Cross* (London, 1936); François Veuillot, *La Rocque et son parti* (Paris, 1938); Charles Vallin, "Le P. S. F.," *Sciences Politiques,* Aug., 1937; Doriot, *La France avec nous* (Paris, 1937); *Refaire la France* (Paris, 1938); also *Emancipation Nationale,* Nov. 14, 1936 (Congress of the P. P. F.). The program of the P. S. F. included increased au-

the spirit that animated each as well as the composition of
their memberships seem to justify a differentiation. The new
character and following of the former Croix de Feu place this
group halfway between the old-fashioned conservatives and the
revolutionary Fascists, while the P. P. F. may be considered
the best copy in France of the Italian and German models.
This distinction is particularly evident in the field of foreign
policy. Doriot defended isolation for France and free play to
Germany in the East, in contrast with the new foreign policy
of La Rocque and the P. S. F., who advocated a policy of conditional resistance to Pan-Germanism.

The P. P. F. of Doriot advocated a policy of retrenchment
and *rapprochement* with Germany. "We must disengage ourselves from any exterior obligation not contributing to this
aim [the defense of the French Empire]. Our Polish friends
have recognized that France will sooner or later be forced to
renounce her policy of responsibility in Central and Eastern
Europe. Our other allies should understand this too. Our
interests are in the Mediterranean, and this greatly facilitates
a definitive reconciliation with Germany, whose natural line
of expansion is toward the East of Europe."[74] This policy of
retrenchment was essentially based on the anti-Marxist dogma
of the P. P. F., the keystone of their political philosophy. They
insisted that communism was Public Enemy Number One, not
Germany, and the logical consequence was the complete acceptance of the anti-Bolshevist crusade instituted by the Fascist

---

thority for the executive (the power of the President of the Republic to name
the cabinet, and to address and dissolve the Chamber; ministers answerable to
him), and reform of the electoral system (proportional representation, woman
suffrage, *vote familial*). In the economic life it advocated occupational representation (local, regional, and state groups of employees of the same industry; at the
top of the pyramid, a national economic council). The program of the P. P. F.,
similar in many respects, dwelled on political and economic antiliberalism. The
Right emphasized authority, at the expense of liberty more than ever after 1936.
Cf. Louis Reynaud, *La Démocratie en France* (Paris, 1938), pp. 285 ff.; J. Montigny,
France, libère-toi! pp. 155 ff.; Bardoux, *L'Ordre nouveau,* pp. 164 ff.

[74] Bertrand de Jouvenel, "Le P. P. F.," *Sciences Politiques,* Oct., 1937, pp.
368 ff. Also Jacques Doriot, *La France ne sera pas un pays d'esclaves* (Paris,
1936), pp. 22 ff.; *La France avec nous,* pp. 72, 76.

states. As M. Pierre Brossolette wrote in *L'Europe Nouvelle:* "The struggle against fascism explains all the foreign policy of the Communists; the struggle against communism explains all the foreign policy of M. Jacques Doriot. . . . After having stated as an axiom that the interests of France and of peace were, everywhere and always, identical with the struggle against communism—which makes things much easier—all M. Doriot has to do to get out of an embarrassing situation is to avoid considering the question of the immediate, material interest in each concrete case. And *la boucle est ainsi bouclée*— everything is logically deduced therefrom."[75] The group of Resigned Nationalists, or isolationsists,[76] was thus strengthened by the support of the P. P. F.

The majority of the Right, the Conditional Nationalists, continued to take a *"Ni pour Berlin ni pour Moscou"* atti- tude.[77] The P. S. F. was one of the champions of this policy, which did not entirely reject *rapprochement* with Germany, but subordinated it to the maintenance of the European *status quo.* Colonel de la Rocque, as leader of the P. S. F., gave less emphasis to the necessity of an understanding with the Reich, and showed a firmer attitude towards possible German expan- sion than he had as head of the Croix de Feu.[78] It is signifi- cant that his mouthpiece in the Chamber, Ybarnégaray, as well as his sympathizer, De Kerillis, were both keenly aware of the danger of Pan-Germanism.

The ideological struggle between the socialist and liberal forces of the Left and the authoritarian and conservative forces of the Right thus appears to have been crystallized by the Spanish Civil War, which followed France's shift toward the Left. Fear and bias speeded the evolution toward the extremes at the expense of the Center, in both foreign and domestic

[75] "Leur politique étrangère," Aug. 20, 1938.

[76] See above, pp. 71-73. The main agency for direct Franco-German *rapproche- ment* was still the Comité France-Allemagne under the direction of Fernand de Brinon.

[77] *Le Temps,* June 4, 1937 (Congress of the Fédération Républicaine).

[78] Charles Vallin, "Le P. S. F.," *Sciences Politiques,* Aug., 1937; Pierre Dominique, "Le front de la liberté," *L'Europe Nouvelle,* May 29, 1937, p. 515.

policy. The neutrality of Great Britain and France distorted the character of the International Civil War in making it appear as exclusively a duel between the two totalitarian systems; as a result, many Frenchmen became convinced that the choice was not only between a pro-German or a pro-Russian foreign policy, but between a Fascist and a Soviet regime in France. It was too late to convince many patriots that the struggle for national security was still paramount and that the ideological war was substantially a camouflage for German ambitions.

CHAPTER VIII

THE *ANSCHLUSS*

THE RIGHT's belief that the Popular Front would have a short life was soon justified by the facts. The rift between the Radical-Socialists and the Communists, which had started in 1936 over the question of intervention in Spain,[1] widened during 1937; M. Blum's inauguration of *la Pause,* the breathing spell in the economic and social program of the Popular Front, satisfied the Radicals but drew the anger of the Extreme Left. A climax was reached at the beginning of 1938. The Communists withdrew their collaboration from the cabinet of M. Chautemps, who had replaced Blum as premier the preceding June. M. Chautemps resigned but, upon request, formed a new government, which this time was almost entirely composed of Radical-Socialists. "Parliamentary wits declared that if this went on much longer, Popular Front government number six would be composed of M. Tardieu, M. Laval, and the Cagoulards."[2] Although the Leftist parties had won the elections, the force of events installed a government of Moderates—for the third time since the war of 1914-1918. Except for the short-lived Blum cabinet (March 13-April 8) the Popular Front government had come to an end.[3] The official burial, however, did not take place until October, 1939, when M. Daladier's cabinet was given the full support of the Right.

The foreign policy of the Popular Front government was at

[1] The Communists abstained from voting confidence in the Blum cabinet's foreign policy on December 5, 1936, almost causing the resignation of the Popular Front government.

[2] Werth, *France and Munich,* p. 114. The Cagoulard plot had been opportunely discovered by the Minister of the Interior, M. Dormoy, at the reassembly of Parliament in the fall of 1937.

[3] The Socialists and Communists voted for the ministerial declaration, but since the Right also voted for it, the large majority was actually a demonstration of weakness. When M. Chautemps asked for plenary powers, the Socialists refused them, exactly as the Radicals had denied them to M. Blum in June, 1937. He resigned almost frivolously on March 10, without inviting a debate on the subject.

best timid and unimaginative. As M. Paul Reynaud had told
the Chamber in December, 1936, there were only two logical
policies for France to follow: to abandon Central and Eastern
Europe to their fate, or to strengthen the Franco-Soviet Pact to
form a nucleus for the *status quo* coalition. The first policy
was unacceptable, and the second difficult, for since the remilitarization of the Rhineland France had become the none too
brilliant second of Great Britain; she had meekly followed
suit when the British had decided to relinquish the sanctions
against Italy, and again when they had opposed intervention
in Spain. M. Delbos, foreign minister in the Blum and Chautemps cabinets, was most careful not to antagonize London
by a Franco-Soviet military agreement. He chose a middle
course, a dangerous policy of resistance to German expansion,
not backed by sufficient force and not bold enough to convince
and unite the potential victims.[4] Collective security within
the frame of the League of Nations had lost its reassuring
former glamour, Italy had been alienated, Britain's immediate
military help was negligible, and the Rhineland was being fortified and defended by fast-growing legions. France's smaller
allies, with the exception of Czechoslovakia, were worried
about the French Army's ability to protect them, and were already in the process of reorienting their foreign policy: Belgium had declared her neutrality in October, 1936, and Poland,
Yugoslavia, and Rumania were accepting French money while
obviously hesitating between neutrality and collective resistance.[5] Moreover, the foreign policy of the Popular Front
government satisfied neither the Extreme Left, who wanted
intervention in Spain and a military agreement with the
Soviets, nor the Right, who insisted on Franco-Italian *rapprochement* and the abandonment of the Franco-Soviet Pact.
In December, 1937, M. Delbos followed in the footsteps of M.

---

[4] Cf. *JO. Ch.*, June 23, 1936, pp. 1553-1554; Dec. 4, 1936, p. 3327.
[5] Poland was given 2,600 million francs and Rumania 272 million. Yet they
were reluctant to collaborate with the Franco-Russian entente against Germany.
Blum desired the members of the Little Entente to sign a pact of mutual assistance
among themselves before signing a similar pact with France, but they refused since
they suspected German designs on Czechoslovakia.

Barthou by touring the capitals of the Little Entente, but had considerably less success. Only Czechoslovakia could definitely be counted on the French side.

This country was the cornerstone of France's postwar security. Should the *Anschluss* be realized she would be threatened from three sides, and her independence would be imperiled. French intervention on behalf of Austria could therefore have been expected, although Great Britain and Italy had gone a long way from the days of the Stresa Front. Since France was the main obstacle to the *Anschluss,* the coup against Austria had to be calculated to reduce the risks of French reaction to the minimum. The appearance of a "legal" absorption of a willing Austria was one means to this end; another was to seize upon a psychological moment when France was off guard, as during a ministerial crisis. Both conditions were realized to a point of perfection by Herr Hitler's superb timing.

On February 12, 1938, the German Führer called Dr. Von Schuschnigg to a meeting at Berchtesgaden. There he forced upon the Austrian chancellor a set of demands destined to weaken and overcome quickly the resistance of the Vaterländische Front. Not only was a general amnesty to be given to the Austrian Nazis; they were to be allowed to engage in "legal activity," and one of their leaders, Dr. Seyss-Inquart, was to be given the key post of Minister for Public Order and Security. The terms of the Berchtesgaden ultimatum were accepted by the Austrian Government a few days later, and during the next weeks Nazi demonstrations in the principal cities grew in vigor, until on March 9 Schuschnigg made the courageous and fateful decision to hold a plebiscite four days later. On the tenth France found herself without a government: M. Chautemps had left to others the responsibility for the coming events. The invasion of Austria was further facilitated by the resignation of Dr. Schuschnigg, who had yielded to another ultimatum; Seyss-Inquart was able to request officially that German troops be sent into the country. On

March 11 they crossed the border unimpeded, and the next day the first German detachments were already on the Italian frontier at the Brenner Pass.

Since France was caught without a government and since the mechanism of intervention was not geared to automatic action, especially in case of a "legal" invasion, it was improbable that France would fight for Austrian independence. The foreign policy of the Right before and after the crisis is significant mainly in terms of the resistance they would offer to a German aggression against Czechoslovakia, which the *Anschluss* made almost certain.

The Berchtesgaden ultimatum announced the probability of Austrian incorporation into the Third Reich, and the resignation of Mr. Anthony Eden on February 20 from the British cabinet indicated that Great Britain would not attempt to stop Germany from realizing her aims. The majority of the Right was relieved by the government's indifference toward Hitler's demands on the Austrian chancellor;[6] they also approved the foreign policy of the Chamberlain government toward Spain and Central Europe—and were delighted that Mr. Eden, the fly in the ointment, had been removed. Chamberlain's speech of February 21 could be interpreted as an invitation to a Four Power Pact between Germany, Italy, France, and Great Britain, while his speech of February 22 was an admission of the impotence of the League in protecting the small nations, and might be construed as giving Germany a free hand in Central Europe.[7] M. Georges Suarez in *Le Matin* (March 6, 1938) went so far as to liken the proposed Four Power Pact to Locarno and to hail Chamberlain as the true heir of Briand, by contrast to Mr. Eden, who had always defended the League of Nations against "the spirit of Locarno."

[6] Only the minority of Traditional Nationalists regretted that France did not protect Austria; cf. Pertinax, *L'Echo de Paris*, Feb. 16, 1938. Here again the French Government seems to have followed the British lead. Chamberlain had announced on February 28 and March 2 that Britain did not consider any action against Germany justified from "the judicial point of view."

[7] Werth, *France and Munich*, pp. 40-41.

The new British policy, based on the open admission of the failure of collective security within the frame of the League of Nations, left the French with only two choices: either to follow Great Britain in her policy of noncommitment in Central and Eastern Europe or to take the lead in organizing resistance to Pan-Germanism, with the quasi-certainty that England would have to come to France's rescue. Although the Traditional Nationalists themselves were reluctant to admit it, the policy of resistance would necessarily have to be based on the acceptance of Russian aid in the coming diplomatic and military struggle.

Facing the dilemma of German expansion or resistance with the help of the Soviets, the Right maintained their positions in 1938. The three general trends already present in 1936 manifested themselves clearly during the important Chamber debates on foreign policy of February 25 and 26, shortly after the Berchtesgaden ultimatum; the same trends continued after the *Anschluss* and can easily be traced in the reactions of the press toward the Czechoslovak problem during the first half of 1938.

During the February debate the policy of unconditional firmness was defended by M. Paul Reynaud.[8] MM. Montigny and Flandin, the latter now the leader of the Resigned Nationalists, urged a policy of retrenchment behind the Maginot Line; and MM. Louis Marin and Ybarnégaray expressed the Stresa policy of the Conditional Nationalists, who seemed to include the majority of the "Right" and "Center."

At first glance it seemed that the policy advocated by this third group was as firm as that of the Traditional Nationalists. M. Marin stated that "we cannot back out of the promise that we have made," and that "we will not abandon our friends when we have made them a promise"; he criticized the "cynical imperialist ambitions" of Germany. But his policy of

[8] MM. Delbos, Chautemps, and Pezet also reaffirmed France's obligations to Czechoslovakia. The Chamber endorsed their policy of collective security by a vote of 439 to 2.

resistance was based on a problematic entente with Rome. "Among the countries menaced by Germany, there is Italy. That nation knows that it has always been menaced by Germany throughout the course of the centuries. . . . The obvious interest of Italy, which cannot escape her statesmen, will be to return one day to the policy of Stresa." M. Marin, however, rejected the idea of *rapprochement* with Germany and a new Four Power Pact: he warned the Chamber not to accept the idea of conversation with Germany at its face value and he condemned "in the most vehement manner" the Four Power Pact as a "butchers' club." "It is impossible for France and Germany to be in this quartet . . . France having nothing to ask of Germany, and Germany wanting to demand a great many things from each and every one."[9]

Similarly M. Ybarnégaray, after criticizing M. Flandin's trip to Berlin and stressing the strategic importance of Austria, patriotically declared: "To those faint-hearted and blind who go about saying: 'We will never mobilize for Austria and Czechoslovakia,' it is my duty to reply, at the risk of an unpopularity which I disregard: 'it is not for Austria and Czechoslovakia that we will mobilize, for it is on the shores of the Danube, at this very time, that the fate of the frontiers of our country is being decided.'" According to him, all hope of preserving the independence of Austria was not dead, and an energetic reaction on the part of France and Great Britain could still prevent the *Anschluss*. If France and Great Britain were ready to unite on the Danube, then they must declare it loudly, and everything could still be saved. But in order to oppose Pan-Germanism he advocated the re-establishment of the Stresa Front, which he said had been sacrificed to the Negus of Abyssinia. It was not certain that Mussolini had abandoned France. "It is difficult for me to think so. . . . Italy's friendship was precious to us in the hour of peril, it can be precious to us again today." He concluded by outlining his program, which was also that of Colonel de la Rocque's

[9] *JO. Ch.*, Feb. 25, 1938, p. 613.

Parti Social Français: "In summary, I am for a policy of vigilance and firmness toward Germany, a policy of support for Austria and of the *status quo* in Central Europe, a policy of friendship toward Italy while we stay on the side of Great Britain and, under the conditions that I have defined, for an immense effort to lessen the antagonism between two groups of powers and to save peace."[10] Thus the firmness shown in the first part of his speech had lost much of its meaning when he reached his conclusion: reconstruction of the Stresa Front and even a policy of *rapprochement* between the dictatorships and the democracies. The defense of Eastern Europe was not mentioned in conjunction with that of Central Europe, and the only alternative to the Stresa Front that would allow France to defend Austria and Czechoslovakia victoriously—that is, a Russian alliance—was dismissed in one sentence at the end of his speech.

The leaders of the Resigned Nationalists based their arguments on "realism." "France can no longer follow the policy of her preferences," said M. Montigny, "she must follow the policy of necessities and of her possibilities." Mobilization alone would not stop Hitler, as it would have done in 1936. War would be necessary. In 1936 Germany had just begun to rearm, and the Rhineland was demilitarized, but in 1938 fortifications had been built, Belgium was no longer France's ally, the German Army was now more numerous than the French, and German industry was ready for total war. While convinced of the "immense strength of the French Army for the defensive," M. Montigny did not believe that it possessed the shock troops necessary for an offensive. According to him, there had been for years a contradiction between France's foreign policy and her military policy. Because of the pacts of mutual assistance signed with particularly exposed countries, France was faced with the necessity of intervention, therefore of taking the offensive, while at the same time "the instinct of our people has imposed on us the organization of

[10] *Ibid.*, pp. 595 ff.

a purely defensive army." After suggesting the organization of a plebiscite in Austria—which did not meet with a favorable response in the Chamber—he argued that in any case France could not act without Italy and that *rapprochement* with this country should precede conversations with Germany.[11]

Although the case for a realistic policy of retrenchment was much better in 1938 than it had been in 1936, M. Montigny advanced another argument which showed that it was not only realism that directed his thinking. He criticized the Communist deputy, M. Péri, for his ambition to "encircle the spirit of aggression," which, he declared, would really mean encircling one hundred and eighty million people in Central Europe, for Poland and Yugoslavia would join Germany and Italy; and then, to the applause of the "Right" and the "Center," he referred to the dark designs of the Soviets: "Everything is happening as if certain elements, far from here, wanted the war that stalks over Europe to burst forth in the West (applause at the 'Center' and 'Right'), and the *abcès de fixation* to be on our soil. . . ."[12]

During this same debate M. Flandin advocated a similar policy of a free hand to Germany in Central and Eastern Europe, which had already been indicated in his speech in the Chamber on December 5, 1936, and made clear by his speeches to the Congress of the Alliance Démocratique at Nice on November 7, 1937,[13] and at La Teste on February 13, 1938.[14] On the latter date he had condemned the Communists for their anti-German and anti-Italian attitude, because they were "inspired by the desire to make our country the soldier of a *mystique.* . . . If they hold power more completely tomorrow, even at the price of a national unanimity that would unwisely associate them with the government, we can get ready to grease our shoes and put on our gas masks."[15]

This accusation emanating from the lips of the president

[11] *Ibid.,* Feb. 26, 1938, p. 633.
[12] *Ibid.,* p. 635.
[14] *Ibid.,* pp. 190-192.
[13] *Paix et liberté,* pp. 173-175.
[15] *Ibid.,* p. 190.

of the Alliance Démocratique was surprising, for two years before he had eloquently defended the ratification of the Franco-Russian Pact against the Right with the support of the Left and Extreme Left. M. Péri did not miss the opportunity of reminding the Chamber of this about-face.[16]

In his speech to the Chamber on February 26, 1938, M. Flandin relied on the authority of Chamberlain to point out that the League of Nations was in no position to insure the security of small nations. He reminded his fellow deputies that as early as December, 1936, he had told them that "France should not accept the risk of playing the role of the *gendarme* of Europe alone," and added that France must align her policy in Central and Eastern Europe with that of Great Britain. Yet he pretended that he did not advocate *renoncement;* France must prepare economically and militarily to be able to resist some day with the help of England.[17] Flandin then quoted Chamberlain as saying that the nations who were still members of the League could not be held responsible for assuming risks that they were not ready to undertake, and told the Chamber that Great Britain would not intervene in Central and Eastern Europe. After asking whether the Chamber would still accept the risks resulting from France's pacts of mutual assistance, since they were dependent on the dead Covenant of the League, he finally came to the point when he stated: "If French security can no longer be assured by the League of Nations, will you shape your policy on that of England, or on that of Russia which M. Péri set forth with such clarity yesterday? If you choose the English formula, why don't you, too, start conversations with Italy and with Germany?"[18]

According to Flandin, the *Anschluss* could be stopped only with Italian aid, and *rapprochement* with Italy should be started immediately. As for *rapprochement* with Germany, it was the intention of the British Government to start Anglo-German as well as Anglo-Italian conversations, and therefore,

[16] *JO. Ch.*, Feb. 25, 1938, p. 605.
[17] *Ibid.*, Feb. 26, 1938, p. 639.　　　　[18] *Ibid.*, p. 640.

why should France wait to defend her own interests? There was no third way besides his formula and that of M. Péri, he declared, for the policy advocated by the Foreign Minister M. Delbos was based only on "the old, out-of-date formulas of the League of Nations, of collective security, and of mutual assistance." France, moreover, should not be afraid of an understanding with Germany; no attempt to gain European hegemony had a chance of success. If she were attacked, France would be strong enough to resist behind the Maginot Line until other freedom-loving countries would come to her rescue. But war would be inevitable if a policy of *rapprochement* with Italy and Germany were not started; and he was opposed to the theory of an inevitable as well as a preventive war.[19] Flandin correctly predicted what would happen if the Chamber should hesitate: "If you delay your choice between this policy [intervention] and our own a little longer, a day will come when you will no longer be able to maintain this attitude because, by waiting, you will every day increase the risk of humiliation and of war, and you will precipitate the very ruin of the regime" (loud applause on several benches at the "Center" and the "Right").[20]

M. Flandin was indeed right in declaring that there were only two policies for France to follow. As M. Reynaud later stated: ". . . either she maintains the balance of power in Europe, or, as a first step, she retreats behind the Maginot Line."[21] The policy of M. Reynaud and the Traditional Nationalists was that of opposition to any German aggression, not only on the stipulation of British and Italian aid, but unconditionally, in the belief that Great Britain, Russia, and the smaller countries would inevitably come to the help of France. As Le Grix interpreted it in the *Revue Hebdomadaire*, Reynaud represented the policy of Mr. Eden and accepted the risk of war, while Flandin's attitude might be likened to that of Chamberlain; the latter was for the "policy of the London-

[19] *Ibid.*, p. 645.
[20] *Ibid.*, p. 646.   [21] *Ibid.*

Paris-Berlin axis, while Reynaud was in favor of the Barcelona-Paris-Prague-Moscow axis."[22]   But M. Paul Reynaud himself quickly passed over the question of Russian aid. After stressing the strength of France and stating that in case of war she would not be alone, he added: "I have purposely said nothing of Russia because my information is fragmentary. But I must say that personally I am struck by one fact: Those who complain of the efficacy of the intervention by the Russians in Spain are the very ones who declare that, if Russia were engaged beside us with her immense forces, she would not be of any help at all to us" (loud applause at the "Extreme Left," at the "Left," and on several benches of the "Center").[23]

Reynaud went on to develop the policy of firmness toward Germany as the only one for France to follow. In leaving a free hand to Germany in Central and Eastern Europe, France would only delay war: "A day will come when the demands of the colossal neighbor will appear intolerable to the pride of a noble people, and, on that day, you will be thrown into war, without honor and without friends."[24]   He correctly emphasized that Great Britain would find herself obligated to come to France's rescue in case of war; according to him, the resignation of Mr. Eden did not change British diplomacy, which had always refused to make any commitments in Central Europe, although it had always maintained the threat of possible action against the aggressors. It was France who should therefore take the lead in protecting Austria and Czechoslovakia: "England cannot afford to see France crushed, whatever may be the personal feelings of the men in charge of her public affairs. But when it is a question of Central Europe, it is France who must take the initiative and assume her responsibilities."[25]

When M. Reynaud spoke of the *"faux réalistes,"* he was applauded by the Left and Extreme Left, and only on a few benches at the "Center." Apparently, the policy of integral

---

[22] *Ibid.*, March 5, 1938, p. 190.
[24] *Ibid.*, p. 648.
[23] *Ibid.*, Feb. 26, 1938, p. 647.
[25] *Ibid.*, p. 649.

firmness was supported by only a small minority at the "Right" and "Center," while the policy of conditional firmness and even that of retrenchment appeared to have an important following.[26] Under these conditions it was to be expected that most Rightist leaders would not ask the government for reprisals against Germany if they were faced with a *fait accompli* in Austria.

After the German coup in Austria on March 11, which caught France without a government, only the Traditional Nationalists took a firm attitude. De Kerillis, who was now one of their leaders, wrote in *L'Epoque* (March 15) that Hitler was a great gambler and would have backed down if France had been firm:

"Then what? Would we mobilize?"

"Certainly."

"But England, Italy, Poland, Czechoslovakia would not have followed. Hitler would have seen us isolated in front of him, and he would have seized upon the opportunity to crush us."

"I don't believe any of that talk. In international affairs bravery is just as contagious as cowardice. If France had shown herself courageous, she would have crystallized the resistance of a Europe which no longer has any delusions about the German menace."

Pertinax urged France and England to take a strong stand in the Czechoslovakian matter: "Having disposed of Austria, Hitler's Germany will easily dominate Hungary. If France and England do not declare clearly and firmly that they will defend Czechoslovakia, German hegemony will be completed

[26] A relatively accurate measurement of the reaction of the deputies to the speeches can be established by the description of the applause in the *Journal Officiel*: *applaudissements sur divers bancs à Droite (et au Centre); applaudissements sur de nombreux bancs à Droite (et au Centre); applaudissements à Droite (et au Centre); vifs applaudissements à Droite (et au Centre).* Another indication of the number adhering to the policy of unconditional firmness at the Chamber was given by the fact that only 50 deputies of the "Right" and "Center" accepted the *union sacrée* later proposed by M. Blum. It is also significant that on February 26, 150 deputies of the Right abstained from endorsing the foreign policy of the Chautemps government, which was based on collective security and respect for France's obligations to Czechoslovakia.

in a short time."[27] The same attitude was taken by Buré in *L'Ordre*[28] and by Georges Bidault in *L'Aube.*

At the opposite extreme the Resigned Nationalists and especially the pro-Fascist press started a violent campaign against the newly formed Blum government. Maurras accused the Socialist leader of wanting war in order to be the master of the country (*L'Action Française,* March 13) and on the fourteenth, under the title "Un ministère de catastrophe," he pointedly recalled that at the time of the Ethiopian Affair he had threatened with death the men who should be responsible for a war with Italy.

The first reaction of the majority of the Rightist papers, however, was one of moral indignation and apparent firmness. *Le Temps* stated in its editorial of March 13 that "the realization of this *Mittel Europa* which would establish the hegemony of Germany in Central and Eastern Europe appears more and more clearly as the real goal of the policy of Hitler's Reich. . . . One is indeed obliged to admit that these events mark the end of a political order on which the peace of Europe was founded for twenty years." Wladimir d'Ormesson wrote in *Le Figaro* (March 12) that "faced by perils that are, alas! only too visible, there is now only one party which has the right to exist and to act, and that is France. There is now only one Front to which one has the right to claim allegiance: the National Front. . . . Enough of retreats. The hour has struck for a 'political Marne'." Yet it soon appeared that their conception of a *Front National* was in conflict with that of M. Léon Blum, who was trying to build a coalition cabinet comprising representatives of all parties, from the Right to the Communists. Obviously a cabinet of national union had to be formed quickly, representing the great majority of groups and parties. But the Right turned a deaf ear to M. Blum's proposals. With the exception of the Traditional

---

[27] *L'Echo de Paris,* March 12, 1938. This paper was bought by Léon Bailby, proprietor of *Le Jour,* a few days later; both sheets were combined under the name: *Le Jour-Echo de Paris,* from March 28 on. Pertinax withdrew his collaboration.

[28] Cf. *L'Ordre,* March 12, 15.

Nationalists, the Rightist press opposed entering a coalition cabinet with the Communists:[29] the reason advanced was that Communist ministers would present a grave danger for France since they "were entirely in the hands of a foreign government and did nothing without having received their instructions from Moscow."[30]   On March 17 M. Flandin spoke in the Chamber for the groups of the minority which refused the *rassemblement national* proposed by Léon Blum[31] and gave the reason for the attitude of the Right. He pointed to the "fundamental opposition between our conceptions and, especially, those of the Communist party, principally in the field of foreign policy," and emphasized the dependence of the latter upon the Komintern.[32]   Later in the debate Flandin made his position even clearer in answering Léon Blum: "But what we dread most is that a misunderstanding might result from the formation of a government, supposedly of French unity, that would partly conceal a profound disagreement over a policy of peace or of war. . . . *M. le Président,* you invite us to union, to collaboration. Will it be to follow the policy of the Communist party or our own?"[33] He added that if M. Blum, after consulting the Communist leaders, could promise a policy of nonintervention, there would be a possibility of union. Otherwise the *rassemblement national* would be impossible. Other speakers of the Right took up the same arguments. "Union with all the French classes, yes!" said M. Fernand

[29] According to *L'Action Française* (March 13), only De Kerillis, Reynaud, Champetier de Ribes, and the Démocrates Populaires in the Chamber, and the newspapers *L'Aube* and *Le Petit Parisien* were in favor of Blum's proposed *Union sacrée.* De Kerillis was accused of bellicism under the influence of Reynaud and the Jews, but it especially charged Paul Reynaud of "ostensibly carrying on the intrigue for the Soviets, who, for their part, were pursuing only these objects: War, the ruin of France, and on her ruins, the Revolution." Cf. *ibid.,* March 16, 22, 23; also *Le Jour,* March 22.

[30] D'Ormesson, *Le Figaro,* March 13, 1938; also La Rocque, *Le Petit Journal,* March 13, 1938; *L'Action Française,* March 13, 1938; S. Lauzanne, *Le Matin,* March 12, 13, 14, 1938; Marin, *L'Echo de Paris,* March 15, 1938; *Le Temps,* RP, March 14, 1938; *La République,* March 13, 1938.

[31] M. P. Simon supported Blum's proposal in the name of fifty deputies of the "Right" and "Center" including MM. Mandel, Reynaud, Pezet, de Kerillis, but the majority followed Flandin.

[32] *JO. Ch.,* March 17, 1938, p. 840.   [33] *Ibid.,* p. 843.

Laurent. "Union with chiefs taking their orders from Moscow? No! Neither in peacè, nor in war, nor above all in government, the essential aim of which is to avoid war" (*Applaudissements à Droite, vives exclamations à l'Extrême Gauche*).[34]

Whether or not the fear of being dragged into war by Communist participation in the government was sincere, it brought many dangerously close to playing the game of the Axis, as M. Blum told the Chamber; according to him, Germany and Italy had succeeded "in transforming the old antinomy that we know: democracies against dictators, or pacific powers against warlike powers, into that of Communist and anti-Communist powers." It was against France's interests, he added, to "see everything in relation to this criterion, make it a rule for judgments, for discriminations, for actions."[35]

Fear of the "bellicism" of the Communists was certainly not the only reason for the refusal of the majority of the Right to enter a government of national union under M. Blum. As M. Xavier Vallat declared in the same debate, M. Blum was not the leader who would inspire confidence, and a man was needed who would symbolize the national reconciliation and present a program acceptable to all.[36] The press of the Extreme Right, of course, rejected the idea of a government headed by the Socialist leader; and Daudet did not miss the opportunity for an insult: "We need a man, not a Jew."[37] On April 7 Pierre Gaxotte wrote in *Candide* an article of personal abuse directed against Léon Blum, in which he zestfully recorded all the worst slanders against the French Premier. Similarly Le Grix wrote in the *Revue Hebdomadaire* (April 2): *"Renverser Blum d'abord,"* and spoke of an extra-parliamentary government headed by the *"glorieux vieillard,"* an obvious allusion to Marshal Pétain. The academician Henri Bordeaux also asked in *L'Echo de Paris* (March 13): "Why not entrust power to a man above parties and discus-

---

[34] *Ibid.*, March 22, 1938, p. 841; also Vallat, p. 845, Montigny, p. 876, Scapini, p. 881. [35] *Ibid.*, March 22, 1938, p. 838.
[36] *Ibid.*, p. 845. [37] *L'Action Française*, March 13, 1938.

sions? Don't you guess his name?" Others hoped for a *"cabinet restreint d'hommes de gouvernement,"*[38] and for a "handful of experienced, resolute men."[39]

It was clear that the Right believed the Popular Front to be dying and that, if M. Blum could be stopped from forming his cabinet of national union, he would soon be succeeded by a moderate Leftist government, which in time would necessarily break with the Socialists and Communists and rely on the support of the Right and Center. This interpretation is confirmed by the warm welcome which the Daladier government was to receive three weeks later in the press of the Right.

The Rightist minority in the Chamber, wittingly or unwittingly, had played into the hands of the Axis by refusing to collaborate with the Left and Extreme Left in the government of national union proposed by Léon Blum; but immediately after the fall of Austria a number of Rightist papers went even further. "A formidable press campaign, started by the pro-Nazi papers, but which has spread to certain organs among the most serious or the most patriotic, has been suddenly unleashed against Czechoslovakia," wrote Henri de Kerillis in *L'Epoque.* "They point out that Czechoslovakia is not viable, not defendable. They proclaim that the independence of the Czech State is not worth the life of one French soldier. In short, they say and write everything needed to give Germany the impression that she really does not have to hesitate if she wants to devour the prey that she covets."[40]

This campaign against Czechoslovakia began in the press of the Extreme Right immediately after the formation of the second Blum government on March 13. The next day Maurras bitterly criticized M. Corbin, the French ambassador to London, who was supposed to have told Lord Halifax that France would fight for Czechoslovakia. On March 15 he declared in

[38] Lauzanne, *Le Matin,* March 16, 1938.
[39] D'Ormesson, *Le Figaro,* March 13, 1938.
[40] Quoted by *L'Europe Nouvelle,* May 7, 1938; see also Werth, *France and Munich,* pp. 118-123.

L'Action Française that France should not fight unless her morale were prepared for war and unless the political regime were revised, and on the sixteenth he warned M. Blum and M. Paul-Boncour, the new foreign minister, against encouraging Czechoslovakia to show firmness toward Germany. M. Bailby in *Le Jour* went just as far in his defeatist attitude. On March 16 he asserted that in case of a "pacific conquest" by Germany the Prague government would not find any help coming from Soviet Russia. "Occupied as Russia is at this moment shooting her leaders, she has other irons in the fire besides getting into a war with Germany." He continued pessimistically:

As for us, we shall execute our pact of allegiance by invading the Rhineland.

We will then be the ones that have declared war on the Reich. "Unprovoked aggression." England will immediately declare that she cannot join us.

And Italy, knowing that we are busy in the East, will start out by sending her troops on a Cook's tour through Nice and into Tunisia. . . .

M. Bailby's article drew upon him the wrath of Emile Buré, who answered him in *L'Ordre* the next day. "Léon Bailby is sure that Russia would not help Czechoslovakia if Germany attacked her. He does not know what he is talking about. . . . M. Bailby is ill-advised in making such a statement since he is the one who, on general principles, has always opposed the Franco-Soviet Pact and is always accepting and spreading all the rumors about the Soviets which are instigated by Hitler and Mussolini to cover their own imperialistic militarism." He then expressed his bitterness about the attitude of many Rightists: "Nationalists, who believed that Mussolini would reappear on the Brenner Pass after the Ethiopian victory which Pierre Laval let him get away with, Nationalists, who believed that Mussolini and Hitler entered Spain only to save her from communism, you can give no one any lesson on farsightedness and perspicacity. The only hope of my distressed heart is that the nation will not be obliged to pay too dearly for your blindness."

The extremist papers, *La Liberté, Candide, Je Suis Partout,* and *Gringoire,* with the *Revue Hebdomadaire,* followed suit in the neo-pacifist campaign. On April 16 *Gringoire* printed an anti-Czech article across seven columns under the title "Will you fight for the Czechs?" according to which Czecho-slovakia did not exist as a nation but was only "an intellectual construction without geographic unity and without ethnic unity." On March 31 Pierre Gaxotte signed another anti-Czech article entitled "What is Czechoslovakia?" in which he stated that this country was a recent invention, the creation of a few Freemason professors, a fragile construction composed of a "mosaic of nationalities" for which "war would be suicide and which, moreover, was responsible for its present troubles." Le Grix entitled one of his weekly interpretations of the news: "Shall we accept the Jewish war?" According to him, the situation was not too hopeless because Mussolini seemed to accept a policy of collaboration with Great Britain as well as with Germany, and because "the Blum ministry seems more and more powerless to mobilize French opinion in favor of an intervention for Red Spain and for Czechoslovakia; and still more [powerless] as regards English opinion and the British cabinet."[41] He went on castigating the "war party" composed of "criminals, madmen and fools," who accepted the terrible risk of war "to save dying bolshevism."

The campaign did not limit itself to the press of the Extreme Right. The climax was reached with an article by Professor Joseph Barthélemy in *Le Temps* on April 12. Under the title "Agonized Conscience" Professor Barthélemy first covered Czechoslovakia with laurels, described her beautiful landscape and the lovely city of Prague, and arrived at the problem of the minorities. "Is it necessary that three million Frenchmen, all the young people of our universities, our schools, our countryside and our factories, be sacrificed in order

[41] *Revue Hebdomadaire,* March 26, 1938, pp. 494 ff.

to maintain three million Germans under Czech sovereignty? I reply with sorrow but with firmness: No!" He then put forward the diplomatic and military argument according to which Great Britain would let France fight alone against Germany and Italy; Russia was not to be trusted and could not move her armies through Poland and Rumania, or land her planes on the airfields of Czechoslovakia which would soon be destroyed by the Germans. The Siegfried Line was as impregnable as the Maginot Line, and in any case France's military organization was planned for the defensive and not for the offensive.

After reviewing the economic argument according to which Czechoslovakia depended for two thirds of her exports upon Germany, Barthélemy finally arrived at the core of his article, the legal argument that France was not bound by her treaties with the Czechoslovak State. He undertook to prove that the Franco-Czech treaty of January 25, 1924, was dependent upon the Covenant of the League of Nations and that the pact of October 16, 1925, was part of the Locarno system of treaties. After a detailed argumentation, Barthélemy concluded: "One does not even need to invoke the formula: *'Accessorium sequitur principale'*; the Covenant dead, the accessory of the Covenant is dead; Locarno dead, the accessory of Locarno is dead. The very letter of the text expressly foresees that the pact will enter into operation with Locarno and will die with Locarno. . . . Indeed, it is urgent to repeat it, because our compatriots are particularly sensitive to the consideration of signature, honor and the given word: *France is not obliged to make war* to keep the Sudetens in allegiance to Prague." He then enumerated the points of a realistic policy for France to follow[42] and concluded his article: "There is a

[42] According to Professor Barthélemy the French Government should not act as long as it did not have the means of doing so, but should wait to take a firm stand until France's rearmaments (air force) would be sufficiently advanced. Yet he contradicted himself in patriotically stating that the French Army was the first in the world. The reconstruction of the Stresa Front was part of his program; he hinted at the support that the Right would give to M. Daladier if the Radical-Socialists should break with the Socialist and Communist majority.

war party; it enrolls the pacifists, always ready to make war under the fine pretext of preventing it. As for us, *we* want peace, as rapidly as possible, by all legitimate means.

"It has been very painful for me to write this article, but I considered it my duty to do so. And now, as in the time of Valmy: *'Vive la Nation!'*"

Although a few days later *Le Temps* replied to the legal argumentation of Barthélemy, and restated France's obligations to Czechoslovakia under the treaties of 1924 and 1925,[43] the fact remained that Barthélemy's arguments were to be widely used by the neo-pacifist *Munichois.*[44]

One indication of how far the campaign for appeasement went during the first half of 1938 is given by M. Flandin's speech at Vienne on June 12; he stated that France must not mobilize as long as she "is not attacked and all the methods of conciliation and arbitration have been exhausted in order to prevent war. The people of France will not let themselves be dragged into a new European conflict by sly intrigues and odious machinations."[45]   Commenting on this declaration, Pertinax wrote in *L'Europe Nouvelle:*

What can this sentence mean if not that we must dismiss all our allies and let Germany, according to her own ideas, regroup all Central and Eastern Europe, and even in the West, Holland, Belgium, Switzerland . . . provided that in the general upheaval the French frontiers be not touched. . . . Such a doctrine defies good sense. The Extreme Left never went so far in their pacifism.

But what can one say of this disintegration of the conservative elements which separate in opposite camps what was formerly always united: patriotism and the conservative spirit?

Words like those which M. Flandin has uttered conspire to precipitate war.[46]

The majority of the Rightist papers did not join the anti-Czech campaign, but maintained their awkward position, half-

[43] *Le Temps*, BJ, April 18, 1938; cf. also Werth, *France and Munich*, p. 122.
[44] See below, pp. 171 ff.
[45] Quoted in *L'Europe Nouvelle*, June 18, 1938, p. 653.
[46] *Ibid.*, pp. 632-633.

way between the Traditional Nationalists and the advocates of retrenchment.[47] Their resistance to Pan-Germanism seemed to be conditional upon English firmness and the friendship or at least the neutrality of Italy, and they carefully left the door wide open for negotiations with Germany.[48] The result, as expressed by Colonel de la Rocque, in *Le Petit Journal* (March 23), was a "prudent and firm diplomacy." "When France, again mistress of herself, has simultaneously assured her collaboration with London and her liaison with Rome, she will then be able to broach the decisive conversation with Berlin."

The acceptance of the British lead was the first element of this policy. Mr. Eden's resignation and Chamberlain's attitude toward Spain and Central Europe had reassured the majority of the Right; by its noncommittal character the British policy appeared to justify their own irresolution.[49]

[47] M. Louis Marin, the leader of the Fédération Républicaine, criticized the neo-pacifist campaign of a section of the Rightist press in *La Nation*, June 18: "After the annexation of Austria, the Third Reich is considering a blow against the Sudetens. That is perfectly obvious.

"Yet Frenchmen who are not of the Left spend their time carrying on the German game by publishing amazing articles which are much exploited in the National-Socialist papers."

He congratulated the British Government for its firm stand during the crisis of May, 1938, and emphasized "the importance of firmness in international negotiations." According to the Leftist political writer M. Brossolette, "M. Louis Marin finds himself led to a position infinitely nearer that of M. Blum than that of M. Flandin" (*L'Europe Nouvelle*, Aug. 27, 1938; see also D'Ormesson, *Le Figaro*, April 10, 1938; Pinon, *Revue des Deux Mondes*, April 1, p. 719, May 1, pp. 415-416).

[48] *Le Temps*, April 15, 1938. Cf. Pinon, *Revue des Deux Mondes*, April 15, pp. 955 ff.; May 1, 1938, pp. 233 ff.; Recouly, *Revue de France*, April 1, 1938, p. 419; May 1, 1938, p. 129; D'Ormesson, *Le Figaro*, March 20, 1938; May 4, 15, 1938; La Rocque, *Le Petit Journal*, March 13, 14, 20, 1938.

[49] Thus in the editorial of March 25 *Le Temps* congratulated Chamberlain on his last speech, in which he had opposed the Soviet Government's proposal for the convocation of an international conference to negotiate a pact of mutual assistance, on the ground that it would divide Europe into two rival groups of powers. It then gave a clear statement of British policy toward Czechoslovakia. "The British did not want to make any commitment in regard to a possible German aggression against Czechoslovakia; they intended to remain master of their own decision and not to be automatically dragged into a war. . . . It is not at all impossible, however, that they would come to the assistance of France if the latter were led to fulfill her obligations under the Franco-Czechoslovak treaty of 1925."

During the short-lived Blum cabinet (March 13-April 8) Chamberlain's "realism" was often contrasted with the "anti-Fascist," interventionist policy attributed to Blum and Paul-Boncour. As M. d'Ormesson stated in *Le Figaro* (March 24): ". . . the foreign policy of England is sensible: she does not intend to be dragged beyond certain limits which seem to her unreasonable. Now the French foreign policy, such as an important part of the majority [governmental majority] describes it, seems to her to be trying to go beyond these limits. . . . It is said in London that, if the British Government gave this majority the impression that England would support France without reservation, France would be rushed into any adventure." It is not surprising, therefore, that Chamberlain's realistic foreign policy should have induced the Right to follow the lead of Great Britain in the Czechoslovak affair. The signature of the Anglo-Italian agreement on April 16[50] and the conclusion of a Franco-British military alliance during the London conversations (April 27-29) received the almost unanimous approval of the Rightist press as two important steps toward the realization of the new version of the Stresa Front and toward the consolidation of peace in Europe.[51]

The fact that most Rightists had made their attitude contingent on that of England became apparent after the crisis of May 21 when the firm attitude of the Czech and British governments was supposed to have averted a German invasion of Czechoslovakia. For several days there had been ominous rumors of German troop concentrations near the Czech border; on May 21, after a grave incident at the frontier, Prague mobilized several thousand specialists, while the British ambassador to Berlin, Sir Nevile Henderson, was said to have warned the German Government that Great Britain would support France if Czechoslovakia were attacked. Whatever the seriousness of the threat to the latter country might have been, it was admitted then that the firmness of the British and the Czechs had obliged Germany to back down. Pertinax

---

[50] *Le Temps,* BJ, April 16, 1938.   [51] *Ibid.,* BJ, RP, May 1, 1938.

could declare in *L'Europe Nouvelle* that May 21 was a "turning point." "But," he added, ". . . it is only a turning point and not an end . . . and it is not certain that our British friends who saved peace by an act of firmness the other day will not try, at some critical moment, to save peace by an act of weakness."[52]

For several days before the denouement of the crisis the neo-pacifist campaign grew in intensity in the majority of the Rightist papers.[53] However, after it became apparent that the attack against Czechoslovakia would not materialize, the neo-pacifist campaign subsided, and the press assumed a firmer tone toward Germany. Even Léon Bailby appeared quite determined; on the twenty-fifth he explained his sudden change by distinguishing between the "preventive war" which was "the war sought and desired by Stalin and by the Franco-Russians" and the "defensive war" which "almost happened on May 21." The great difference between these two types of war, he declared, would be that in the latter case Great Britain would side with France. On May 26 he wrote: "The Franco-Russians, who are sometimes rascals, sometimes poor, thoughtless people overtaken and swept along by the storm, are astonished that the French Nationaux have now changed tactics and urge resistance. What has been changed? they say. Oh nothing, or nothing very important! Just that thanks to the British decision French isolation has been broken since Saturday, the twenty-first of May."

This change of attitude is significant. Although the recrudescence of the neo-pacifist campaign during the crisis of May could be interpreted as only a proof of the unwillingness of many Rightist leaders to defend Czechoslovakia and as a means of pressure upon the government, their firmer position following the English stand on May 21 also indicates that the Right might have maintained it had London kept the initiative in resisting German threats.

[52] Quoted by Werth, *France and Munich*, p. 155.
[53] See *Le Matin*, May 21, 1938; *Le Petit Journal*, May 20, 1938; *Le Jour-Echo de Paris*, May 20, 22, 1938.

The British lead was definitely accepted by the majority of the Rightist press when Lord Runciman was sent to Prague on August 3. From then on France followed Britain. As Pertinax remarked in *L'Europe Nouvelle* of July 30:

> France had affirmed her resolution on every occasion to execute the treaty of 1925, to go to the rescue of Czechoslovakia if the political independence or territorial integrity of this country were attacked. This determined attitude on the part of France carried England along, who announced it to Berlin. Henceforth French resolution will probably cease to be the *ressort fondamental*. The eventual report of Lord Runciman will replace it: whatever its nature, it will certainly govern the conduct of Great Britain and indirectly that of France. It is a very striking innovation. The "leadership," the direction of Franco-British co-operation, has been in fact transferred from Paris to London.

The second element of the conditional firmness of the majority of the Rightist press was the emphasis put on a Franco-Italian *rapprochement*. Even after Italy had accepted the *Anschluss,* the majority of the Right refused to admit the clear evidence that "Italy has decided to let *Mittel Europa* develop in Central Europe in the belief that a Germany more powerful economically and with great military strength would help Italy find prizes in and around the Mediterranean."[54] The responsibility for the *Anschluss* was traced back to the breaking of the Stresa Front during the Italo-Ethiopian War, and especially to the anti-Italian policy of the Popular Front governments. Yet everything was not lost, they declared; although his prestige had greatly suffered from the *Anschluss,* Mussolini could not accept German hegemony in Central and Southeastern Europe. With the alternative left to him between German hegemony and European equilibrium, he would necessarily choose the second and ultimately side with Great Britain and France.[55] As the first step in re-establishing normal relations with Italy it was necessary to send an am-

[54] Pertinax, *L'Echo de Paris*, March 12, 1938.
[55] Cf. Pinon, *Revue des Deux Mondes*, April 15, 1938, pp. 955-956; Recouly, *Revue de France*, June 1, 1938; Dominique, *La République*, March 16, 1938.

bassador to the "King of Italy and *Emperor of Ethiopia.*" "When you come to think that the two countries no longer have normal diplomatic relations because of three little words (and, what is more, three little words related to the extinct League of Nations), you certainly have reason to be astonished. . . ," wrote Wladimir d'Ormesson in *Le Figaro* (March 20). "And you have every reason to be raving mad when you think that, if this semirupture had not occurred eighteen months ago, it is practically a positive fact . . . that the Austrian affair would not have taken the turn that it has."

The *rapprochement* with Italy, however, was not expected to bring about a re-establishment of the anti-German coalition of Stresa.[56] The fact that the Rome-Berlin Axis had resisted the strain of the *Anschluss* apparently led the Right away from their old dream of the Stresa Front to the new conception of a Four Power Pact.[57] The explanation was given by St. Brice in the *Revue Universelle* (May 1):

The *rapprochement* with Rome cannot appear to be directed against Berlin. The past cannot be changed. . . . Only a few months ago one could have saved Austria by returning to the Laval plan [Stresa Front]. Now it is too late, the *Anschluss* has been made. Italy has accepted the organization of Central Europe based on the idea of a strong Germany. One can think of preventing the future developments which Italy must fear more than any other power. But the idea of abruptly separating Italy from Germany would be crazy.

Instead of an ally against Germany, Mussolini was now presented as the possible arbiter between the Western democracies and the Third Reich. "Italy can play a role of primary importance in the rational evolution of European affairs," wrote D'Ormesson in *Le Figaro* (May 4): "Rome is today at an intersection where great currents cross. To act in such a way that

[56] Cf. *Le Temps*, April 20, 1938: The Anglo-Italian agreement of April 16 had brought about "an atmosphere favorable to a more general co-operation of the principal powers, and it thereby avoids, to a certain degree, the menace of seeing Europe divided into two rival blocs."

[57] Cf. *Le Matin*, April 23, 27, 30, 1938; *Le Figaro*, May 4, 15, 17, 1938; *Le Petit Journal*, March 23, 1938; *Revue des Deux Mondes*, May 1, 1938, p. 236.

they will not clash, but will for the safety of Europe come to subside little by little, is a task worthy of the diplomatic activity of Italy and the prestige of Mussolini."

This desire to re-establish normal relations with Italy may, therefore, be interpreted as a manifestation of the eagerness of many at the Right to reach an agreement between the four Great Powers concerning Czechoslovakia, an agreement which would serve the double purpose of avoiding a European war and establishing a new concert of Europe without Soviet Russia.

It is obvious that the Right's eagerness to reach this agreement was conditioned by their opposition to the Franco-Russian Pact. The two policies were in direct opposition; a Four Power diplomacy was now the only alternative to a policy of resistance necessarily based on the Paris-Prague-Moscow axis.[58] With Austria gone, and Czechoslovakia apparently next on the German list of conquests, the part of Russia in the present diplomatic battle was essential for the preservation of the *status quo;* Italy, on the contrary, could be expected to support German ambitions.

The refusal of the majority of the Right to accept Soviet help was in part based on military and diplomatic arguments. It was often contended that the internal crisis in the U. S. S. R. (the famous blood purge of 1938) had weakened her military strength, or that Poland and Rumania would never let the Russian armies cross their territory to go to the rescue of Czechoslovakia. Irrespective of the basis of such arguments, the ideological objection most frequently raised seems to have been all significant. The Right's unwillingness to accept the *Union sacrée* proposed by Blum because of Communist participation has already shown the importance, and the danger,

[58] "Soviet diplomacy had thought that the Spanish affair would definitely prevent any chance of conversation between the 'democratic' Anglo-French group and the 'totalitarian' German-Italian group and that thus the Soviets would escape the risk of isolation. On the contrary, it is the Spanish conflict that led England to treat with Italy and to make the first step toward negotiations between the four powers, England, France, Italy, Germany, the system of negotiations which is most feared by the Russians" (Lucien Romier, *Le Figaro,* June 7, 1938).

of the antagonism between the Right and the Extreme Left.
The continuation of the anti-Soviet and anti-"bellicist" campaign after the *Anschluss* only added to the evidence of the
ideological struggle.

The violence of the anti-Soviet campaign was of course
greater among the advocates of retrenchment than among the
Conditional Nationalists; not only were the Russian Government, the Third International, the French Extreme Left, and
the C. G. T. attacked, but the Traditional Nationalists as well,
who were labeled "bellicists" or *"Franco-Russes."*[59] Indicative
of the complete disharmony between the foreign policy of the
neo-pacifists and that of the Extreme Left was the statement
of M. Pierre Dominique[60] in *La République,* March 22: "M.
Gabriel Péri, Communist deputy and diplomatic editor of
L'Humanité, speaks of the 'criminal' policies of Mr. Chamberlain.

"M. Péri can say that, for what is right and just for us is
criminal for the Communists. And the reverse is just as true;
what is right and just for the Communists appears criminal
to us."

Evidently, the fear of social revolution voiced by the majority of the Rightist leaders, a fear which was partly sincere
and partly the expression of their hatred of the Popular Front,
made it safe for Hitler to wage his war of nerves during
September. Even some sincere patriots expressed their dread

[59] During the crisis of May, M. Léon Bailby wrote of M. Reynaud's trip to
London (*Le Jour-Echo de Paris,* May 22): "The ideas of M. Reynaud concerning
foreign policy are known. They are clearly oriented toward the defense and, if
possible, the extension of the Franco-Russian Pact. They are hostile to the Italy of
Mussolini and the Spain of Franco. . . . What is going on at Prague and Berlin
is taking such a curious turn that not one mistake can be made. One trembles
when one thinks that Lord Halifax may take seriously the suggestions of a French
minister who speaks in his own name only and in opposition to the opinion of the
national majority of his country." Violent criticism of the *"Franco-Russes"* continued after the apparent conversion of the Right to a firmer attitude following
the crisis of May 21. Cf. *Le Jour,* May 28; *L'Action Française,* May 26; *Le Matin,*
May 28.

[60] M. Dominique, formerly a Leftist, had been drawn to the Right since 1936
by his violent opposition to the Communist party, especially to its foreign policy.

of War-Revolution, while admitting that German propaganda was taking full advantage of the Communist menace. Typical of this attitude were the conflicting statements of René Pinon. On June 1 he declared that "Fighting bolshevism is for Hitler's policy only a pretext, a useful fiction, an article of propaganda . . .";[61] yet on May 1, he had affirmed, concerning the fall of the second Blum government, that France was "at the crossroads" and had the choice "of either heading towards revolution and communism, thereby unleashing the proletarian war, a war of nations and a war of classes . . . or else of negotiating, without consideration for ideological preferences, the establishment of an equilibrium in Europe that will assure peace."[62]   On June 15 he again showed his indecision; the two perils of communism and German invasion were "equally to be feared" and "increased by reciprocal action and reaction."[63]   Apparently the only way out of the dilemma—German hegemony or War-Revolution—was to find a peaceful solution to the Sudeten problem that would be "compatible with the sovereignty and independence of the Czechoslovak State."[64]   Many, however, neglected this condition for a settlement of the Czech crisis and were ready to accede to any demand on the part of Hitler.

[61] *Revue des Deux Mondes*, p. 716.

[62] *Ibid.*, p. 233.   [63] *Ibid.*, p. 956.

[64] *Ibid.*, May 15, 1938, p. 477.   The same indecisive policy was followed by D'Ormesson, who defended a policy of firmness while criticizing the Franco-Russian Pact (cf. *Le Figaro*, April 28, June 18, 1938). The awkward position of the Conditional Nationalists was best expressed by Colonel de la Rocque, who succeeded in presenting the terms of the dilemma without even attempting to find a way out.   To him the danger number two was to be feared as much as the danger number one: in fact, they were identical (*Le Petit Journal*, May 20, 1938).

CHAPTER IX

MUNICH

To EUROPE, the important issue behind the claims of the Sudeten Germans was not the national problem of their autonomy inside Czechoslovakia; it was the international problem created by Hitler's attempt to use the demands of the German minority in order to reduce the Bohemian bastion and thus to dominate Eastern and Southeastern Europe. No one opposed a settlement of the question of autonomy for the Sudeten Germans, provided that this was compatible with the maintenance of the integrity of the Czech State and its security, but on the international question public opinion was divided.

The Czech crisis, which had started almost immediately after the *Anschluss,* became more acute after the German military preparations of August. It reached the explosion point during September, with the refusal of Herr Henlein to accept Prague's Plan Number Four, which appeared to be the limit of concession compatible with the security of the nation, and with the Nuremberg Congress, which dramatized the situation and made German intervention appear more imminent.

The first of these periods of international tension ended on September 14 with the announcement that Chamberlain was going to fly to Berchtesgaden the next day. Significantly enough, on this date Henlein for the first time proclaimed that the Sudeten Germans no longer wished autonomy within the Czechoslovak State but incorporation within the German Reich. Chamberlain's acceptance of this demand at Berchtesgaden seemed to settle the Czechoslovak crisis to the complete advantage of the Third Reich, which thus gained three million people and an important industrial region, and at the same time reduced the Czech fortress to impotence and put Czechoslovakia within the economic and political orbit of Germany. A second crisis, however, followed Chamberlain's failure to reach an agreement with Herr Hitler at their Godesberg meeting. This period of the "scare days" lasted from September 23 to September 28, when the conference of Munich was announced. The reactions of French opinion before and after each of these three landmarks—Berchtesgaden, Godesberg, and Munich—throw much light on the main causes of the Right's policy of appeasement.[1]

The Traditional Nationalists[2] were willing to accept a reasonable compromise on the question of autonomy for the Sudeten Germans, but refused any solution incompatible with the unity and security of Czechoslovakia. They wanted France to show an unmistakably firm hand in this matter and to take the measures necessary to win the diplomatic and, if need be, the military contest. The limits of possible concessions were described by Pertinax in *L'Ordre* of July 27, 1938, when Runciman's mission to Prague was announced. After pointing out the difficulty of local autonomy and the impossibility of uniting all the Sudeten Germans into one separate territory, he opposed Point Eight of the Karlsbad program, which demanded full liberty to profess the German political philosophy. "Here Lord Runciman will have to choose between democracy and Hitlerism, the rights of Man in the Western sense and those of the 'people' which, in the last analysis, are the rights of a Führer, the Führer on the spot or the one in Berlin, the chances being that, in spite of the window dressing, they will be the same person." Pertinax then opposed the idea of neutralizing Czechoslovakia, for, he said, "An inert and defenseless Bohemia where Czechs and Germans have been at odds for seven centuries would thereby be practically tied hand and foot to the Pan-German offensive which does not fear to be neutralized."

[1] The best treatment of the September crisis has been given by Werth, *France and Munich*. For the books on Munich, see *Politique Etrangère*, June, 1939. The point of view of the *Munichois* was expressed by Fabre-Luce, *Histoire secrète de la capitulation de Munich* (Paris, 1938): the opposite point of view by P. Nizan, *Chronique de Septembre* (Paris, 1939).

[2] They were still represented by *L'Aube*, *L'Ordre*, and *L'Epoque* in the press, and De Kerillis, Mandel, and Reynaud in the Chamber.

The policy advocated by the Traditional Nationalists during the first crisis was expressed by an article of De Kerillis in *L'Epoque* of September 9, 1938, in which he criticized the French Government for not taking any measures to counterbalance German military preparation.

The German game is successful beyond all Hitler's hopes. France and England have failed to learn a lesson from their great victory of May 23. Impressed by Germany's military display, they have been trying to keep her quiet with concessions. . . . Paris and London are afraid of answering Germany's military preparations by equal preparations. . . . The moral side of the drama is being neglected. . . . If this goes on, Germany will believe that she can do everything. She will no longer be content with the Sudeten's autonomy within Czechoslovakia: she will want to annex the Sudetenland. . . . Before it is too late we must warn Hitler.

The next day he cautioned the German Government against the belief that France would tolerate such a solution of the Czechoslovakian problem. "Hitler's error would be colossal if he founded his policy on France's capitulation. France will no more give way in 1938 than did Belgium in 1914."

In direct opposition was the policy of peace-at-any-cost urged by the Resigned Nationalists.[3] During the first crisis of September they were always ahead of the governments and even of the Sudeten Germans in proposing solutions that were hardly compatible with Czech sovereignty and security. Thus as early as September 6, a day before the famous editorial of the London *Times* which proposed the transfer of the Sudetenland to Germany, M. Emile Roche had already made the same suggestion in *La République*.[4] A few days later Stéphane Lauzanne defended the same idea. He wrote in *Le Matin*

---

[3] Among these were the papers of Jacques Doriot, *La Liberté* and *L'Emancipation Nationale;* the extreme Rightist dailies *Le Matin, Le Jour,* and *L'Action Française* (although the last two defended a contradictory policy difficult to define); the weeklies *Candide, Choc, Je Suis Partout, Gringoire* (although André Tardieu's articles contradicted its editorial policy), and the periodicals *Revue Hebdomadaire* and to a lesser extent the *Revue Universelle*.

To the press of the Extreme Right must be added *Le Journal* and *Paris-Midi* and the former Leftist *La République*.

[4] Werth, *France and Munich*, p. 240.

(September 9) that France could not oppose the plebiscite demanded by the Sudeten Germans. "How can a war—we must utter the word—resolve the problem of a cohabitation that has become impossible between two races? Would it make the Czechs and Sudeten Germans get on better to-morrow. . . ? In the light of tradition France cannot deny one of the principles of her history: the principle of the right of peoples to dispose freely of themselves."

At this early stage most of the papers of this group did not advocate the dismemberment of Czechoslovakia, but rather a federated and neutral state, which nevertheless would have left the Czechs in a subservient position toward Germany. M. Léon Bailby became the chief advocate of the *"helvétisation"* and neutralization of the country. He made the reason for his project obvious when he stated: "Only Soviet Russia and those among us paid by Russia can combat such a project, because it will take away from Stalin any pretext for interfering with European affairs."[5] Thanks to this system, he wrote on September 11, the Czechoslovak State "would no longer be the ally of Russia, but neither would it be the subject of Germany." The main result of the plan would have been, of course, that the link which Czechoslovakia formed between France and Russia would be broken and that the U. S. S. R. would be ejected from European affairs. M. Emile Roche made this aim clear when he wrote in *La République,* the day after Hitler's speech at Nuremberg: "Perhaps this is the time for the four great nations who hold in their hands the heritage of Occidental civilization to act in full agreement." Thus the Four Power Pact policy excluding Russia from European affairs and ending the postwar system of collective security was already present in the minds of the Resigned Nationalists even before Berchtesgaden.[6]

[5] *Le Jour,* Sept. 9, 10, 11, 12, 1938; the same idea of federalism was defended by most papers of the Resigned Nationalists: *Paris-Midi,* Sept. 9; *La République,* Sept. 10; *La Liberté,* Sept. 10; *L'Homme Libre,* Sept. 13; *L'Action Française,* Sept. 11, 1938.

[6] Bailby was explicit as to the means of convincing the Czech Government to follow the road of its "best interest." After reminding his readers that France

Plainly, their neo-pacifist campaign was designed to exert pressure on the government. M. Flandin even went so far as to refuse the government the right to mobilize. In *Le Journal* (September 15) he wrote: "I do not contest the legal right of the government to issue a decree for mobilization. I deny it the moral right, as long as France is not attacked, since mobilization is almost equal to a declaration of war and since, according to Article 9 of the constitution, war cannot be declared without the previous consent of the Chambers." One of the main elements of this neo-pacifist campaign was the violent criticism of the *"parti de la guerre,"* or *"bellicistes,"* at the Right as well as at the Extreme Left. The Traditional Nationalists, like Buré and Pertinax, were "bandits" or *"vendus aux Soviets";* but it was the Extreme Left under the orders of Moscow that constituted the really important menace to peace.

If there is a war party at Berlin, there is another at Paris. That of Berlin can be stopped by the fear of catastrophe. That of Paris wants catastrophe because defeat is the means of implanting bolshevism in the Occident. . . .[7]

The usual argument, that the Soviets were doing their best to bring about war by "poisoning the conflict" between the Czechs and Sudeten Germans and by spreading rumors and *fausses nouvelles,*[8] was much in evidence. But it was rather difficult to make the public admit that only the Third International was a danger for peace; Germany also had to be presented as accepting the possibility of war, though for quite different reasons than the Soviets. "The more or less underhanded actions of the two camps," wrote J. le Boucher in *L'Action Française* (September 14), "conspire equally against Czechoslovakia. The Soviets are aiming at World Revolution;

---

was not bound by her treaty to Czechoslovakia, as Professor Barthélemy had said, he added: "France and England have only one obvious and decisive way out of it, that is, to impose on Czechoslovakia what she promised in 1919 to do." On September 14 he warned the Czech Government that if it did not accept the principle of federation "the coming days will surely inflict on the Prague leaders sacrifices that are much harder than those they did not agree to in time."

[7] *Candide, L'Action Française,* RP, Sept. 10, 1938.

[8] See *L'Action Française,* Sept. 10, 12, 1938; *ibid.,* RP, Sept. 14, 1938.

Germany at Teutonic hegemony in Europe." Similarly Bailby declared in *Le Jour* (September 13): "Germany will go as far as war if she cannot do otherwise to impose her hegemony upon Europe. Russia wishes for war because she calculates that all the States touched by the cataclysm will decay internally and will thus, by the same stroke, be handed over to Communist revolution."

The presentation of the two dangers—German hegemony and Communist revolution—was the favorite theme of the press of the third group, the Conditional Nationalists. Colonel de la Rocque castigated both Berlin and Moscow, both the *bellicistes* and the pacifists, while appealing to the *anciens combattants* across the border: "Hitler, Mussolini, you veterans of the front lines, call up your memories, measure your responsibilities. . . . The cabal of Moscow is known to you. It poisons every dispute, every suffering. . . . Will you open our old continent, devastated by battle, to Bolshevist orgies?"[9]

This group, however, still pretended to oppose German demands incompatible with the security of Czechoslovakia. On July 27 the editorial in *Le Temps* had already made this clear: "The very nature of Lord Runciman's mission demands exclusion from discussion of these bitterly contested problems relating to Czechoslovakia's foreign policy, national defense and independence, and sovereignty as a State. Any interference, however friendly, by a foreigner in these touchy subjects could hardly be imagined."[10] During the first half of September the press of the Conditional Nationalists declared that a German attack on Czechoslovakia would automatically mean war. Raymond Recouly patriotically stated in the *Revue de France* of September 15: "It is no longer a question of discussing whether or not we should fight for the Czechs. The question put this way is put as badly as possible. No country

---

[9] *Le Petit Journal*, Sept. 11, 1938.

[10] D'Ormesson wrote that the *Drang nach Osten* was all right if it meant only a peaceful expansion by Germany. "On the other hand, no Frenchman in his senses could conceive this expansion being made by way of conquest, that is to say, by iron and by fire, above all because the conflagration would inevitably spread over all Europe" (*Le Figaro*, Aug. 1, 1938).

goes to war for a foreign country, but only for itself. . . .
Moreover, even if we were willing to pay the price of certain
dishonor, we could not escape the obligation of intervention."
In *Le Petit Parisien* (September 10) Lucien Bourguès asserted
that, if Germany used force against Czechoslovakia, "France
would not hesitate a second to give her promised help to the
Czechs. And Berlin knows that England and all her resources,
as Chamberlain has clearly indicated, would immediately support France. From the start the American resources would be
at the disposal of the Franco-British combine with a probable
active participation by America later on, as she could not
remain aloof very long." His firm attitude lost much of its
meaning, however, when he added that "if the Reich really
shows it means peace and desires a friendly settlement for
which France and Great Britain are striving, then such a
settlement will soon be reached. The two Western powers
stand ready to redouble their efforts to insure successful negotiations."

The firmness of the Conditional Nationalists was open to
question. It should be determined whether they would fight
only if Czechoslovakia were actually attacked, or would oppose a definite "no" to any attempt whatsoever to reduce the
Czech bastion—as by the "legal" annexation of the Sudetenland or even by the federalization and neutralization of the
Czech State. In the first case, their firmness would be based
on their conception of honor, the moral obligation for France
to abide by the letter of her treaties. In the second case, it
would go further and would respect the spirit and not the
letter only of the treaties, by maintaining at all costs the
integrity and independence of this ally and, as a consequence,
what was left of the postwar system of defense against Germany. Although up to Berchtesgaden their attitude was rather
confused, it could generally be interpreted as one of opposition to German demands incompatible with the integrity and
sovereignty of the Czechoslovak State.[11] But this firmness

[11] Thus in *Le Figaro* (Sept. 18) Lucien Romier opposed not only the separation of the Sudetenland from Czechoslovakia but even the dangerous neutralization

of the Conditional Nationalists was partly contradicted by their efforts to serve as arbiters between Berlin and Prague and by their too obvious desire to reach a peaceful compromise. Their neutral attitude was bound to further the game of Germany by applying pressure on the Czech Government to make still greater concessions instead of backing it resolutely in the defense of its essential rights. Their indecision, born of the conflicting desires to stop German expansion and to avoid war, gave a great advantage to the Third Reich in the diplomatic and psychological battle.[12] The ease with which the Berchtesgaden deal was accepted by the Conditional Nationalists is additional proof that their desire for peace was stronger than their fear of German expansion.

The transfer of the Sudetenland to Germany, which was demanded for the first time by Herr Henlein on September 14 and accepted by Chamberlain the next day at Berchtesgaden, and by the French Government on September 18, obviously changed the Sudeten issue from a national problem to an international one. The balance of power in Europe was dangerously modified to the benefit of Germany. The French postwar system of collective security was definitely doomed; Czechoslovakia could no longer be counted as an ally, and the main barrier to German expansionist policy was removed. Chamberlain's decision to confer with Herr Hitler at Berchtesgaden was received with enthusiasm by all the Right-

---

of this country which would put it under the economic and even political domination of Germany. In the same paper, however, D'Ormesson unsafely stressed peace with honor while apparently taking a firm stand: "Everything that is compatible with honor must be tried to find a pacific solution to the problem that weighs on the world, and to avoid a catastrophe. . . . But let everyone, Good God, stop confusing the idea of peace and the idea of weakness. . . . We desire peace with all our force. But we do not fear anything" (Sept. 13, 1938). Cf. René Pinon, *Revue des Deux Mondes*, Sept. 15, pp. 476 ff.

[12] Typical of this indecision was the editorial in *Le Temps* of September 15 written at the height of the crisis, just before the announcement of Chamberlain's flight to Berchtesgaden: "Before this sinister perspective of war the duty of statesmen is indicated, as is that of all citizens: to keep cool, foresee the worst, put oneself in position to face it, but at the same time to neglect nothing to keep Europe from slipping into the psychosis of war and to maintain peace."

ist papers save those of the Traditional Nationalists.[13] The "Revue de la Presse" of *Le Temps* (September 16) emphasized the "quasi-unanimity of the press in applauding without reserve the courageous initiative of Mr. Neville Chamberlain. In general the failure of the sensational discussions that are going to start between the British Premier and the Führer is not envisaged even by the pessimists." It was obvious that French public opinion as a whole, that is, the great majority of the Right and an important section of the Left, was ready to accept whatever decision would be reached at Berchtesgaden, for it was psychologically too late for the French Government to resume the leadership temporarily granted to Britain when Lord Runciman went to Prague in August, a leadership now definitely confirmed by the meeting of Chamberlain and the German Führer.

The easy acceptance of the dismemberment of Czechoslovakia by the Right, confirmed by their often-expressed impatience to see Prague accept the terms of the Anglo-French plan, was nevertheless remarkable, especially in view of the firm stand taken by many papers in the preceding months. For the Right, the sacrifice of Czechoslovakia on the altar of peace was an immense concession, "going beyond anything that could be imagined,"[14] yet necessitated and justified by the desire "to spare the world the frightful ordeal of a general war."[15] In spite of apologies, reservations, and *ex post facto* justifications,[16] the great majority of their papers did not hide their joy at avoiding war, even at such a heavy price. Since it was at Berchtesgaden that Czechoslovakia was aban-

[13] *L'Ordre, L'Epoque, L'Aube;* see also Robert d'Harcourt's article, *La Croix,* Sept. 18, 1938.

[14] D'Ormesson, *Le Figaro,* Sept. 19, 1938. The day before, however, he had apparently accepted far-reaching concessions and had attempted to justify them: "Now it is in the interest of our Czech and Slovak friends themselves that their future be henceforth removed from internal convulsion and solemnly guaranteed by Europe."

[15] *Le Temps,* Sept. 23, 1938; cf. Pinon, *Revue des Deux Mondes,* Oct. 1, 1938, p. 718.

[16] Cf. *Le Temps,* RP, Sept. 20, 21, 22, 1938; only *La République* (Sept. 20) seemed entirely satisfied and hoped for complete European collaboration in the near future.

doned by France and Great Britain, the arguments used to vindicate her ordeal were similar to those justifying the greater concessions granted at Munich, and will be analyzed at that time.

It is only fair to add that the majority of the traditionally pacifist Left, with the exception of the Communists, also accepted the verdict. Their mood was well described by M. Blum's reaction in *Le Populaire* (September 10): "War is probably avoided. But under such conditions that I, who have never ceased fighting for peace and for many years have sacrificed much in my life for it, can feel no joy about it, but am torn between cowardly relief and shame."

A second crisis followed the interview of Hitler and Chamberlain at Godesberg and the breakdown of negotiations on September 23 resulting from further demands on the part of the Führer. The Czech Government ordered general mobilization and two days later declared the terms of the Godesberg memoranda unacceptable. In France another class of reservists was called up on the twenty-fourth, and in Germany Herr Hitler threatened in his speech at the Sports Palace on the twenty-sixth to invade Czechoslovakia unless the Sudetenland were immediately ceded. On the twenty-seventh he announced mobilization for the next day. The period of tension was finally ended on September 28 by Chamberlain's statement in the House of Commons that Hitler had invited him, Mussolini, and Daladier to confer in Munich the following day.

This second crisis is interesting only so far as it shows the degree to which the Right were willing to yield when it came to a question of "national honor" and resistance to German threats; the defense of the postwar system of collective security was in reality no longer an issue, since for all practical purposes Czechoslovakia had already been given up as an ally after Berchtesgaden. Even the Traditional Nationalist paper *L'Ordre* stated on September 25 that "since the sacrifice is made, since it was thought that the Sudetens must be given to Germany, the occupation of a small portion of the region scarcely matters any more and does not seem, in any case, to be a reason for justifying an international conflict."

The campaign for appeasement was rigorously carried on in the press of the Extreme Right after the Godesberg meeting. Bailby wrote in *Le Jour* (September 25): "I shall repeat here without wearying that France will not march into an offensive war on the orders of the Soviets. . . ." According to him, war had to be avoided because France would lose the British alliance if she took the initiative of an armed intervention. The next day he congratulated M. Bonnet on his foreign policy, the "only one that combines wisdom with care for French honor"; and on the twenty-seventh Bailby and the other Resigned Nationalists denounced as a *fausse nouvelle* the declaration made by the Foreign Office on September 26 that in case of German aggression in Czechoslovakia, France would be bound to come to her assistance and that Great Britain and Russia would certainly stand by France. Their argument was that the document could hardly be authentic since the word "Russia" was no longer used in diplomatic language and since the Foreign Office had no way of knowing that the Soviets would fight.[17]

Illustrative of the campaign for appeasement was Maurras's angry reaction to the partial mobilization of September 24 (*L'Action Française,* September 26):

Our young people leave, shoulder their knapsacks for Czechoslovakia, for Moscow! Blows, blood and death for Prague and Moscow.

And afterwards?

To an absurd objective and disastrous result![18]

The next day under the title "Down with war!" he stated: "Must we make war because that miserable Pierre Cot, the

---

[17] For a discussion of the *fausses nouvelles* see Werth, *France and Munich,* pp. 288-293; also Hamilton Fish Armstrong, *Foreign Affairs,* Jan., 1939; and *L'Europe Nouvelle Documentaire,* brochure No. 8. Other papers which denounced the declaration of the Foreign Office as a *fausse nouvelle* were *La Liberté,* Sept. 30, 1938; *L'Action Française,* Sept. 29, 1938; *La République,* Sept. 20, 1938; *Le Matin,* Sept. 20 and Oct. 2, 1938; also *Revue Hebdomadaire,* Oct. 8, 1938.

[18] Lauzanne, *Le Matin,* Sept. 25, 1938.

destroyer of our aviation and agent of the Soviets, has wrung
a promise of assistance to Czechoslovakia from the weak
Daladier . . . [a promise] which has . . . never been inscribed
in the treaties?" On the twenty-eighth the title of his article
was: "No! No war!" and on the twenty-ninth: "No war!
No! No!"

On September 27 a poster opposing mobilization without
the convocation of the Chambers, which M. Flandin had had
printed, was on display for a short time. "French people,"
it read, "you are being deceived. You are being made to
believe that an impassable moat separates the demands of
Hitler from the concessions already agreed to. That is false.
The only disagreement is over a question of procedure." After
denouncing the ideological war desired by the Extreme Left
and the "clever machine set up for weeks and months by
occult forces to make war inevitable," it declared that there
must be no mobilization and that Parliament must be called to
discuss the situation objectively. It concluded: "At this hour,
I see only one single legal means of maintaining peace. Let
all those who want to save it address their petition against
war to the chief of the State." Although the poster was torn
off by the police and the issue of *La Liberté* of September 28,
which had printed it, was confiscated, *Le Jour* and *L'Action
Française* praised the "eloquent appeal" on the next day.

An important section of the press, however, mainly the
Conditional Nationalists, reacted more patriotically to the ultimatum of Godesberg and accepted, although reluctantly, the
idea of war in case Hitler refused to reconsider his new
demands. Speaking of the success of the partial mobilization,
René Pinon wrote that the people of France would have fought
"if there were no other way out but battle," and that it would
not have been "war for Czechoslovakia," but war against
Pan-Germanism to save France from a new invasion.[19]

Colonel de la Rocque also made, in his confused style, a
patriotic appeal: "In these whirlwinds of contradictory pas-

[19] *Revue des Deux Mondes,* Oct. 15, 1938, pp. 952-953.

sions, let us be ourselves among the exhausted and the *belli-cistes,* the defeatists and the timid; let us remain strictly Frenchmen. Let us do everything to maintain a realistic and dignified peace. If honor or security demands it, let us be ready to raise France in a single leap against the aggressor." Even Emile Roche, who had been one of the extreme advocates of peace at any cost and who had been the first to ask for dismemberment of Czechoslovakia, took an attitude of outraged patriotism after the failure of the Godesberg meeting. On September 25 he wrote in *La République:*

> If Germany thought that she could take advantage of the situation to force her demands and use brutality and menaces to further them, not only the risk of a conflict would arise, but the certitude of one would be impressed on the minds of all, English and French alike.
>
> Perhaps it has not been useless to write that in this paper, where we have ceaselessly defended and will always defend peace.
>
> But with honor and dignity!

It is quite remarkable that a number of those who had accepted the essentials of the capitulation, the cession of the Sudetenland, should stand up to the German demands of relatively secondary importance made at Godesberg. The question of national honor and prestige, the moral obligation to abide by the treaties in case of German aggression against Czechoslovakia, as well as the readiness to follow the British Government whatever position it took, may explain the relative firmness of a section of the press. As D'Ormesson stated in a later book apropos of Hitler's demands: "Suddenly the problem had been raised from the political to the moral plane. . . . On every hand the storm of protest increased in volume. France, though she had done everything in her power to avoid a conflict, felt that she had now no choice but to take military measures."[20]

It seems that a mixture of patriotism and pacifism was the diet required by the readers of the Rightist press. In some

[20] *France,* p. 206.

cases, such as *Le Petit Journal* of Colonel de la Rocque, the mixture led to an entirely incoherent policy; in others, like *Le Jour* and *L'Action Française,* it was cleverly used alternately to flatter the patriotic impulses and pacific longings of the readers and to screen the defeatist campaign of the papers behind patriotic declarations and a show of apparent firmness—whenever the international situation allowed it without risk. Thus from the crisis of May 21 until the beginning of September, M. Bailby patriotically criticized the demands of the Sudeten Germans and declared that Hitler wanted European domination.[21]   When the crisis approached, however, his attitude quickly changed, and he was the chief advocate of the *"helvétisation"* and "neutralization" of Czechoslovakia and a violent critic of the *bellicistes.*   Again, when the first crisis of September subsided after Berchtesgaden and all danger of war seemed past, his patriotism was allowed to raise its head.   On September 20 and 22, he affirmed that the French would fight with the same ardor as in 1914 if Hitler refused a pacific solution of the Czechoslovak crisis.[22]   But during the "scare days" of the second crisis of September and until Munich, Bailby resumed his pacifist argument and stood in the front line of the appeasers.   Finally after Munich he could safely admit that France was paying a high price for peace, and that only the future would tell whether or not the government had been right in yielding to the German demands.[23]   The same offended and pessimistic nationalism was shown after Munich by *L'Action Française.*   On October 2 Charles Maurras described Hitler as "Europe's mad dog," now more alarming than ever; "optimists who figure that giving him satisfaction in the East would make him less dangerous on the other side, get a laugh out of me as they forget two little things, namely, the passions of men and the age-old customs of history." This patriotic attitude taken by the Extreme Right after the crisis

[21] *Le Jour,* July 14, 18, Aug. 19, Sept. 3, 1938.

[22] On September 23 he blamed the U. S. S. R. for having abandoned the Czechs and wrote, serenely unperturbed: "In view of the efforts we have made to circumscribe the mutilation of Bohemia, the total abandonment by Russia has no excuse."   [23] *Le Jour,* Oct. 1, 1938.

may be interpreted as a psychological compensation demanded by their Nationalist following after France's diplomatic defeat at Munich, as well as a clever defense against the charge of "pro-Fascist appeasement."

The reaction of the press and Parliament to the news of the Munich conference showed an indecent enthusiasm hardly justified by the Franco-British sacrifice of Czechoslovakia: "Victory! Victory! Hundreds of thousands of Parisians went down into the street to greet it with frenzy, without any word of command from any group or political cell. Peace is won. It is won over the crooks, sell-outs and madmen. It is won for old and young, for mothers and their little ones."[24]

Jean Prouvost was almost as enthusiastic in *Paris-Soir* (October 1):

Yes, we are going to live. But thanks to whom? Thanks to Neville Chamberlain. . . . Thanks to President Roosevelt. . . . All honor to them. All honor also to our own. Honor to Edouard Daladier, to Georges Bonnet. . . . Our Premier and Minister of Foreign Affairs have preserved peace for us. That is well. They preserved peace with dignity and honor. That is better. Thanks to them France can continue living her beautiful and glorious destiny as a peaceful and democratic nation.

Colonel de la Rocque joined in the chorus of praise, exclaiming proudly: "What a marvellous and extraordinary people we are! Neither war blustering nor exhibitionist defeatism registers with us. We were ready to fight enthusiastically if our honor and security so demanded. We wanted peace and refused to pour a single drop of oil into the flames of the Sudeten conflict. This shows prodigious firmness, good sense, and wisdom."[25] *Le Journal* of October 1 waxed lyrical: "Peace passed over Paris yesterday like a torch to rekindle in the heart of every Frenchman the love of other Frenchmen."[26] The fact that the majority of the French public, with the important exception of the Extreme Left, a number of Moderate

---

[24] Lauzanne, *Le Matin*, Oct. 1, 1938.   [25] *Petit Journal*, Oct. 1, 1938.
[26] See also *Le Temps*, RP, Sept. 30, Oct. 1, 2, 1938.

Leftists, and a minority of Nationalists, felt an intense physical relief at the news of Munich seems above discussion.[27]   The Leftist pacifist Galtier Boissière was as enthusiastic as the neo-pacifist Stéphane Lauzanne:

If the peoples did not march, as in 1914, to the great profit of the munitions makers and all the profiteers, it is because they no longer believed in a gay and joyous war, because they no longer believed that a new order can come out of human butchery.   And if the Four hastily made a provisional peace, it is because they were afraid of these peoples who no longer believed in the virtues of war . . . (*Le Crapouillot,* November, 1939).

While the debate in the Chamber on October 4 may not prove the sincerity of the pacifism of many deputies, at least it showed that they were convinced that their constituents were over-whelmingly opposed to war.   With the exception of M. de Kerillis, one Socialist, and the Communist deputies, the Chamber voted unanimously in favor of the Munich Pact.[28]   In the debate, M. Léon Blum, after expressing his "profound joy at peace" and his "sorrow for Czechoslovakia," voiced his belief that everything should be done to avoid war. He revealed the *cas de conscience* of the pacifist Socialists when he added: "In the present crisis we have been logical with ourselves.   We have never admitted the fatality of war.   We were inspired by the heroic lesson left us by Jaurès." Yet he made it clear that his pacifism was not absolute and unconditional: "But this considered and passionate desire for peace does not lead a people to submit to everything . . .; it does not abolish the distinction between just and unjust; it does not annul the validity of contracts on which any organization of collective security is based."[29]

On the opposite side of the House, M. Ybarnégaray and other Rightist deputies expressed a similar distaste for war. The former spoke of the "tragic dilemma, on the one hand, to save the little peoples, on the other, to be unable to save them except by dragging France and Europe into the most

[27] Cf. Werth, *France and Munich,* p. 315.
[28] 535 to 75, with 3 abstentions.   [29] *JO. Ch.,* Oct. 4, 1938, p. 1535.

horrible catastrophe. You have chosen. . . . You were right."[30]
It seems difficult, however, despite the conformity of view,
to compare the doctrinal pacifism of the Leftist leaders to the
opportunist neo-pacifism of the Rightists, even when the
powerful antiwar feeling of the public is taken into account.
M. de Kerillis, after voicing his "sorrowful protests" against
the peace of Munich which "annuls forever the benefits of the
victory of 1918,"[31] made it clear that the leaders of opinion and
the representatives of the people had failed in their duty by
letting themselves be carried away by the "understandable but
unconsidered enthusiasm of the crowds."[32] While it is quite
possible that in September, 1938, the leaders could not have
gone against overwhelming popular feeling, even had they
tried, they were themselves partly responsible for this wave
of pacifism which they had encouraged rather than discouraged
during the three previous years. It may be that for each individual the peace of Munich was a *cas de conscience,* a struggle
between his patriotism and his love for peace. The public could
not properly weigh the pros and cons of the situation, however,
when the scales had consistently been weighted on one side.
The honor of France was not a sufficient incentive for waging
a cruel war on behalf of a small and unhappy state; but had
the leaders of opinion emphasized instead that the security of
France was at stake, the necessary impulse for a policy of resistance might have been created.

It cannot be denied that the pacific mood of the French
might be largely attributed to the immense lassitude born of
the World War and to the feeling of inferiority toward Germany, especially after the creation of the Third Reich. It was
felt that even another victory would be useless and could
not change the *rapport de forces* between France and Ger-

[30] *Ibid.,* p. 1539.

[31] M. de Kerillis eloquently showed that "this peace signifies the renunciation
of our historic policy, pursued without interruption for centuries, to maintain the
European equilibrium. This peace consecrates the triumph of Hitler, that is, at
the same time that of Germany and of international fascism" (Exclamations at
the "Right."   Applause at the "Extreme Left" and on several benches) (*ibid.,*
p. 1538).   [32] *Ibid.*

many; many believed that their country could no longer compete with the enormous economic and military strength of their neighbor for the leadership of the new Europe that would have to be rebuilt after another war. This inferiority complex explains the negativism of French foreign policy, which manifested itself both at the Right in a policy of abandonment and at the Left in a passive and purely formal adherence to the principles of collective security. Self-confidence was lacking: when deeds were needed, only words were uttered by timid leaders who reflected the state of mind of a weary nation.

Fabre-Luce in his book, *Le Secret de la république,* expressed this pessimism of an old nation doubting its destiny and afraid of standing up to the threats of the "hereditary enemy": "Above all, let us not hope to save ourselves by war. . . . In spite of the victory of 1918, our strength, compared to that of Germany, is today not so great as in 1914. Even supposing that the exploit could be repeated tomorrow, we would none the less continue to slide further down the scale. A military victory that is not prolonged by a permanent effort, by a startling increase in the birth rate, by the triumph of work, is only an episode. It does not settle the fate of a nation."[33]

Although the argument has often been advanced that it is impossible to make any distinction between the reactions of the Right and those of the Left to the Munich peace, the difference between the motives that actuated the Socialists and those that governed the Nationalists is obvious. It would be more difficult to determine the causes of the acceptance of Munich by the Moderate Leftists, like the Radical-Socialists and the Union Socialiste Républicaine, who were not, in general, doctrinaire pacifists. Quite possibly the antiwar feeling in September influenced the leaders of the Moderate Leftists, like those of the Center, more readily than either the Extreme Left or Extreme Right, since they were fundamentally opportunists and lacked a positive doctrine in foreign policy.[34] On

[33] P. 231.

[34] A significant comparison may be made between the firm attitude of some Moderate Leftists in the beginning of 1938 and their pro-Munich stand in the

the other hand, both Traditional Pacifism and Rightist Neo-Pacifism were likely to meet in the Center and contribute in varying degrees to their attitude toward the Czechoslovak affair.

It seems, however, that neo-pacifism, that is, "realism" and fear of War-Revolution, was the determining factor in the attitude of the right wing of the Radical-Socialists (to which belonged M. Bonnet) and of some prominent National-Socialists at the Left, such as MM. Déat, Bergery, and Marquet. It must be kept in mind that the breaking up of the Popular Front, which had started at the beginning of the year, became more apparent at the time of Munich and was an accomplished fact with the failure of the general strike at the end of November. As early as October 13 the bureau of the Radical-Socialist party passed a declaration against the domestic and foreign policy of the Communists, thus ending their unenthusiastic collaboration with the Extreme Left. Undoubtedly the Popular Front had already been broken before September in the minds of many Moderate Leftists who could, therefore, be considered as belonging to the future anti-Marxist coalition behind Daladier after November, 1938. A new definition of the Right based on opposition to socialism rather than to the principles of the French Revolution would have preceded only by a few months what actually took place at the end of the year.[35]

Thus in order to have a clearer picture of the attitude

---

month of September. See Mistler, *JO. Ch.*, Feb. 26, 1938, pp. 600 ff. The contrast is especially striking for M. de Monzie, who defended a policy of defense of Austria and Czechoslovakia in February and was a convinced *Munichois* in September.

[35] See below, pp. 201 ff. Other reasons that could explain the pro-Munich attitude of the majority of the Left were: the belief that France was incapable of waging a long war, the parochial patriotism of many, according to which only a defensive war was justified, the influence of the principle of self-determination on some idealists, the long-established revisionist foreign policy of some (cf. Four Power Pact in 1933), the love for compromise of the opportunists who had gladly accepted Lord Runciman's mission and Chamberlain's deal at Berchtesgaden, and the policy of keeping in close union with Great Britain, regardless of the shifts of policy of the British Government. Finally, the failure of the League discouraged many former disciples of collective security and made them take a chance with a return to the Four Power Pact policy.

toward Munich assumed by the leaders of opinion, it is useful
to consider the *anti-Munichois* as composed of the Communists,
the Left wing of the Socialist party, as well as of the C. G. T.,
a minority of Radical-Socialists, and the Traditional Nationalists.[36]   The majority, the *Munichois,* could be divided into
two main groups, the borderline, of course, not being rigid:
those attracted by the traditional pacifism of the Socialists and
those drawn to the opportunistic neo-pacifism of the Right.
The real test of the acceptance of Munich was not the overwhelming vote of confidence by the Chamber immediately
after Daladier's return from Munich but acceptance of the
Four Power diplomacy, in terms of a free hand to Germany
in the East or of conditional resistance without Soviet Russia.
Those who defended a policy of integral resistance after
Munich may be classified as *anti-Munichois,* although they
voted for the government in October.

Before reviewing the outstanding causes of the neo-pacifism
of the Rightist leaders, it will be useful to eliminate some of
the arguments most frequently used in the press as of secondary importance.   As has been said, the pacific temper of
the public during September can only partly explain the attitude of the leaders; the spectacular use of the emotional chord
of pacifism during the crisis by many Rightist papers proved
merely a very effective device in defense of the policy of
appeasement.

Neither should the right of self-determination of peoples
be considered a sufficient incentive for the leaders to accept
the dismemberment of Czechoslovakia.   Although this argument was often used in the press and quite likely with success, it is doubtful that such a lofty principle had much to
do with their desire to accept peace at almost any cost.   The
issue at stake surpassed greatly the question of self-determination since France's own security was directly threatened; more-

---

[36] The Jacobin patriotism of some Radicals, like MM. Herriot, Cot, Chappedelaine, Campinchi, and Archimbaut, led them to defend a foreign policy similar to
that of the Traditional Nationalists of the type of Buré, Pertinax, or De Kerillis.

over, a compromise could have been easily found between self-determination and the maintenance of the European balance of power that would have satisfied the German minority had not the government of the Reich been behind the scene.

It was also stated in the press that France had to follow Great Britain and could not resume the initiative without the risk of being left alone against Germany. It was doubtless the purpose of the campaign of *fausses nouvelles* in the Rightist press to lead the public into this convenient belief since the communiqué of the British Foreign Office on September 26 had made it clear that, in case of war over Czechoslovakia, Great Britain would come to the rescue of France.

We must also reject the "legal" argument as expressed by Professor Barthélemy and others that France was no longer bound to help the Czechs since the demise of the League Covenant had invalidated her pacts of mutual assistance. Whatever its technical value, the argument was obviously without influence on the Right, who had always opposed the principle of collective security, with its concomitant indivisible peace, and had accepted the League only as a system of potential alliances against German aggression. The failure of the League should have been interpreted by them as the failure of an ineffective instrument for the maintenance of the European *status quo,* to be replaced by a more adequate one.

It was frequently argued that the fate of Czechoslovakia did not directly—or even indirectly—affect the security of France and that therefore it did not justify a war. The belief, if sincere, that Germany would not or could not attack France if left free in Eastern Europe would, of course, justify Munich for the Right. In all logic the wishful thinking of men like Montigny and Flandin of the Center, who believed that Germany could be appeased, was more defensible than the opportunism of M. Maurras or M. Bailby of the Extreme Right, who after the crisis expressed their profound distrust of Germany, although throughout the period of tension they had been the first to clamor for appeasement. However, even those who thought that German expansion would take place toward the East did not affirm that it would never be directed against France, or would leave her perfectly safe.[37]   Moreover, the Right had never before Munich been inclined to sacrifice French security to the good will of the German Führer. In terms of their traditional anti-German policy their abandonment of Czechoslovakia can hardly be explained by a sudden belief in Hitler's good intentions and in the value of his word.

In the last analysis, the main causes of the Right's easy acceptance of a policy of a free hand to Germany in Eastern and Southeastern Europe seem to be similar to those examined with respect to the crises of March, 1936, and March, 1938, which may be ranged under the heading of "Realism" and "Ideology."

Maurras pretended that France's unpreparedness was the fundamental cause of her abdication when he stated (*L'Action Française,* September 20): "Certainly Germany, Enemy Number One, gains an enormous increase in power, but whatever the future dangers, they are preferable to the danger of an immediate disaster.   By gaining time, we shall be able to re-establish the European equilibrium."   As in 1936, the statement that the French Army was actually inferior to that of Germany and would necessarily have been defeated even in an offensive war was seldom found; rather it was declared that war would be long and exhaustive, since the French Army, defensive in character, could not give immediate and effective help to the Czechs.[38]   France could not afford a costly victory, it was argued; the loss in men necessary to pierce the Siegfried Line would be enormous, even disastrous for a country with a low birthrate. France would for a long time have to bear the brunt of the fighting, since Great Britain had only small forces to land in France and since the help of Russia and the other Eastern countries was doubtful or, if rendered,

[37] See Montigny, *France, libère-toi!* p. 136.
[38] Cf. *JO. Ch.,* Oct. 4, 1938; Miellet, p. 1529; Frossard, p. 1539.

of doubtful efficiency. The geographic and military arguments concerning Russian aid used in 1936 were used again in 1938, reinforced by the argument of the purges suffered by the Red Army.

Essentially, it was the low state of French morale, the inadequate production in war industries, especially that of airplanes, and the nature of France's military organization that were held responsible for the government's acceptance of unfavorable conditions of peace. These arguments were summarized by Raymond Recouly:

A diplomatic defeat, if there is a defeat, is still, without question, much better than a military defeat. . . .

Even if defeat could have been avoided . . . victory would have had to be paid for by hundreds of thousands, if not millions of human lives, which would risk dangerously weakening a country like ours where the birthrate has already fallen so low. . . .

To maintain the treaties against Germany a strong France was needed. France, alas! has grown weak and this weakness has, since 1936, taken alarming proportions, not so much with regard to the army itself, as to material, aviation, industrial production, and economic and financial conditions.[39]

It must be admitted—especially in the light of recent events —that these excuses were far more valid in September, 1938, than they were in March, 1936, at the time of the remilitarization of the Rhineland, since Germany had had thirty months to rearm at full speed and to fortify her Western frontier. But the fact that these arguments were used then, when the situation apparently did not justify extreme caution, throws some doubt upon their sincerity, and the general belief that France would ultimately have won the war leaves the realistic argument without its main justification.

The conviction often expressed that Soviet Russia would not be a reliable ally but might let France fight alone against Germany cannot be dismissed too lightly. Still this belief cannot be separated from the fear of War-Revolution which usually accompanied it.

[39] *Revue de France,* Oct. 15, 1938, pp. 559-560.

The main argument against accepting the risks of war was still the classic one of the Communist menace. It was used and abused in 1938 as in 1936: Moscow, helped by a war party in Paris, wanted France to fight Germany in order to save Russia from a German invasion and at the same time to bring about the Bolshevist revolution in Europe. The campaign against Russia and international communism was of course most active at the Extreme Right.[40] Colonel de la Rocque continued to affirm that Public Enemy Number Two was just as dangerous as Public Enemy Number One, and *Le Matin* stated on September 29: "No people has anything to gain by war. All the peoples have something to lose by it. Only one man, only one doctrine, would, in the end, be the beneficiaries. The man is the one, already covered with blood, who stays buried in the Kremlin. The doctrine is that which would destroy the bases of civilization for the satisfaction of that man's dream of anarchic hegemony." The same fear of postwar revolution was also frequently voiced by the *Modérés*. Thus a former minister of finance, M. Germain Martin, exposed the plan of the Communists in *Le Capital:* "to engender a war through which, whatever happens, the people of Moscow will be the winners. The Communists, in accord with the Soviet Government, want their war. It is important to unmask the diabolic project, nurtured methodically for years."[41] And the serious M. Pinon warned his readers of the *Revue des Deux Mondes* as much against the Communist menace as against German ambition.[42]

The attack on the Russian Government and the Third International might be partly interpreted as an all-out assault on the French Communist party, in the hope of destroying the Popular Front. But the coalition of the three Leftist parties was fast disintegrating, and its collapse was well-nigh inevi-

[40] *Le Jour,* Sept. 6, 13, 1938; *L'Action Française,* Sept. 10, 20, 1938; *La Liberté,* Oct. 21, 1938; *Choc,* Sept. 13, 1938; *Le Petit Journal,* Oct. 8, 11, 30, 1938.
[41] Sept. 27, also Nov. 23.
[42] Oct. 1, 1938, p. 720; see also Recouly, *Revue de France,* Oct. 15, pp. 558-559; Georges Prade, *Revue Bleue,* Oct., 1938, p. 363; Montigny, *France, libère-toi!* pp. 113 ff.

table. Rather than to finish off an already impotent Popular Front, the anti-Bolshevist campaign was apparently intended to add a powerful argument against the policy of resistance to Germany, and further to discredit Moscow, thus ruining any chance of a Franco-Soviet alliance in the future. The Extreme Right was not reluctant in admitting their purpose— to exclude the U. S. S. R. from the new Europe.

Whatever the sincerity of the leaders who manipulated the argument of the Bolshevist revolution, it must have been quite efficacious to sustain the heavy use made of it for three years, and to justify three major diplomatic defeats. A weighty section of French conservative opinion must have earnestly believed that a European war would ultimately bring economic chaos and a social upheaval, although they may have refused to admit that their fear of revolution was synonymous with fear of victory.[43] There is much truth in Mr. Louis Fischer's comment: "A war would have ended in the political death of Hitler and Mussolini, and it could only have been successfully waged by the democracies with the political support of the working classes and the armed support of the U. S. S. R., and after the rescue of republican Spain. The ruling classes of England and France regarded this as too high a price to pay for national security. The bourgeoisie of the Western democracies feared to win the war." This alleged reason might not be true as to Great Britain, but it certainly was one of the main elements of the appeasement policy in France.[44]

[43] It was also argued that the Third International wanted France's defeat at the hands of Germany, who would then find in Western Europe, in Africa, and South America her field of expansion; Soviet Russia would thus be saved (cf. Montigny, *France, libère-toi!* p. 114).

[44] *Nation*, Oct. 29, 1938, p. 448. It is significant that in September and October, 1938, anticommunism was the common denominator of neo-pacifism and was by no means limited to the Right. The neo-Socialist Adrien Marquet made it clear after Munich where his sympathy lay in the struggle between fascism and communism (cf. *Le Temps*, Oct. 4, 1938). The right wing of the Socialist party under M. Paul Faure and that of the C. G. T. under M. Belin were openly anti-Communist as well as pacifist at the time of Munich. During the debate on the Munich Pact, M. Bergery (*JO. Ch.*, Oct. 4, 1938, p. 1540) made his position plain by bitterly criticizing the policy of the Communists. Although the U. S. R., the party of Déat, Frossard, De Monzie, Pomaret, all ardent *Munichois*, based

For the Extreme Right, democracy was the enemy as much as communism; the coming war appeared to them as a struggle between the democratic ideal of the Republic that they had always condemned, and their own conception of authoritarian government, which was defended by the enemies of France. Thus Stéphane Lauzanne wrote in *Le Matin* on October 3 that "Frenchmen were asked to declare and make war for an awkward, uncomprehending, intolerant regime," and Le Grix spoke of the "world war of religion," the "ideological crusade of the democracies against the dictatorships, . . . which is only deferred, but which a certain number of dark minds continue patiently to prepare, indeed to make inevitable, in the United States, in England, in France (let us not insist any more on the question of 'race'), minds that are much more dangerous for peace—as I see it—than that of Hitler. No, war is not inevitable, except for those people."[45]

The relative importance of what appear to be the two main causes for the policy of abdication culminating in Munich cannot, of course, be established accurately. From the past record of the Rightist leaders' attitude toward Germany, however, the theory may be advanced that the realistic arguments had a greater impact on the *Modérés* than on the Extremists, who were apparently most influenced by their ideological bias. Significantly, the position of Conditional Nationalism was left more or less intact in spite of the loss of Czechoslovakia: an important section of the Right still believed, at least outwardly, in the possibility and desirability of opposing any further German aggression. Only the Resigned Nationalists saw in the capitulation of Munich the culmination of their policy of retrenchment; in their eyes the success of the Reich sealed not only the fate of the Czechs, but also that of France's postwar policy of Eastern intervention. Both groups interpreted

---

its attitude on pacifist grounds (*Le Temps*, Oct. 3, 4, 1938), its anti-Marxism was well known. As to the Radical-Socialists, their declaration of October 13 and their Congress of October 27 mark the end of their short collaboration with the Communists.

[45] *Revue Hebdomadaire*, Sept. 3, 1938, p. 124.

differently the meaning of the "Munich spirit" and the Four Power diplomacy, yet both agreed on two points: they fully accepted, even glorified, France's major diplomatic defeat, and they congratulated themselves on its main advantages, the rout of the *bellicistes,* especially the Communists, and the elimination of Soviet Russia from European affairs.

PART IV

BACK TO RESISTANCE?
(1938-1939)

CHAPTER X

THE FOUR POWER DIPLOMACY

WITH THE Munich capitulation, France's diplomatic retreat on the European Continent had become a rout. She had lost a powerful and dependable ally, and her entire chain of alliances had been severed, for none of her allies could count on aid against Germany or Italy unless France herself was directly threatened. King Carol of Rumania received no support from the Quai d'Orsay when he visited Paris in November; Yugoslavia had left the French camp and had been drawn into the Italo-German orbit. After the disintegration of the Popular Front and Daladier's rupture with the Communists, relations with the Soviets progressively worsened. France was appeasing not only Hitler but Mussolini and Franco as well: an ambassador was sent to the "King of Italy and Emperor of Ethiopia," and General Franco was recognized, with the approval of the governmental majority.[1] France and Germany signed a declaration of amity on December 6 in which they pledged themselves to recognize as definitive their common frontiers. From this agreement it was inferred that the Reich would relinquish its colonial claims so long as France permitted it to pursue an expansionist policy in the Eastern part of Europe, a state of affairs already implied by Munich.

Yet not all *Munichois* interpreted the Franco-British diplomatic defeat as the legalization of German hegemony east of the Rhine; the positions of the Rightists in foreign policy were still the same during the months following Munich as they had been since 1936.

The Right's first emotional reaction to the Munich Pact and the nervous strain of the September crises, as has been

[1] The foreign policy of the government was upheld by a Chamber vote of 323 to 261 on February 24, 1939. The Spanish frontier had been closed in June, thus sealing the fate of the Loyalists; the recognition of Franco was the logical outcome of this policy of nonintervention.

shown, translated itself into an optimistic outburst. "As a sequel to the Munich agreement a sense of almost physical relief came about in European relations. Nerves had been strained to such a point that a reaction was only natural. The hope was indulged that the agreement between the four great powers might mark the dawn of a new era."[2]

Then followed what might be termed the rational reaction to the Munich Pact. This reasoned acceptance of the agreement between the four powers by the majority of the Right was much more significant than their enthusiastic approval of Chamberlain's policy during and immediately after the crisis. While the minority of Traditional Nationalists or *anti-Munichois* either opposed Munich, as did De Kerillis, or accepted it as a "necessary but disastrous accident,"[3] the great majority actively defended the agreement with the Führer and its projection into the future; that is, they viewed the Four Power diplomacy as a means to settle European problems. This policy, however, was not necessarily synonymous with giving Germany free play in the East; many *Munichois* continued to advocate conditional resistance to German hegemony and hoped to find the elements for a new balance of power in Europe.

The abandonment of Czechoslovakia had given the Reich an obvious economic supremacy and political preponderance in the Danube basin and Eastern Europe. Nevertheless, it was hoped that this preponderance would not lead to complete hegemony. "The question is to know whether Germany will tackle the problem of exploiting *Mittel Europa* in a spirit that

[2] D'Ormesson, *France,* p. 210; see also *Le Figaro,* Oct. 2, 1938. This reflex was not limited to the Right; M. Blum himself was not too gloomy about the future of Europe after Munich, and hoped it would lead to a general settlement of European difficulties. He wrote on October 1 in *Le Populaire:* "Europe is not out of the danger zone. No state has yet enjoyed lasting security. Shall we go no further than to complete and hasten war preparations. . . . Will the respite be devoted to this? Or will the Munich agreement be seized upon at once as a point of departure and support for enlarged negotiations aiming to settle general economic and political European problems, thus leading toward real, solid, equitable, indivisible, and disarmed peace?"

[3] Ernest Pezet, *JO. Ch.,* Jan. 20, 1939, p. 136.

one could qualify as American, or with the traditional spirit of political hegemony," stated Lucien Romier in *Le Figaro* on October 11.   In the first case, Germany would have to "equip and transform the economy of Europe," and could not do so as long as her industry was geared for war; she would therefore need a definite agreement for security with France and Great Britain.   In the second case, "Germany would use her new resources solely to prepare a vast enterprise against the Western powers whom she would first try to divide.   It would be a frightful catastrophe for her and for all.   For no system can make three hundred million true Europeans abdicate their past and their future in favor of eighty million."[4]

Consequently it was over the question of complete German hegemony that the *Munichois* were divided.   The trends of Conditional and Resigned Nationalism can be clearly traced in the press and in Parliament at the end of 1938 and at the beginning of 1939.   It was evident, however, that whether willing or unwilling to abandon Eastern and Southeastern Europe, the *Munichois* saw in the Four Power Pact diplomacy the means of eliminating Soviet Russia from European affairs and of turning the Franco-Soviet Pact into a useless instrument.

The group of Resigned Nationalists interpreted the peace of Munich as the consecration of their policy of retrenchment: France would have to give up her pacts of mutual assistance with her Eastern allies and, fortifying herself behind the Maginot Line, would have to concentrate on her Empire.   The policy of the "Retreat to the Empire"[5] was thus described by Stéphane Lauzanne: "France should not conclude military

[4] René Pinon discussed the same question (*Revue des Deux Mondes*, Oct. 15, 1938, p. 957): "As for the Munich agreements, only the future will show their value.   If they are to be only a stage, a period of respite, on the road that is leading the Germans, as they hope, to dominate the other peoples, they will only appear as an onerous expedient to gain a few months. . . . If they inaugurate a new equilibrium, if they arouse a new spirit, they can become the origin of a better era. . . ."

[5] This policy was defended by *Le Matin, Le Jour, Je Suis Partout, L'Action Française, Candide, Gringoire, La Liberté, Le Journal, La République*, in various degrees; often the policy of a paper was contradictory, Germany would be still talked of as the enemy and yet a policy of a free hand for the Reich, or at least no commitments in the East for France, would be advocated.

alliances which even on the map represent impossibilities. Above all, she should not take the part of the gendarme of Central and Eastern Europe. . . . Security is not on the Danube, on the Vistula, on the Bosporus. It is along the Vosges, the Alps, the Pyrenees, and even the Atlas Mountains. Her effort must be concentrated there. Her preoccupation of every hour must be there. France has two capitals: Paris and Algiers."[6]

The chief leader of this policy was M. Flandin, who expressed his views at the Congress of the Alliance Démocratique in November. According to him, France should renounce intervention on the Continent. "Let her turn away from Central Europe and let two other Europes be established near the Europe that we call Franco-English: that of Germany and that of Russia."[7] The final declaration of the Congress unmistakably approved a policy of nonintervention in the East. It stated that French security could no longer be .assured by the League and the doctrine of collective security, but only by national defense, and that France "must follow up the German and Italian negotiations begun at Munich" and "revise all the pacts by which she would risk being engaged in conflicts foreign to her vital interests."[8]

MM. Flandin and Montigny expressed the policy of a free hand in the East in greater detail at the important Chamber debate on foreign policy of January, 1939. Their arguments were the same as those used before Munich, with emphasis on a policy of colonial defense and colonial self-sufficiency based on the belief that the French and British Empires together were sufficiently strong to insure their own security, regardless of the growing strength of the Axis.[9] The fate of the two

[6] *Le Matin*, Oct. 17, 1938.   [7] *Le Temps,* Nov. 13, 1938.

[8] *Ibid.,* Nov. 15, 1938. It is significant to note that M. Flandin, the foremost advocate of a policy of retrenchment, was re-elected president of the Alliance Démocratique by 1,626 out of 1,745 votes, apparently on the issue of foreign policy. After being criticized by M. Charles Reibel for his antiwar poster of September and his telegram of congratulation to Hitler upon Munich, he faced the issue of foreign policy squarely: "The battle is going on in this country between two parties, the peace party and the war party. It is up to you to choose. . . ."

[9] Cf. Flandin, debate of Jan. 17, 1939, p. 67; M. Montigny expressed the same belief (*JO. Ch.,* Jan. 13, 1939, p. 28).

Empires was not to be decided in Eastern Europe. "Other great powers have to protect more direct interests in these parts than we," said M. Flandin. "It is up to them to do so, and if their strength, especially as far as Soviet Russia is concerned, is indeed what our Communist colleagues describe it to be, I think that the ambitions attributed to Germany, notably in the Ukraine, will not be very easily realized."[10]

While the Resigned Nationalists were willing to let the Reich expand freely as long as France was not directly threatened, the majority of the Right still continued to advocate conditional resistance. After resuming the position of those who would "let Germany find a field of expansion in Russia on the pretext of crushing communism," René Pinon stated his own position, that of the Conditional Nationalists:

Others on the contrary, without mistaking the importance of the Empire and the value of its resources, have maintained that France should look for the bases of a new European equilibrium. While recognizing, as Mr. Chamberlain has said, the preponderant position of Germany in Central Europe, which her geographic position and the mass of her population assure her, this new balance would guarantee the independence and the security of the small and medium-sized states.[11]

The Congress of the Fédération Républicaine in November supported this policy. The final resolution stated that the Congress "considers that the constantly increasing German danger makes it a duty for France to neglect nothing in order to re-establish the friendships necessary to her security and the European equilibrium," and "affirms its fidelity to its traditional principles, which tend to maintain and seek an effective and loyal collaboration with Great Britain, Italy, and the

[10] *Ibid.*, Jan. 17, 1939, pp. 66-67. At the same time M. Flandin did his best to convince the Chamber that his policy was fundamentally similar to that of the Conditional Nationalists, as expressed by Louis Marin, since the advocates of "la politique de l'Empire" had always reserved the right for France to intervene eventually in Eastern Europe (*ibid.*, pp. 66-67, Jan. 26, p. 200; see also Montigny, Jan. 13, p. 28).

[11] *Revue des Deux Mondes*, Nov. 15, 1938, p. 472. This policy was clearly advocated by *Le Figaro*, *Le Petit Parisien*, *Le Petit Journal*, *Le Temps*, and others.

countries of Central and Eastern Europe."[12] *Rapprochement* with Germany was not mentioned, nor was the Franco-Russian Pact. It was the Stresa Front that was still advocated as the only effective means of opposing Pan-Germanism.

The same policy of conditional resistance was defended at the Congress of the Parti Social Français on December 4. "The P. S. F. declares that, France and Europe having a respite from war, no other issue can be envisaged but a more or less stable equilibrium between France and Germany, or an armed conflict with its tragic consequences. . . ." But the declaration could not resist the temptation of stressing the danger of Public Enemy Number Two. "The most serious and most immediate menaces hanging over France are those of a civil war attracting invasion and those of a foreign war followed by this World Revolution which the demonic power of the Soviets is preparing from afar." The declaration condemned the Franco-Soviet Pact and advocated the reconstruction of the Stresa Front, strengthened by collaboration with the Eastern states and the Spain of Franco.[13]

It was during the debates of January, 1939, in the Chamber, that the policy of conditional resistance to Germany was best expressed. Its advocates still saw the Reich as a great potential danger to France: "Since our Western civilization began," said Louis Marin, "Germany has always repeated the same attempts at hegemony. From the Germanic Holy Roman Empire . . . to Hitler, she has always followed the same policy."[14] Yet only the smaller states threatened by Germany should build a league of protection; M. Marin never mentioned the U. S. S. R. in the possible systems of alliance which he reviewed and even made it quite plain that his party would not enter a government divided over the question of a Russian alliance.[15] Characteristic of this policy of Conditional Nationalism was also the speech of M. Oberkirch, one of the most outspoken critics of the Russian alliance. After lengthily enumerating the con-

[12] *Le Temps,* Nov. 18, 1938.   [13] *Ibid.,* Dec. 5, 1938.

[14] *JO. Ch.,* Jan. 24, 1939, p. 193; see also X. Vallat, Jan. 20, 1939, p. 170; Ph. Henriot, Jan. 10, 1939, p. 142.   [15] *Ibid.,* Jan. 24, 1939, pp. 196-198.

ventional arguments against the Franco-Soviet Pact, he declared
that France should not disinterest herself in the fate of Europe
and that it was "Poland who must become the pivot of our
policy in the East of Europe."[16] Other orators also defended
the necessity of building an Eastern barrier to Pan-Germanism
around this country and criticized the government for not
having attempted after Munich to help Poland and Hungary
obtain a common frontier through Ruthenia.[17] In the Senate
M. Lémery spoke of a "Warsaw-Bucharest axis, the only one
capable of grouping around itself all the forces for stabiliza-
tion which today are drifting and disconcerted in Central and
Eastern Europe."[18] The advocates of resistance were thus
obliged to court small and illusory friendships and patch them
together in a mythological coalition.

Besides, their will to resist was curiously linked with the
acceptance of the Four Power diplomacy. The speech of M.
Philippe Henriot in the Chamber showed how confused was
the state of mind which, while opposing German hegemony,
accepted the spirit of Munich. He objected to giving the Reich
free play in Eastern Europe, yet, according to him, Munich
was not only a *pis aller* and "the end of an established order,"
but "should be the point of departure for a new and bold

[16] *Ibid.*, Jan. 26, 1939, p. 219.

[17] Cf. *JO. Ch.*, X. Vallat, Jan. 20, 1939, p. 170; Ph. Henriot, Jan. 20, p. 143.
M. Pinon suggested that the Ukrainian problem should be settled in favor of the
Ukrainian patriots. But in order to avoid war it would be essential that Poland,
instead of Germany, should take the lead in building an independent Ukraine,
which in turn would become an important element of the league of defense
against Germany (*Revue des Deux Mondes*, Jan. 1, 1939, pp. 237-239). Such a
solution to the problem would have had the advantage of both weakening Russia
and strengthening the buffer states, thus putting a stop to the danger of German
hegemony, as well as to the threat of bolshevism.

[18] *JO. S.*, Feb. 7, 1939, p. 98. The emphasis in these pages has been on the
Chamber debates; the trends in foreign policy were similar in the Senate. The
deputies, being more direct representatives of the people, gave a better picture of
public opinion than the senators. Moreover, the Chamber had a much greater influence on the foreign policy of the government than the other House, whose debates
on foreign affairs were infrequent and presented little danger to the government.
The position of Conditional Nationalism was prevalent in the Senate. An *ordre
du jour* signed by MM. Caillaux, Bérenger, Fabry, Hennessy, and others "affirmed
the traditional policy of France of insuring the development of peace in a stable
European order" (Feb. 7).

policy. . . . We must make up our minds: either take our place among the builders of the Europe of tomorrow or else resign ourselves to joining the long line of mourners who will make the ruins of the Europe of yesterday their 'wailing wall.' "[19] Similarly Senator Lémery affirmed that Munich was *"un moindre mal"* and opposed Germany's military hegemony on the Continent, but he carefully added that "we do not want to molest or curb her in the prosperity she is seeking. . . ." A policy of resistance to German aggression had to be reconciled with the Franco-German declaration of *"bon voisinage."*[20] Thus the league of defense against Pan-Germanism had to be compatible with the Munich policy; Germany should not feel that she was being encircled and must break the new barrier in order to realize her *Lebensraum.* Her peaceful expansion implicitly recognized at Munich had to be left unimpaired and only actual military conquest was to be discouraged. This policy necessarily led to a half-hearted advocacy of resistance and was an awkward and dangerous compromise between integral resistance and complete resignation. As M. Ernest Pezet expressed it in criticizing M. Bonnet's policy: "The government seems to me to use empty words when it affirms that it is not sacrificing the former friendships of France. For the spirit of the Munich agreement, Mr. Secretary of Foreign Affairs, if you are faithful to it, requires that you support them only cautiously and not completely. The reparation of the ethnic-political mistakes existing in Europe, which will be required one day and which you will be unable to prevent, concerns precisely those old friends whom you do not want to sacrifice to new friends."[21]

Obviously the policy of conditional resistance to Pan-Germanism was still founded on the formula: *"Ni pour Berlin ni pour Moscou."* Advocacy of the reconstruction of the Stresa Front had been the way out of this dilemma for a long time, but by now *rapprochement* with Italy had become

[19] *JO. Ch.,* Jan. 20, 1939, pp. 143-144.
[20] *JO. S.,* Feb. 7, 1939, pp. 97-98.
[21] *JO. Ch.,* Jan. 20, 1939, pp. 134-135.

synonymous with the acceptance of the Four Power diplomacy, that is, of a deal with Berlin at the expense of Moscow.

In November, when it seemed likely that France would be crippled by a general strike, the Italian dictator, taking a leaf out of Hitler's book on diplomatic technique, pressed his demands. A demonstration in the Italian Chamber of Deputies on November 30, 1938, offensive in tone, clamored for Tunisia, Corsica, Nice, and Savoy. The show had evidently been planned at this psychological moment in order to induce Chamberlain to act as mediator between the enemy sisters during his proposed visit to Rome. Soon afterwards, in the middle of December, the Italian Government abrogated the 1935 agreement between France and Italy. Thus the advances made by M. Bonnet after Munich in recognizing the conquest of Ethiopia and in appointing an ambassador to Rome were rewarded by an expression of brutal greed. The answer to the Italian challenge was the triumphant trip of M. Daladier to Corsica, Tunisia, and Algeria at the beginning of January, 1939, to strengthen imperial patriotism, inspect the defenses of the threatened territory, and warn the Italians. The Chamber approved the cabinet's foreign policy on January 28, 1939, by a vote of 379 to 232, and the Senate on February 9 by 287 to 15.[22]

The unanimous resistance to the Italian territorial claims in both the French press and Parliament was no less remarkable than were the efforts of the Right to maintain intact the prestige of the Four Power diplomacy, which, they declared, was not affected by the Italian pretensions.[23] Those

---

[22] The deputies in opposition were the 156 Socialists, the 72 Communists, one Independent Republican (De Kerillis), and two members of the Union Sociale et Républicaine (*Le Temps,* Jan. 28, 1939). The senators in opposition were 13 Socialists (the other two Socialist senators abstained from voting) and the two Communists.

[23] Typical of the attitude of the Right was D'Ormesson's statement that "This time the French are unanimously resolved not to be walked on. . . . The hour of integral resistance has come. . . . We are not yet in a state of material mobilization . . . but we are in a state of moral mobilization" (*Le Figaro,* Dec. 25, 1938).

The manifestation in the Italian Chamber was at first played down by the press and presented as not engaging the responsibility of the Italian Government (*Le Temps,* Dec. 2, 1938). It did not appear to interfere with the reactions of

contradictory attitudes can be reconciled only if we admit that the majority of the Right had accepted the deal with the Axis over Czechoslovakia in order to keep the Soviets out of European affairs, and not under the illusion that harmonious relations would endure between the four Western countries. Italian colonial claims would therefore have nothing to do with a general agreement between the Big Four. They were a question apart, to be settled between France and Italy, unless, and this eventuality was improbable, Germany should back her Axis partner. Since Great Britain was firmly on the side of a resolute France and since German expansion was most likely to continue toward the East, the Italian claims were not to be taken too seriously.[24]

M. Scapini, one of the most prominent members of the Comité France-Allemagne and thus advocate of direct *rapprochement* with the Reich, told the Chamber that, if Germany backed Italy in her demands, *"c'est la guerre."* In the other eventuality, on the contrary, conversations should be started for "the settlement of the immense economic problems of Europe," i.e., the satisfaction of German revendications.[25] On December 6 the "Bulletin du Jour" of *Le Temps* made clear the Rightists' geopolitical conception of the Four Power Pact diplomacy as an agreement over spheres of influence, according to which the maritime Empires of France and Great Britain could peacefully coexist with the continental Empire of Germany.

---

the Right to Herr von Ribbentrop's visit to Paris a week later, or with the signing of the Franco-German declaration. Compare the "Revue de la Presse" of *Le Temps,* Nov. 25, 1938, with that of Dec. 9, 1938.

[24] "The interest, the aspirations of Germany, are turned at this moment not toward the West of Europe, but toward the East. In spite of her recent triumphs . . . Germany . . . is not satisfied. . . . Under these conditions we must not be astonished that her eyes, her desires, turn in another direction, towards the Ukraine. . . ." M. Recouly concluded that Hitler would not want a war in the West to help Mussolini and that France should refuse any substantial concession to Italy (*Revue de France,* Jan. 15, 1939, pp. 274-276).

[25] *JO. Ch.,* Jan. 26, 1939, p. 247. MM. Elbel and Delauney also gave emphasis to the economic needs of the Reich, which would have to be settled to its advantage if war were to be avoided (*ibid.,* Jan. 19, 1939, p. 103; Jan. 24, pp. 166 f.).

Any imperialistic policy may be conceived under two aspects. . . . There is the conception, which is that of England and of France, of an empire bathed by all the seas. There is the conception of the vast political and economic empire as a solid whole, which Russia has realized in Europe and Asia and which Germany is at present in the act of realizing in the center of the Continent. These two conceptions are imposed by the geographic positions of the so-called imperial powers. It is therefore of prime importance that the Germans understand the necessities that are required for the free development of the French imperial policy and the British imperial policy, without which there could be no real equilibrium of strength and influence.

In other words, if Germany abandoned all colonial ambitions outside Europe she would be entitled to rebuild a modern version of the Holy Roman Empire in Europe. The Four Power diplomacy was an instrument for the adjustment of Eastern European problems to the benefit of Germany, but not for satisfying the colonial aspirations of the Axis partners.

In spite of the "bitter disappointment"[26] of the pro-Mussolini press, hopes for the reconstruction of the Stresa Front had not disappeared. M. Bailby spoke of a "lovers' quarrel," and M. Vallat affirmed in the Chamber that "the nature of things must lead France and Italy to carry on a policy of friendship."[27] But the myth of the Stresa Front had been exploded once more, and this time with loud reverberations. Talk of friendship with Italy was obviously no more than the expression of the desire to maintain the appearance of an agreement between the four Western powers and thus to avoid the con-

[26] St. Brice, *Revue Universelle*, Dec. 15, 1938, p. 728: "The disappointment is bitter for those who have taken such pains to struggle against the sectarian campaigns by maintaining that there is an intelligent and reasonable force in the new Risorgimento, to which great credit can be extended."

[27] *JO. Ch.*, Dec. 9, 1938, p. 1720. Even a month later, after the Franco-Italian treaty of 1935 had been denounced by Italy, M. Louis Marin told the Chamber that he still believed in the possibility of resurrecting the Stresa Front (*ibid.*, Jan. 24, 1939, p. 197). Cf. Philippe Henriot, p. 142. *Rapprochement* with Italy was advocated at the Congress of the P. S. F. on December 4 (*Le Temps*, Dec. 5, 1938). See also *Le Temps*, BJ, Dec. 7, and *Paris Midi*, RP, Jan. 15, 1939.

sequences of a policy of integral resistance to Germany based on a Russian alliance.[28]

The campaign following Munich against the Russian pact and the Communist party supplied abundant proof of the continued hatred of Public Enemy Number Two. The backbone of the campaign was the usual argument that "a conflagration which would hurl the great European nations against each other is the only way for Moscow to make the World Revolution break out."[29] The Traditional Nationalists, although they had no love for bolshevism, were the only Rightists who defended the necessity of a military agreement with the Soviets.

"Eastern alliances, the union of French and Slavic strength," De Kerillis told the Chamber, "are the essential conditions for European equilibrium.

"The regime of Soviet Russia, I assure you, my dear colleagues of the Right, is as repugnant to me as to all of you. But when it is a question of appraising the permanent laws of the foreign policy of my country, I do not allow the bourgeois to speak louder in me than the patriot" (loud applause at the Communist Extreme Left, at the "Extreme Left," and on some benches at the "Left," the "Center" and the "Right").[30]

The anti-Bolshevist campaign carried on by the majority of the Right in the press and in Parliament[31] was not limited

[28] M. Jean Fabry urged in *Le Matin* (Jan. 26, 1939) that the Franco-Russian Pact be not renewed and added: *"Il serait fou de penser que nous pourrons faire à la fois deux politiques contradictoires, celle du pacte franco-soviet de 1935 et celle de l'accord allemand de 1938."*

[29] Raymond Recouly, *Revue de France*, Nov. 15, 1938, p. 128. Also *Le Temps*, Nov. 15, 22, 1938; *Le Figaro*, Nov. 21, 1938; *Le Jour*, Nov. 5, 7, 1938; *Le Matin*, Jan. 26, Feb. 20, 1939.

[30] *JO. Ch.*, Jan. 13, 1939, p. 33. The neo-pacifist *Munichois* were condemned in the Chamber by the advocates of a policy of total resistance to Germany (P. Cot, Jan. 20, 1939, p. 148; F. Grenier, Jan. 26, 1939, p. 215; Grumbach, Jan. 24, 1939, p. 188). While the Leftist opposition was not unanimous in defending a policy of intervention in favor of the Spanish Government, it is significant that, in spite of the danger to France's lines of communication in the Mediterranean caused by the presence of Italian forces in Spain and the Balearic Islands and in spite of the open Italian ambitions in North Africa, the Rightist deputies still defended the policy of nonintervention and asked for an ambassador to Franco.

[31] Criticism of the Soviet pact (especially of the military agreement suggested by

to the field of foreign policy. It was logically extended to domestic politics in the form of a campaign against the "bellicists" in general and the Communists in particular. Immediately after Munich the "bellicists" were the main enemy of the neo-pacifists:[32] there were "accounts to settle" with the war party, which was at first composed, as M. Flandin put it, of the Communists, the anti-Fascist fanatics, and the old-fashioned anti-German Nationalists.[33] This heterogeneous group had in common the policy of integral resistance to the dictators and the belief in the necessity of a Franco-Russian alliance, as opposed to the belief of the neo-pacifists in the Four Power Pact diplomacy. The complete victory of the pro-Munich neo-pacifists, however, made it unnecessary for them to press any further the issue of "bellicism" and "pacifism." The *Munichois* of the Right knew that the moderate government of M. Daladier, even with a minority of "bellicist" ministers, would nevertheless follow the Munich policy while reassuring the privileged classes by its orthodox economic and social policy as well as by its energy and promise of longevity. Therefore the Rightist press soon concentrated on an all-out attack on Marxism which provided an easy platform for the regrouping of parties in the new conservative coalition; the union of

---

De Kerillis), and denunciation of the revolutionary aims of Moscow, were voiced by most Rightist speakers in the Chamber debates of January, 1939 (cf. *JO. Ch.,* Montigny, p. 30; Flandin, p. 66; Deschizeaux, p. 68; Henriot, p. 144; Jacquinot, p. 151; Riou, p. 179).

[32] It is noteworthy that the most fervent *Munichois* of the Right objected to the participation in the government of socially conservative politicians who had been anti-*Munichois*, like Reynaud, Mandel, and Herriot. Bailby, protesting against the nomination of Reynaud as Minister of Finance, frankly admitted his fears: "With Reynaud, his immediate group, his friends—Mandel, Herriot, Campinchi, and others —will regain hope in the constitution of a newly constructed ministry, from which would be excluded, naturally, men like Bonnet and De Monzie and in which Daladier himself would be sacrificed. . . . In reality we are witnessing a resumption of the offensive by the Popular Front; for Reynaud is Blum, and Herriot is Thorez." For the Right, the pro-Munich and anti-Communist Radical-Socialists became "Nationaux" by opposition to the "bellicist" minority who were still "Popular Front Radicals" (cf. D'Ormesson, *Le Figaro,* Dec. 16, 1938). Even the pacifist and anti-Communist section of the Socialist party under Paul Faure was greeted with the title of "National" (Bailby, *Le Jour,* Dec. 31, 1938; also, *Le Jour,* Nov. 4, 6, 1938).

[33] *Le Temps,* Nov. 15, 1938.

French bourgeoisie against the Socialist proletariat was the logical outcome of the evolution of French politics in the preceding years.[34]

Unfortunately anticommunism was usually synonymous with neo-pacifism. The Right objected as much to the suspicious patriotism of the French section of the Third International as to its aim of social revolution.[35] In their opinion, the Communist party, whose influence multiplied the dangers of the pact with the Soviets, had to be eliminated from the governmental majority if peace was to be maintained. Their prayer was soon answered. The opposition of the Communist deputies to the peace of Munich had transformed them into a minority. The Socialists themselves, although they upheld the government's foreign policy on October 4, abstained from

[34] With delight D'Ormesson quoted an article of Gaston Jèze, the Radical-Socialist professor of law, in *L'Ere Nouvelle*, Dec. 15, 1938: "At the point we have reached, there must henceforth be only two parties in France: the anti-Marxists and the Marxists (SFIO and Communist). There is no conciliation possible between them. The French democrats must unite their efforts to strike down the national enemy, Marxism. The restoration of the nation can only be attained by the complete defeat of Marxism, a revolutionary doctrine of civil war and demagogic dictatorship.

"There are some Radicals who do not understand this. They have no place in the ranks of democracy. To tell the truth, don't electoral preoccupations draw them near to the Marxists? Without their voices they will not be reëlected." D'Ormesson went on to criticize the twenty-nine Radical deputies who abstained from voting on the general policy of the government (*Le Figaro*, Dec. 16, 1938).

In April, 1938, M. Etienne Fournol had already given as a definition of the *Modérés* all the republicans opposed to Marxism, thus including an important section of the Left whose anticommunism was leading to a coalition with the Right (*Sciences Politiques*, April, 1938, p. 123).

[35] Thus the patriotic Alexandre Millerand told the Senate: "I, for my part, have never thought of reproaching the former governments for having concluded or maintained a Franco-Russian Pact with the Soviet Government. What I do not forgive them is to have allowed the Communist party, because of internal politics, to exercise an unacceptable influence on the affairs of France" (*JO. S.*, Feb. 7, 1939, p. 106).

During the same debate, M. Charles Reibel criticized the Communist party's patriotism. It was "all the more excessive," he declared, "because at the moment when the Communist party envisaged, with a serene eye, a European catastrophe, this same Communist party, by slowing down the production in the war factories, impeded as much as possible indispensable armaments (*vifs applaudissements sur de nombreux bancs à droite et au centre*), to a point even that some journalists could say that this party wanted both war and the defeat of France on which it hoped to base the World Revolution" (*ibid.*, p. 97).

voting the next day on Daladier's request for an extension of his decree powers until November 15.[36]   As events proved, the rift between the Extreme Left and the new majority was deep and lasting.   The general strike on November 30, supposedly organized as a manifestation against the government's foreign policy, marked the complete defeat of the "bellicist" proletariat by the "neo-pacifist" bourgeoisie.   It was the definite triumph of the advocates of the Munich policy over the advocates of integral resistance.   On the domestic plane it was the logical consequence of the Munich Pact, just as the visit of Herr von Ribbentrop to Paris and the signing of the Franco-German declarations of December were the logical consequence on the diplomatic plane.

For the majority of the Right, therefore, the main advantage of the Munich policy was negative rather than positive, the elimination of Soviet Russia from European affairs and of the Extreme Left from the government, rather than the certainty of a fruitful collaboration with the Axis.   As Léon Bailby frankly admitted in *Le Jour* (October 3, 1938): "In order to regulate the great problems of the hour, it is useful for them [the four great powers] to form a sort of 'European *Directoire*,' before which their personal disputes as well as those of others would be brought. *The primary advantage of this assemblage is that Russia is evicted from it.*   Too much could not be done to remove her from Europe, to send her back to her Asia, to her internal struggles.   The barbed wire in which old Clemenceau dreamed of enclosing her is still ready to serve.   Let it be used.   And let the contagious Bolshevist propaganda, which has put our country in a state of least resistance, be crushed by all possible means."

Only a minority was logical with itself in following up the policy of retrenchment which the abdication of France in September seemed to have implied; in spite of their reservation, the Resigned Nationalists obviously accepted German hegem-

---

[36] The government obtained 331 votes.   There were 203 abstentions and 78 votes against the cabinet.

ony east of the Rhine as the inevitable consequence of
Munich. The majority on the contrary, although convinced
of the desirability of the Four Power diplomacy, was losing
the few illusions it might have entertained concerning the
good will of the Axis and was ready to advocate resistance to
further aggressions. Two conditions, however, were necessary
for a new orientation on their part: Germany had definitely to
prove her determination upon military hegemony, and France
—at last cured of the Popular Front disease—had to form a
coalition of conservative powers with a determined and powerful Great Britain.

CHAPTER XI

THE END OF THE TRUCE

THE IMMEDIATE reaction of the Rightist press to the occupation of Bohemia and Moravia by German troops in March, 1939, appeared to be one of disappointment and anger; there was no general agreement, however, upon resistance to future German aggression. It was only in the latter part of April and at the beginning of May, after the Franco-British guarantees had been given to Poland and Rumania, that a quasi-unanimous determination to resist was reached.

The Conditional Nationalists were apparently shocked by the German chancellor's betrayal of faith. The new German aggression had made it glaringly certain that Herr Hitler aimed at the complete domination of Eastern and Southeastern Europe in the near future; he had dramatically proved that his ambition was not confined to the creation of a purely Germanic Reich. "The doctrine of German racial unity on which the whole National-Socialist regime is based has been abandoned for that of living space," stated the "Bulletin du Jour" of *Le Temps* on March 16, "[and] the whole new system of permanent co-operation on the part of the four principal powers [has been destroyed by Germany's unilateral action]."

The invasion of Bohemia brought an early death to the "Munich spirit" that had been accepted by the majority of the Right. Although it is hard to believe that the French Nationalists, with their traditional distrust of their neighbor across the Rhine, could have fallen prey to Hitler's promises, their reaction to the German occupation of Prague seems to indicate that their disillusionment was sincere. "How can one henceforth negotiate," demanded René Pinon, "with a government whose signature and whose word are of no value, and whose political doctrine changes in accordance with its interests of the moment?"[1] The disappointment apparent in most papers was reflected by D'Ormesson's article in *Le Figaro* on March 16:

Nothing more remains of the Munich agreements . . . nor does anything remain of the assurances solemnly uttered after Munich. Chancellor Hitler then declared that German demands were satisfied in Europe. And neither does anything remain of the racial doctrine which the Führer formerly championed, and in the name of which he was carrying on the regrouping of the Germanic family, but of the Germanic family alone.

D'Ormesson's policy toward Germany underwent an obvious change, as did that of the majority of the Right. The next day he patriotically stated: "Before such a situation, there is only one possible policy: resist, resist to the utmost, resist even to the supreme sacrifice if it is necessary"; and on March 23 he declared: "Any attempt, direct or indirect, to put hands on Rumania or disrupt Rumanian territorial integrity would create an immediate *casus belli* in Europe."[2]

The lesson of Prague for the Conditional Nationalists was that Pan-Germanism must now be opposed at all costs.[3] While

[1] *Revue des Deux Mondes*, April 1, 1939, p. 709. Yet M. Pinon admitted that the British had been more indignant than the French over the new German coup, because more than the French they had believed in the promises of the German Führer (*ibid.*). It is, however, significant that some of the advocates of direct understanding with the Reich, like Jean Goy and Henri Pichot, both presidents of war veteran organizations, admitted their mistake and became convinced of the necessity of standing firm (cf. *Le Jour-Echo de Paris*, April 10, 1939). Others, like Montigny and Flandin, were silenced by the reaction of public opinion. The Comité France-Allemagne, which grouped the main advocates of Franco-German *rapprochement*, decided at the end of March to suspend its activity (cf. *L'Europe Nouvelle*, April 1, 1939).

[2] Similarly the "Bulletin du Jour" of *Le Temps* declared on March 21 that not only the fate of Central Europe was at stake but "the problem of the domination of the world by the German-Italian-Japanese bloc. . . ." The next day the necessity of opposing *Mittel Europa* was again emphasized; however, it was admitted that France and Great Britain could not alone stop *"la ruée vers l'Est"* and that the most threatened nations must act in concert. The two main difficulties, it was pointed out, were the fact that Russia was a Bolshevist state and that Italy was now on the side of the Reich. The implication was that resistance to Pan-Germanism would have been an easy matter, had Italy been friendly and Russia socially conservative. Obviously the Right felt it difficult to reconcile their contradictory aims and find a way out of their old dilemma.

[3] *Le Temps*, RP, March 16, 17, 18, 19, 20, 1939; *Paris-Midi*, RP, March 20,

Le Petit Parisien clearly stressed the necessity for a permanent effort on the part of France to mobilize all her military and economic resources in order to "re-establish the equilibrium of forces in Europe,"[4] Raymond Recouly, speaking of the Reich's "scandalous and cynical disregard for law and justice," showed the danger of German expansion in Poland, Rumania, or Yugoslavia. He emphatically stated that "France and Great Britain must not and cannot allow the German Government to extend its sovereignty in any one of these three directions. If they committed the mistake of not resisting, Germany would draw such an increase in economic and military strength from her new acquisitions as would thereafter make it impossible for us even to think of entering into a struggle with her. We are at a decisive, pathetic moment. If we hope to restrain and to limit Germany, this barrier against her must be built without delay—today, for tomorrow might be too late."[5]

The attitude of the Resigned Nationalists, although equivocal, indicated that, despite the occupation of Bohemia and Moravia, they had not abandoned their policy of laissez faire. The leader of this group was *Le Matin,* which immediately put forward arguments against the possibility of Franco-British intervention.[6] On March 21 Stéphane Lauzanne regretted that Great Britain did not start "new negotiations with Berlin"; he worried about "pressure being exercised upon the British Government to include the autocracy of Moscow in the defense line of the democracies." On March 24 he was even more explicit: "Wisdom would counsel not extending the Franco-British line of security beyond the Rhine, and including in it only France, England, Belgium, and Holland."

22, 24, 26, 1939. The "Revue de la Presse" of *Le Temps* (March 22) reflected the temper of the majority: " 'The mobilization of the world,' 'the ideological bloc for peace,' 'coalition of the forces of peace,' 'the democracies on the alert,' such are the headings printed in heavy letters in this morning's papers. The intensive diplomatic activity in which England has taken the initiative is loudly approved."

[4] *Le Temps,* RP, March 17.

[5] *Revue de France,* April 15, 1939, pp. 151-155.

[6] March 14, 15, 1939.

This neo-pacifist isolationism was reflected in other papers of the Extreme Right,[7] although it did not always extend to granting Germany full sway in the East. It manifested itself mostly in a renewed campaign against the bellicists. On March 17 *L'Action Française* spoke of the offensive by the *va-t-en guerre* that the events in Central Europe had launched in the Chamber. The next day the paper attacked the bellicists again and opposed the formation of a new cabinet of National Union; *"Attention aux Juifs"* was its slogan. On March 19 Maurras openly expressed his preference for a policy of retrenchment: "We must avoid rushing to suicide. France is ready for a defensive war, but an offensive war would be suicide." According to him, it would be impossible to pierce the Siegfried Line; France should reach an agreement with Italy and not threaten Germany since "it is the desire of the enemy to have war declared against him. . . . The more we define, the more we delineate the scope of our action, the more chances and means we give the adversary; he will know where to get us and when to catch us." France, he concluded, should not make any commitments to Poland and Rumania since she would either break them at the last minute or fight an offensive war as Hitler wanted.[8]

Emphasis on a *rapprochement* with Italy and criticism of Soviet Russia were other expressions of the neo-pacifism of the Extreme Right, since they clearly meant that the Four Power Pact diplomacy should go on, regardless of the consequences for Eastern Europe. The significance of this policy was pointed out by Léon Bailby in *Le Jour*. Although on March 17 he had attacked Germany as "a predatory and mendacious people," a few days later (March 24) he wrote an article entitled "After London, the Soviet offensive wants to take Paris," with the subtitle: "For the fresh and joyous ideological war in the

---

[7] A section of the Socialist party also continued after March, 1939, to follow their pacifist stand. Its chief representatives were Paul Faure, a leader of the Socialist party, Séverac, an editorial writer of *Le Populaire* and secretary of the S. F. I. O., and André Delmas, head of the schoolteachers' union (cf. *L'Europe Nouvelle*, June 24, p. 695; Aug. 19, 1939, pp. 910-911).

[8] Cf. *Bulletin Quotidien*, March 24, 1939.

interests of Moscow, Frenchmen, you are invited to fight." He clearly stated the relationship between the pro-Italian and anti-Soviet attitudes of the Extreme Right:

France and England are being obliged to choose between the alliance with Moscow and *rapprochement* with Rome. . . . I repeat: we have to choose between Moscow and Rome. Our extremists [of the Left] have chosen the Soviets against Italy. They are thus pushing us toward an ideological war which, no matter what the outcome, can only result in a reinforcement of Soviet Marxism.[9]

The attitude of the Extreme Right began to change only after the Franco-British guarantee to Poland and Rumania and the introduction of conscription in Great Britain. The new firmness of England made the last neo-pacifists, somewhat reluctantly, follow the policy of resistance already adopted by the majority of the Rightist leaders.[10] Thus Jean Fabry, who was in the first row of the appeasers before and after Munich, wrote in *Le Matin* on April 16: "We have never seen more clearly what a catastrophe a conflict in Europe would be. . . . However, *sans phrases, sans menaces,* as M. Daladier has said, we have decided to withdraw no more." On May 2 Léon Bailby sounded like one of the "warmongers" he had so bitterly assailed: "The cleverness of Chancellor Hitler has con-

[9] *Paris-Midi,* RP, March 24, 1939. Characteristic of this anti-Bolshevist neo-pacifism was the article of *Le Matin* on March 25: "The Komintern has given all its representatives in France the formal order to display pro-government sentiments: communism is imperiously invited to take the direction of the national defense of France! . . . Moscow, in fact, sees the German menace against the Ukraine becoming more definite, and is trying to direct the coming storm toward the West." Colonel de la Rocque, although he had defended a policy of conditional resistance, followed *Le Matin* in its criticism of the bellicists and Moscow (*Le Petit Journal,* March 18, 26, 1939). See also *L'Action Française,* March 24, 1939; *La Liberté,* March 23, 1939.

[10] The whole press approved the decision of the British Government to protect Poland (cf. *Paris-Midi,* RP, April 1, 1939, and *Le Temps,* RP, April 5, 6, 1939) and, a few days later, the Italian invasion of Albania strengthened the will to resist (cf. *Paris-Midi,* RP, April 8, 11, 1939). On April 13 *Le Temps* stated that "most of the papers are of the opinion that the time for hesitation has gone and that, in view of the wild speed of the dictatorships, the democracies must not falter before unavoidable decisions." Later, at the beginning of May, when the threat to Poland became more acute, the press made a quasi-unanimous stand for the defense of that country (cf. *Le Temps,* RP, May 2, 13, 1939).

sisted in eating the artichoke leaf by leaf. He has divided and minimized each problem. That is why he thinks that the peaceful powers will come to say: 'No, war cannot be waged for Danzig.' But these repeated ruses do not deceive anyone any longer. And consequently the powers, who have had enough of always yielding to German blackmail, are resolved from now on to answer force by force."[11] It took Maurras longer to clarify his new position, but on June 27 he seemed to have made up his mind. "If you come to tell us that perhaps, after all, an understanding could be reached with Germany, then everything totters, everything gives way, everything crumbles. . . . If in the discussion of the Moscow-Berlin alternatives we lose sight of the fact that Berlin is the most menacing, then, it must be said, everything is lost."

The only exception to the quasi-unanimous determination to come to the help of Poland in case of another German aggression was the famous article of M. Déat in *L'Œuvre* (May 4) entitled "Die for Danzig?" in which he listed his arguments against the automatism of France's commitments.[12]

The reaction to his article indicated that at least outwardly the foreign policy of the Rightist leaders had changed. M. Bailby answered Déat's article in *Le Jour* on May 10:

They would be wrong to believe in Berlin that this opinion is that of the French people. The opposite is true. . . . It is a question of proving our will to resist any attempt at aggression in Europe by defending the integrity of Poland. Danzig? It might just as well be Strasbourg or Metz and Paris. We have said and repeated and proclaimed that we would not yield on the question of the integrity

[11] *Le Jour;* as late as April 17, however, M. Bailby criticized the five "bellicist" ministers in the Cabinet by contrasting them with the defenders of peace, and continued to advocate a policy of *rapprochement* with Italy.

[12] According to Déat, Britain had given her guarantee to Poland with the conviction that the latter considered the annexation of Danzig by the Reich inevitable and would accept it as a pure "formality." He went on giving realistic arguments against intervention; the Polish Army was not heavily armed, the war industries were near the German border, the Poles would not let Soviet armies come to their rescue, and in any case Stalin did not want to send his soldiers to help them. Above all, the decision of war should not be left in the hands of a few Polish statesmen; France should not have an automatic commitment to fight. "It is Paris and London that must have the first word."

of the Polish State. We must keep our word; we must not go back on it.

Several factors seem to have contributed to the changed attitude of the former *Munichois*. The healthy patriotic reaction of the French public during December and January following the Italian threats against France's territory and colonies[13] appears to have created the essential psychological preparation for a policy of resistance to the Axis. Although it was at first, perhaps, subconscious, and more evident among the public than among the leaders,[14] it was the prelude to, and the necessary condition for, the subsequent policy of resistance to German expansion. The leaders could no longer make an awkward distinction between intransigent firmness concerning France and her colonies[15] and a policy of concessions to Italy's partner. The spirit of resistance to the threat from the Axis could scarcely be held within narrow limits; the aggression of Germany in March followed by the Italian invasion of Albania could not be separated from the threats to France's territorial integrity. Moreover, the leaders of the Right could not argue France's "moral unpreparedness" after the public's patriotic reaction to Italy's insulting demands. M. Jean Fabry admitted in *Le Matin* on April 16 that, when the threat of war appeared in the Mediterranean, the will to resist the Axis had risen in France and that international fascism, which had gained the sympathy of many Rightists, was now clearly re-

---

[13] For the French reactions to Italian claims and to M. Daladier's propaganda trip to North Africa, see Werth, *France and Munich,* pp. 394-413.

[14] Indications could, however, be found of the change of attitude of the Rightist leaders before the German occupation of Bohemia. Thus, on February 1, René Pinon wrote in the *Revue des Deux Mondes* (p. 716) that "Europe will not breathe until the day when England and France will answer by a categorical 'no.'"

[15] The spirit of resistance against the "absurd and excessive Italian demands" was contrasted with the pacifist wave during the Munich crises by Recouly in the *Revue de France* (Jan. 15, 1939). He gave the main reason for the intransigent attitude of the Right concerning colonies: France and Great Britain would not have to defend "what did not belong to them, Austria, the Sudetenland, but on the contrary what has belonged to them for a long time, their imperial patriotism. It would be absolutely impossible for them to yield. Even if their governments had the cowardice to think of it, public opinion, no longer divided as it was last year, but on the contrary unanimous, would not permit it" (pp. 272-273).

vealing its aspirations and was obviously becoming the main enemy.[16]

On the other hand, the threat of communism could no longer be successfully advanced by the Rightist leaders against a policy of firmness. After the occupation of Prague it was practically impossible to make the public believe in the good faith of the German Führer and, at the same time, in the menace of the Third International; the Communist danger had been well removed by the moderate Daladier government and could not be used to overshadow the threat coming from the Axis. For one thing, the government could not be accused of wanting an ideological war against international fascism; it had proved its willingness to compromise with Germany at a high price. For another, the Extreme Left had lost all influence in the government, and did not present a serious threat either to the domestic politics or the foreign policy of France. D'Ormesson declared in *Le Figaro* (March 15) that firmness in Eastern Europe was possible now that "the Popular Front no longer exists among us. The majority that upholds the government has relegated the Communist party to a position of impotent opposition. That has changed many things."

The third basis of the new policy of resistance, and probably as strong as any, was the fact that Great Britain had for the first time made definite commitments in Eastern Europe; she had also introduced conscription and was rearming on a large scale.[17] Since she was now willing and to some extent able to help maintain the European *status quo,* England had actually become France's main ally on the Continent. This new factor allowed the Right to look elsewhere than to Italy or the U. S. S. R. for effective help against Germany. Their

[16] Cf. M. Dumont-Wilden, *Revue Bleue,* Feb., 1939, p. 66; also Alexander Werth, "France Means Business," *Nation,* July, 1939.

[17] It is doubtful that many Resigned Nationalists, although they had always advocated a follow-England policy, were swayed to the side of resistance by Britain's new determination. Thus, after Munich, M. Montigny made it clear that his pro-British policy was actually a pro-Chamberlain attitude, and that France should "consider her own interest" in case the British Government should change and include men such as Churchill, Eden, and Duff Cooper (*France, libère-toi!* p. 62).

embarrassing situation resulting from the choice between a desired friendship with an unwilling Italy and an undesired alliance with the willing Soviets was thus nicely solved by the introduction of a third possibility, a coalition with Great Britain and Poland.[18] M. Daladier even told the Chamber on May 12 that it was not the foreign policy of France that had changed, but the "possibilities to realize it." "There are nations going along the same road who finally get into step. Today you can see the common determination of these nations to build a dam against aggression."[19]

There remains the question of the degree of sincerity and determination behind the *Munichois'* new will to resist.

It is not likely that they believed Poland would be able to hold the *Wehrmacht* for a long time, or that France was in a position quickly to overcome the Siegfried Line; emphasis was still put on the invulnerability of fortified lines and the superiority of defensive weapons over offensive arms. If the Allies were incapable of a quick offensive, and the Polish Army of a long resistance, the only hope of victory lay in a war of attrition, in which the U. S. S. R. would blockade Germany in the East while the Allies would blockade her in the West. On the other hand, some leaders of the Right might still have believed in the inevitability of a clash between Germany and

[18] M. Pierre Gaxotte, for example, who had been one of the most ardent *Munichois,* justified the new policy of firmness on the ground that now Great Britain and Poland were the allies of a better-armed France (*Je Suis Partout,* May 5, 1939). It is characteristic, however, that the Resigned Nationalists waited until the British Government had made commitments in Eastern Europe to accept a policy of resistance; quite possibly they were forced to do so by the pressure of public opinion.

[19] *JO. Ch.,* p. 1323. See also Daladier's declaration on January 11 (*ibid.,* p. 1261). It was also argued that France was now better prepared, both materially and morally, than in September, 1938; she was stronger militarily, financially, economically. Above all, she was united politically behind Daladier, now that the Communists had been rejected from the governmental majority. Cf. A. Fabre-Luce, "La France a-t-elle changé de politique extérieure?" *Politique Etrangère,* Aug. 4, 1939. M. Fabre-Luce further stated that at the time of Munich, one could believe Hitler's claims on a purely Germanic Reich and that there was a possibility of reorganizing Eastern Europe to satisfy Germany's need for expansion, perhaps without changes of boundaries; but the occupation of Prague had changed all these hopes. France was obliged to make a firm stand in March, at least temporarily, he cautiously stated.

the U. S. S. R. and in the possibility for France to play a waiting game, to intervene at the last moment or to make peace after the Germans had cut themselves a good slice of Russian territory. The first explanation seems to fit the past and present position of the Conditional Nationalists, while the second was more in line with that of the Resigned Nationalists.

The former group continued to advocate a policy of resistance that would not be anchored to a Franco-Soviet military alliance. In spite of the Munich interlude, when they accepted the dismantlement of the Czech rampart, they had consistently, although conditionally, advocated resistance to Pan-Germanism. It is significant that their former opposition to a Franco-Soviet agreement now appeared somewhat modified; while still refusing a full-fledged military alliance with Moscow, they illogically hoped that Russia would play the part of an effective partner in a blockade. In opposing a military alliance with the U. S. S. R., René Pinon declared:

The Komintern appears as a menace to those whom its army could reassure. What we must ask of them [the Soviets] is not military aid, but that their sources of raw materials and their war industries be ready to supply those who are menaced by aggression with what they might need.[20]

But like most Conditional Nationalists, he made it clear that, although communism was still dangerous, the Axis was France's main enemy. A few papers, like the Catholic *La Croix,* even explicitly accepted the help of the Soviets against the German menace. "We must look at things squarely. If one considers that the Hitler danger is danger number one for the Europe of 1939, use must be made of all the means at our disposal."[21] The majority, however, followed a hazardous policy of compromise. Thus, after warning the French not to bring their political ideologies into the field of foreign policy, M. d'Ormesson characteristically added (*Le Figaro,* March 25): "It is not on the U. S. S. R. that the protection of the

[20] *Revue des Deux Mondes,* April 1, 1939, p. 70; cf. also *ibid.,* April 15, 1939, p. 955.
[21] *Paris-Midi,* RP, March 25, 1939. See also *ibid.,* RP, April 2, 13, 1939.

East must chiefly rest. It is on Poland. Our allies in the East are the Poles. The U. S. S. R. is of secondary importance only."[22]

In spite of its perilous limitations, this policy cannot be assimilated to that of the Resigned Nationalists, who, even after their apparent espousal of a policy of resistance, still unconditionally refused any agreement with the U. S. S. R. The usual argument against Bolshevist Russia, which had been more or less abandoned by the majority, was still much used in the press of the Extreme Right. The Soviets were supposed to be doing their best to bring about a European conflict from which they would carefully stay aside in order to save their country and impose the Revolution.[23]   According to them, an agreement with Moscow would necessarily bring about a war which they were anxious to avoid. "It is obvious," stated Bailby in *Le Jour* on May 2, "that if the two democracies . . . ally themselves with this horrible Russian dictatorship which ever since it has existed has lived in a state of perpetual war against the totalitarian states, France and England, no matter what they say and do, will find themselves dragged into that state of war." Concerning the discussions being carried on for a military agreement between the Allies and Soviet Russia, *L'Action Française* affirmed that "success would be a disaster" (June 25), and Senator Lémery stated: "I consider that it would be folly to try to conclude a normal and honest agreement for peace with a state which represents *'le mal, l'abjection, la guerre permanente à la civilisation.'* "[24]

[22] Cf. Lucien Romier, *Le Figaro*, May 8, 1939.

It is interesting to note the doubts of the Right as to the outcome of the Allies' conversation with the Kremlin, especially after the replacing of Litvinov by Molotov as Foreign Commissar. M. Pinon questioned whether the Soviet Government would actually enter into an alliance with Great Britain and France, since neutrality would bring the U. S. S. R. both increased power and the opportunity to bring revolution to an exhausted Europe (*Revue des Deux Mondes*, Aug. 1, 1939, p. 719).

[23] The most violent criticism of the Soviets came from *Le Matin*, which was also the most hesitant in its new policy of firmness, still curiously tinged with neo-pacifism. Cf. *Le Matin*, May 5; also *L'Action Française*, May 5; *Gringoire*, May 11; *Le Jour*, May 2, 22; *Je Suis Partout*, May 5, 1939.

[24] Quoted by *L'Europe Nouvelle*, July 1, 1939, p. 725.

That their will to resist Pan-Germanism was still dubious was indicated by their indestructible hope in a possible reconciliation with Italy. Since there was no illusion that the Axis could be broken,[25] this may be interpreted as a desire to resume the Four Power diplomacy of Munich. Their neo-pacifism, furthermore, was still alive, and they patently showed that they would welcome a compromise settlement at the expense of Poland. Hope for peace was entertained in *Le Matin* almost daily until the very eve of hostilities; the necessity for mutual concessions was stressed.[26] While this attitude might have been only a pious hope that war could be avoided, it was reminiscent of the neo-pacifist campaigns during previous crises and indicated that their resolution to fight further aggression was open to question.

This interpretation seems to be confirmed by the fact that the determination of the Allied governments was sometimes doubted by the press of the Extreme Right. Some papers spoke of the possibility of a tragic *malentendu*—war might start because Hitler would not believe in the resolution of Great Britain and France to fight over Poland.[27] The impression was often given that the anti-German front was intended to be an intimidating instrument rather than a determined coalition and, if necessary, an effective war machine. The old distinction between a defensive war and an offensive war of democracies against totalitarian states was again made. Thus Charles Maurras showed his eagerness to keep France from being car-

[25] Charles Maurras optimistically stated on April 26, 1939, that he had "confidence in the possibility of Franco-Italian reconciliation because of the identity of interests" (*L'Action Française*). Cf. Bailby, *Le Jour*, May 4; also a speech of Laval quoted by *L'Europe Nouvelle*, July 1, 1939, p. 724.

[26] May 10, Aug. 29, 30, 1939. Jean Montigny, at a meeting organized by the Alliance Démocratique at the beginning of June, characteristically stated: "We refuse to consider as inevitable a war of which, no matter what the outcome, bolshevism would be the only final beneficiary. . . . Must we wait for another war before holding the peace conference Europe cannot avoid?" (*Le Temps*, June 5, 1939). M. Flandin, the chief leader of the Resigned Nationalists, apparently kept quiet after the German coup in Bohemia; however, he made the significant statement in an article written for the *Christian Science Monitor* on May 8 that if Germany were defeated she would become militantly communist.

[27] *Le Journal* (*Le Temps*, RP, May 4, 1939); *Candide* (*Le Temps*, RP, June 2, 1939).

ried too far by her commitments: "We must maneuver according to the vital interests of France and of the French in an exact and precise anti-German line, which is neither perverted nor deflected by Moscow. We must assure our liberty of movement first of all, and not hand over to anyone, at Moscow or elsewhere, our sovereign initiative of action . . . in short, we must always keep the ability and the means of putting on the brakes at the critical moment."[28]   Professor Barthélemy contended in *Le Temps* that war, unless it were waged by a very powerful nation against a very weak one, could not solve anything. "It is therefore necessary to reach an agreement whatever you may baptize it."[29]   After explaining why France was obliged in March, 1939, to go through a *"phase de résistance,"* M. Fabre-Luce stated characteristically: "In reality there is much less chance of avoiding war for a long period of time by 'encircling' Germany than by agreeing with her upon a division of zones of influence. Therefore intransigent resistance could only be a temporary position preceding a return to conciliation."[30]

It seems highly probable that the Resigned Nationalists had not fundamentally changed and that they had not abandoned their hopes of a German victory over the Soviets. Although neo-pacifism and the policy of retrenchment could not be too openly advocated in the press, a pro-German campaign of rumors, adverse not only to the U. S. S. R., but also to Great Britain, seems to have been set afoot. M. Ybarnégaray referred to this campaign in *Le Petit Journal* on April 11, 1939, and indignantly opposed it. Colonel de la Rocque himself, in the role of a good patriot, denounced "a certain sly campaign that we find expressed in peculiar posters and in strange items in the press. Is this really the time for Frenchmen worthy of the name to spread libels in honor of M. Hitler and his methods? What is the origin of the subversive campaigns against England, in which France would be the soldier sacri-

---

[28] *L'Action Française*, June 29, 1939.
[29] Quoted by *L'Europe Nouvelle*, June 24, 1939, p. 695.
[30] *Politique Etrangère*, Aug. 4, 1939, p. 396.

ficed in advance, the mercenary, the cannon fodder? Such actions are not only the doings of the tools of Moscow."[31]

The most dangerous aspect of the half-hearted attitude of the Resigned Nationalists was their absolute opposition to the agreement with Russia which was sought by the French and British governments. Their anti-Soviet campaign, and to a lesser extent the compromise position of the Conditional Nationalists, may even have played a part in the decision of the U. S. S. R. to sign the pact of nonintervention with Germany on August 23. The Communist deputy M. Gabriel Péri exposed the danger of these campaigns which seemed to advise Germany "as an easy venture, to seek the living space she covets toward the East and the Soviet lands." He warned of the dangerous repercussions on the decisions of the Soviet Government:

How could those whose participation in the work of protecting the independence of nations is recognized as necessary, how could they now forget that for months it was considered as the *dernier mot* of diplomatic cleverness to divert the excess fury and ambitions of Nazi Germany towards them?

They wish to be convinced—and this is an elementary precaution—that these schemes have been definitively repudiated.[32]

It is significant that the anti-Soviet campaign should have continued, especially in the press of the Extreme Right, until the very eve of the war. It indicates that at least a section of the French bourgeoisie still put their class fears and prejudices above the interests of the country. The Traditional Nationalists vainly warned them of the dangers of their policy. "In view of this great problem, it is the duty of the French bourgeois," wrote De Kerillis in *L'Epoque* on May 4, "to rise above their ideological prejudices. . . . True enough, the Russian alliance is not an ideal solution, but is the last resource, and we must know how to accept the enormous risks involved." Referring to the anti-Soviet campaigns in the press of the "so-called Nationalists," Emile Buré did not hesitate to call

[31] *Le Petit Journal*, April 23, 1939.
[32] *JO. Ch.*, May 11, 1939, p. 1267.

them traitors by comparing them to the *émigrés* of the French Revolution: "I shall not cease repeating it: Coblenz is born again, an infinitely more terrifying Coblenz than its predecessor, because it exercises its defeatist influence in the interior of the country and under the cover of patriotism." It was obvious that the political prejudices of the Extreme Right still clashed with national security; the belief was even voiced in *Je Suis Partout* that the coming war was not their war: "A war 'for justice and right,' to re-establish a Republic in Germany (but without dismembering her), to assure the prosperity of the Jews, to construct a mythologic Czechoslovakia, to leave the miserable old men of the French democracy in their sinecures? We might just as well capitulate right now and save two or three million young corpses."[33]

Paradoxically, the Munich policy appears to have contributed to the defeatist Right's apparent determination to oppose German expansion. It led many of them to relegate the dreaded ideological war to a secondary place behind the struggle for national security, for Munich had eliminated Soviet Russia from European affairs and had strengthened the conservatism of the Daladier government. It had also been the final test of Herr Hitler's "good will," and after the occupation of Prague, there could no longer be any doubt that his real aim was European hegemony. This realization not only rallied the French behind a policy of resistance but brought France the unconditional support of Great Britain. For the first time since 1935 the elements of an anti-German policy acceptable to the Right had been realized: a strong Western alliance of conservative powers, with an Eastern satellite (Poland) whose main qualification as an ally was the negative one of not being a Bolshevist state. The coalition was considered impressive enough to make the German Government hesitate before starting its *Drang nach Osten,* and if worst

[33] Quoted by Georges Bidault in *L'Europe Nouvelle*, July 29, 1939, p. 906. See his four revealing articles of July 29, August 5, 12, and 19, *ibid.*

came to worst, the U. S. S. R. was expected to support the Poles, if not militarily, at least economically.

But anti-Soviet prejudices, a complacent belief in the strength of the peace front, and in many cases lack of sincere determination led to half-hearted support or open opposition to the only measure that could have saved France: a military agreement with the U. S. S. R. The *"Ni pour Berlin ni pour Moscou"* policy of conditional resistance was still dangerously alive; it induced the majority of the Right to accept the possibility of war while opposing the best condition for victory.

CONCLUSION

As GERMAN strength increased, the temptation grew in France to give up the postwar policy of maintaining the territorial *status quo* of the treaties. Belief in the impregnability of the Maginot Line and propensity to think in terms of national rather than collective security furthered this new orientation. As the protection of the West came to be considered more important than, and independent of, the defense of the East, the British alliance became the backbone of French security. But the "dominion status" of France in foreign policy, which was evident in 1936 and lasted until the war, was not imposed by the necessities of the hour: Barthou had proved that French foreign policy could be independent of Britain, and Laval certainly did not subordinate the decisions of the Quai d'Orsay to those of Downing Street in 1935. Until the Italo-Ethiopian War, the *status quo* was also guaranteed by Italy and Russia, and France was still a leader in international affairs.

It was the remilitarization of the Rhineland which put her in the position of a solicitor toward Britain; the main gate in the elaborate barrier against Germany was forced open by the German coup of March 7, and from then on France's smaller allies were unable or unwilling to stem the tide. It seemed that British protection was needed more than ever. The open gates, however, could not be closed by an ally who was ready to guarantee the West but not the East; they could be shut only by a Franco-Soviet military agreement, and this the Right refused.

The reliance of the Right upon the British guarantee and the British lead in March, 1936, and thereafter, may be interpreted as a *post-facto* rationalization of their refusal to let their country oppose German territorial ambitions. After all, the fate of England was linked to that of France, and whatever the latter undertook, the former was bound to support. A determined France could have taken along a reluctant Britain in crushing Pan-Germanism, but the majority of the Right and a section of the Left found it convenient, in order to further their policy of compromise, to follow Great Britain's guidance. At all times they were in a position to reorient France's policy toward integral resistance by an effective pact of mutual assistance with Soviet Russia. In refusing this necessary condition for the maintenance of the *status quo,* the Right were obliged, willy-nilly, to give the Reich a free hand in Central and Eastern Europe.

The neo-pacifist reaction of the Right to the German *fait accompli* of March, 1936, and their stubborn opposition to an agreement with the U. S. S. R. are better evidence of the reversal of their traditional foreign policy than their defeatism at the time of Munich. After the Rhineland had been fortified and the German Army made formidable, they could claim that resistance presented too great a danger, and in September, 1938, a case could be plausibly made out for nonintervention, since the conditions for victory were only partly fulfilled. But the realistic arguments against a firm stand were obviously inapplicable two years earlier when the opportunity was offered to check Pan-Germanism at small cost; nor could realism have explained the continued refusal of a powerful and determined ally in the vain hope of gaining the support of a weaker and unreliable neighbor.

Emotional factors appear to have been more essential in determining the attitude of the Right than the realistic evaluation of the dangers involved in a policy of firmness. For decades, the driving force behind French nationalism had been the fear of Germany, which was possibly stronger after the victory of 1918 than ever before. This fundamental emotional factor could not suddenly disappear; it could only be overshadowed by another, stronger sentiment, such as fear of war or revolution.

Two elemental and contradictory mass impulses go into the psychological make-up of any civilized people: patriotism and reluctance to fight. Undoubtedly the second was powerful enough in postwar France to dull, and temporarily to over-come, the instinct of national self-preservation. But the lead-ers of opinion, who were the guardians of French interests, had the onerous duty of warning the public against the dan-gers of nonresistance; yet instead of striking the patriotic chord as they had so successfully done before, many began to preach neo-pacifism in 1935, played down the threat of German ambitions, and tried to replace this traditional concern of the French with fear of War-Revolution.

The neo-pacifism of the Nationalists had nothing in com-mon with the sentimental and doctrinal opposition to war of the Socialists. The difference between these two forms of paci-fism was made clear by the Extreme Rightist J. P. Maxence in his *Histoire de dix ans:* "Suppress wars . . . an old and empty dream! Adolescents will have to be killed at the moment their blood begins to pulsate strongly in their veins. As long as there are young men, there will be fighters."[1] After dis-dainfully putting the pacifism of the Left in its place, he indi-cated the real character of the neo-pacifism of the Right: "The essential thing is that war should not be vain, and the ideologi-cal war is vain. Only the Marxists want it, for they see in it an open door to their revolution. A war of honor, even of defense, would be vain if it were only to prolong a little more a regime which makes war inevitable and involves too many chances of defeat. It would be insane to start such wars. But it would be too bad if just the word 'war' could chill the hearts of young Frenchmen and make them tremble."

Fear of War-Revolution was too often and too consistently put forward to be lightly dismissed. As M. Paul Reynaud told the Chamber in December, 1936, the anti-Communist crusade organized by Berlin was evidently a success among the French bourgeois.[2] Many feared a victory over Germany as much as a defeat. M. Thierry Maulnier, a disciple of Maurras and theorist of the monarcho-Fascist movement in France, thus ex-

---

[1] Pp. 305-306.   [2] See above, p. 115.

pressed what he termed "the fundamental reason" for the Right's opposition to war in 1938:

These parties [of the Right] had the impression that in case of war not only would the disaster be immense, not only was defeat and devastation of France possible, but *a German defeat would mean the crumbling of the authoritarian systems, which constitute the main rampart to the Communist revolution, and perhaps the immediate bolshevization of Europe.* In other words, a French defeat would really have been a defeat of France, and a French victory would have been less a victory of France than a victory of the principles rightly considered as leading straight to her ruin and to that of civilization itself.[3]

It was, therefore, clearly admitted that the enemies of France were the allies of the Right in the ideological war.

The Right's apprehension of a social upheaval following a European war was of course a great asset for German ambitions, and the Bolshevist threat was the favorite theme of Nazi propaganda. Some patriotic leaders, whose sincerity and integrity are above doubt, realized this fully, yet continued to warn the people as much against the menace coming from Moscow as against that coming from Berlin. Their distorted appraisal of the two dangers, the immediate and the problematical, is difficult to explain. It may have been caused partly by their mistrust of the Machiavellian policy attributed to Moscow; partly also by their awareness of the class struggle, and by their propensity to think speculatively rather than pragmatically.

Neo-pacifism was strongly anchored to total mistrust in the foreign policy of the Soviet Government, which was itself partly responsible for this lack of confidence; had it been entirely aloof from the activities of the Third International, the ideological argument against a Franco-Soviet coalition would not have carried much weight, for the domestic situation in France never warranted the fear of revolution. But the Rightist leaders could point to the spectacular change in the domestic and foreign policy of the French Communist party

[3] *Combat,* Nov., 1938, quoted in *L'Europe Nouvelle,* July 29, 1939, p. 817.

following the new orientation of Soviet diplomacy in 1934, and argue that Stalin had not abandoned the aim of World Revolution entertained by Trotsky; only the methods had changed. The negative policy adopted by the great democracies further increased the conservatives' mistrust of the U. S. S. R.; the opposition of Downing Street to a military agreement between France and the Soviet Union and to intervention in Spain was not interpreted as "muddling through," but as wise foresight. It lent a respectable air to the "realistic" argument which advocated free play for the Reich against Russia, in order to direct the German threat to the East and to deal a mortal blow to bolshevism.

On the other hand, the subordination of national to class interests may be interpreted as a defensive reflex by the bourgeoisie. Their endemic apprehension of an uprising similar to those of 1848 and 1871 had been greatly increased by the triumph of the Bolshevist Revolution of 1918 and by the electoral successes of the Extreme Left in France, especially during the thirties. While in the United States approximately two electors out of a thousand voted Communist, and four out of a thousand Socialist, in France at the last general elections (1936) one out of seven electors voted Communist, and one out of five Socialist. With the Extreme Left gaining over one third of the electorate, the slogan of the "Red menace" could not but find receptive ears. The increase of almost one hundred per cent in the Communist vote can, however, be attributed to the effects of the depression and to discontent with the domestic and the foreign policy of the preceding governments rather than to mass conversion to Marxism; there was little or no actual danger of a proletarian uprising in France during the decade prior to World War II.

Undoubtedly the anti-Marxist outcry of the conservatives expressed their hatred of the Popular Front, their aversion to social reforms and to the rule of the majority which was accepted only as long as the evolution toward the Left was slow and presented little danger to their privileged position. When it appeared to them that liberalism was doomed, many bourgeois began to look for protection in an autocratic regime that would respect their acquired social and economic position. Believing they were forced to choose between authoritarianism and socialism, they logically sided with the counter-revolution. As M. Benda remarked shortly before the war, the bourgeoisie had abandoned the doctrine of the "rights of man" and of equality of opportunity—the basic ideas of the French Revolution—for the thesis of the "rights of the élite," not *"l'élite-individu"* but *"l'élite-classe,"* whose foundation was heredity and no longer personal ability.[4] This antidemocratic conception led many former *Modérés* to seek refuge in an authoritarian or even totalitarian system of government; they accepted a degree of collectivism, but in a frozen society which would protect them from the threat of the working classes.

The electoral triumph of the Extreme Left and the revolutionary events in Spain may have been a sufficient incentive for them to further, more or less consciously, the aim of the Axis. In their eyes domestic and foreign policy could no longer be separated: victory over Italy, over the Rebels in Spain, even over Germany, meant to them a victory of the working classes in France and of Soviet Russia in Europe, and this victory had to be opposed whatever the effect upon national security. The principal condition for a policy of resistance to Pan-Germanism came to be the elimination of Soviet Russia from France's system of alliances, and of the Extreme Left from a position of influence in the government. Conservatism, both of the government of France and of her allies, was made an essential requisite for a policy of firmness. Until 1935, when the governments were socially conservative and Italy could be counted a likely ally, the bulk of the Right maintained their traditional attitude toward Germany. Soon afterwards, however, with the alienation of the "Latin sister" and the constitution of the Popular Front, a policy either of abandonment or of only conditional resistance was accepted by most Rightist

[4] *L'Europe Nouvelle,* July 22, 1939, p. 789.

leaders. It was only after Great Britain had become the determined and effective ally of a conservative France that resistance to German expansion was again quasi-unanimously advocated.

The bogey of the "Red menace" was obviously used by the Extreme Right to promote the success of the counterrevolution in France and in Europe. It was this positive desire to see the triumph of their own ideology rather than the negative fear of a social upheaval that made them side with the authoritarian regimes of Italy, Spain, Japan, and even Germany; the enemy was not only bolshevism, but liberalism. Characteristically, the firmness of the different political sections of the Right toward Germany was in inverse proportion to their sympathy toward Fascist doctrines. The French National Socialists, like Déat or Doriot, defended direct *rapprochement* with Germany, irrespective of the consequences. Maurras and the authoritarian Traditionalists, although theoretically maintaining their old hostility against the hereditary enemy, actually advanced the aims of the Reich in Eastern Europe. The *Modérés,* on the other hand, generally continued to oppose Pan-Germanism everywhere, although the great majority of them refused the best guarantee against it: a Franco-Russian military agreement. Only a small minority of Rightist leaders subordinated their class prejudices to their traditional nationalism.

After the defeat of France in 1940, the tripartite division of the Right into Resigned, Conditional, and Traditional Nationalists still continued to exist. Many of the last group left France to carry on resistance, and their leaders are to be found in New York and London, unless in jail. On the other hand, the all-out collaborationists, who have constituted a pressure group both in Paris and Vichy, are the direct descendants of the Resigned Nationalists. Their rank and file has been recruited mainly from pro-Fascist elements behind Doriot, Déat, and Laval. The third group of Conditional Nationalists, now labeled *attentistes,* were in power during Laval's disgrace, and apparently comprised the bulk of the French Right. Their anti-Soviet, and frequently antidemocratic, prejudices, together with their "realism," led them to accept a policy of partial collaboration with the hereditary enemy. As long as Great Britain was the sole, and relatively weak, ally of the U. S. S. R., their sympathy in the ideological war was likely to be on the side of the Axis. It is probable, however, that the entrance of the United States into the war has had deep repercussions upon this last group and that today only the determined enemies of democracy favor an Axis victory.

Fundamentally, the passive stand of the Nationalist Right, which made them refuse to take the bold steps necessary against German ambition, may be attributed to fear of the political and social consequences of a major war. Their reluctance to fight was not only a sign of a high level of civilization, but also of a diseased political and social order, whose defenders had lost confidence in its worth and vitality. Lack of sufficient faith in political and even economic liberalism left them without the incentive needed to play a leading part in a revolutionary world: a narrow conception of national security could produce only passive resistance, not active determination. Divided France appeared to be neither conservative nor revolutionary enough to face effectively a situation which required not only military power but a great deal of optimism and self-confidence. For victory might not only leave unsolved the problem of French security in the future, it might also pose the dreaded social problems which the Right were unwilling or unable to solve.

The dilemma of the Right was not limited to France: the same picture of hesitation and confusion could be found in other Continental countries and even in Great Britain, the stronghold of placid liberalism. Nations, classes, and individuals everywhere have been more or less conscious actors in this complex and fearful drama: the world struggle for the triumph of one way of life—democracy, fascism or nazism, or communism. This ideological war has been as real as the fight for national self-preservation. The evolution of French

domestic and foreign policy illustrates the reality of this three-
cornered contest among the three modern ideologies and their
respective champions, the Western democracies, the Axis, and
Soviet Russia.

Until 1935 the struggle was not yet in the open: Italy
was on the side of France, as was Soviet Russia, in a loose
front against the German menace. At home the democratic
forces, that is, the defenders of the political *status quo,* from
the Socialists to the Conservatives, opposed both fascism and
communism, the two revolutionary extremes. The threat of
the authoritarian leagues during 1934 and 1935, however, led
to the formation of the Popular Front, a coalition of the progressive and revolutionary Leftists, which in turn increased
the pro-Fascist sympathies of the Right. The sanctions against
Italy initiated the total opposition of Right and Left over
France's foreign policy: Italy's siding with Germany left no
choice to France but to join with the U. S. S. R., a move that
would have created the anti-Fascist coalition of democracy and
communism hated and feared by the Right. A conservative
government might have reassured them into accepting this
powerful ally; a Popular Front government could not, although in an effort to avoid the implications of the ideological
war at home and abroad M. Blum refused to strengthen the
pact of mutual assistance with Moscow, and even declined to
throw France's weight on the side of the Spanish Loyalists.

Spain was the first battlefield between fascism and reactionary traditionalism on the one side, and democracy and communism on the other. In letting the Axis join issue with
the Soviets, Great Britain and France took a position of neutrality in the International Civil War that could not be limited
to Spain and exposed themselves to future capitulations. Their
stand changed the character of the Spanish Civil War and
transformed it in the eyes of many to a duel between the
two revolutionary extremes; it was believed that the choice
was no longer between democracy and totalitarianism but between fascism and communism, that is, between Berlin and
Moscow.

The less radical elements of the Left were bound to rebel against their bellicose allies, the Communists, and to break the coalition of lambs and wolves. Neutrality in the International Civil War, with its corollary, appeasement, was gaining ground; from the Right it spread to the Left, and the Radical-Socialists looked forward to *rapprochement* with the Front National. The short-lived alliance of democracy and Marxism was broken at Munich, both on the domestic and the foreign front; at home the Communists and the Socialists were thrown into the opposition, and abroad the Four Power Pact diplomacy was the attempt to find a *modus vivendi* between the Democratic and Fascist states.

This new orientation failed when the German armies invaded Bohemia and the Italian troops Albania. An effort was then made to return to the old pre-1935 formula of opposing communism at home while gaining the support of the U. S. S. R. against Pan-Germanism. Daladier's *modéré* government partially convinced its majority to forget its anti-Soviet bias, but the late and timid effort ended in failure: mutual confidence was lacking. Power politics temporarily replaced the ideological struggle, and the Germano-Soviet Pact of non-aggression ended for a time the duel between fascism and communism.

The war did not impress the French Right as exclusively a struggle for survival. Their lack of determination, their mistrust of the French working classes, and their reaction to the Soviet-Finnish War indicate the conflicting purposes and continuing hesitation of the Rightists.[5] The debacle of June, 1940, led to collaboration, the logical evolution of appeasement; and the resumption of the ideological war between fascism and communism furnished the Vichy government with

[5] All the elements of the Right's policy of abandonment, or conditional resistance, were to be found during the period of the "phony war": defensive strategy, hope for a compromise peace, pro-Italian policy, hatred for the Soviets. In November Russia's aggression against Finland unleashed a violent anti-Bolshevist and pro-Fascist campaign. War against the U. S. S. R. was openly advocated, with the obvious aim of uniting the four Western powers in a crusade against bolshevism, and thus insuring the triumph of the counterrevolution in Europe. Cf. Pertinax, *Les Fossoyeurs* (New York, 1943), I, 175 ff., 209 ff.

its most abused slogan in favor of collaboration: the defense of "Western civilization" against "Soviet barbarism."

The resistance of Great Britain and the intervention of the United States aligned the great democratic powers with Soviet Russia and brought the ideological war to its present stage, the coalition of politico-economic liberalism and bolshevism: the realistic conception of an alliance between threatened countries, but not between ideologies, is only a convenient means of escaping an awkward situation. Unless a real and lasting compromise is found during and after the war between the social systems and conceptions of government of the present allies, the ideological war will not be ended by the defeat of the Axis.

APPENDIX

DALADIER CABINET I. (January 31, 1933-October 24, 1933; Foreign Minister, Paul-Boncour)

April 23-28. Herriot visits President Roosevelt to discuss war debts

May 5. Renewal of 1926 Treaty of Berlin between Germany and Soviet Union

June 7. Four Power Pact initialed in Rome.

October 14. German withdrawal from Disarmament Conference and League of Nations

SARRAUT CABINET I. (October 26, 1933-November 24, 1933; Foreign Minister, Paul-Boncour)

CHAUTEMPS CABINET II. (November 26, 1933-January 27, 1934; Foreign Minister, Paul-Boncour)

January 26. German-Polish nonaggression pact

DALADIER CABINET II. (January 30, 1934-February 7, 1934; Foreign Minister, Paul-Boncour)

February 6. Riots in Paris

DOUMERGUE CABINET II. (February 9, 1934-November 8, 1934; Foreign Minister, Louis Barthou; after October 13, Pierre Laval)

April 17. Barthou's note to Britain closing disarmament negotiations

June 27. Memorandum on Eastern Pact

July 25. Murder of Dollfuss

September 18. Entrance of the U. S. S. R. into the League of Nations

FLANDIN CABINET. (November 8, 1934-May 30, 1935; Foreign Minister, Laval)

December 5. Franco-Soviet preliminary agreement on a treaty of mutual assistance

January 7. Franco-Italian agreements

January 13. Saar plebiscite favors Germany

March 16. Reintroduction of conscription in Germany; abrogation of Part V of Versailles Treaty

April 11-14. Stresa Conference on German rearmament

May 2. Franco-Soviet Pact of mutual assistance signed

BOUISSON CABINET. (June 1, 1935-June 4, 1935; Foreign Minister, Laval)

LAVAL CABINET IV. (June 7, 1935-January 23, 1936; Foreign Minister, Laval)

June 18. Anglo-German naval accord

October 3. Italy invades Ethiopia

December 8. Hoare-Laval plan for settlement of Ethiopian conflict

SARRAUT CABINET II. (January 24, 1936-June 3, 1936; Foreign Minister, Pierre-Etienne Flandin)

February 27. Chamber of Deputies approves Franco-Soviet Pact

March 7. German military reoccupation of Rhineland; abrogation of Locarno Pact

April 8. France submits a new peace plan

April 26, May 3. General Elections in France

May 9. Annexation of Ethiopia by Italy

May, June. Sit-down strikes

BLUM CABINET I. (June 4, 1936-June 21, 1937; Foreign Minister, Delbos)

July 11. Austro-German agreement

July 18. Beginning of Spanish Civil War

October 14. King Leopold announces Belgium's policy of neutrality

October 25. Formation of Rome-Berlin Axis

CHAUTEMPS CABINET III. (June 22, 1937-January 14, 1938; Foreign Minister, Delbos)

December 11. Italy withdraws from League of Nations

CHAUTEMPS CABINET IV. (January 18, 1938-March 10, 1938; Foreign Minister, Delbos)

February 4. Ribbentrop, German Foreign Minister

BLUM CABINET II. (March 13, 1938-April 8, 1938; Foreign Minister, Paul-Boncour)

March 13. German occupation of Austria; proclamation of *Anschluss*

DALADIER CABINET III. (April 10, 1938-March 21, 1940; Foreign Minister, Georges Bonnet; after September 15, 1939, Daladier)

April 16. Anglo-Italian agreement

April 27-29. Daladier and Bonnet in London; strengthening of Anglo-French alliance

May 21. Czechoslovak mobilization during Sudeten crisis

July 19-22. King and Queen pay state visit to Paris

August 3. Lord Runciman sent to Prague

September 15. Chamberlain meets Hitler at Berchtesgaden

September 22. Chamberlain meets Hitler at Godesberg

September 29-30. Munich Four-Power Conference on the cession of Sudetenland

November 30. Italian agitation on colonial claims against France; failure of general strike

December 6. Franco-German declaration of friendship

December 17. Italian denunciation of Rome accords of January 7, 1935

March 15, 1939. German protectorate over Bohemia and Moravia declared

March 21-24. President Lebrun pays state visit to London

March 22. German occupation of Memel

March 26. Poland rejects German proposals regarding Danzig and the Corridor

March 28. General Franco's troops enter Madrid

March 31. Chamberlain declaration on behalf of Britain and France guaranteeing Poland

April 7. Italian occupation of Albania

April 13. British and French declarations guaranteeing Greece and Rumania

April 28. German denunciation of Anglo-German naval agreement and German-Polish nonaggression pact

May 22. Signature of German-Italian alliance

June 23. Agreement on mutual assistance with Turkey

August 11. Franco-British military mission arrives in Moscow

August 23. German-Soviet nonaggression pact signed

September 1. Germany invades Poland

September 3. A state of war with Germany is declared to exist

Composition of the Chamber

Fifteenth Legislature, Elections of May 1-8, 1932

La Droite:

Indépendants	14	
Indépendants d'action économique, sociale et paysanne	7	
Fédération républicaine	41	
Groupe républicain et social	18	80

Le Centre:

Démocrates populaires	16	
Républicains du centre	6	
Centre républicain	34	
Républicains de gauche	29	
Gauche radicale	48	
Indépendants de gauche	23	156

La Gauche:

Radicaux et radicaux-socialistes	160	
Républicains socialistes et socialistes français	28	
Gauche indépendante	15	
Socialistes S. F. I. O.	131	
Groupe de l'Unité ouvrière	9	
Communistes	10	353

Isolés*	26	615

* Droite 2, Centre 17, Gauche 3, de nuance incertaine 4.

Sixteenth Legislature, Elections of April 26 and May 3, 1936

Indépendants républicains	13	
Fédération républicaine	59	
Indépendants d'action populaire	16	
Républicains indépendants et agraires indépendants	40	
La Droite		128
Républicains de gauche et radicaux indépendants	44	
Démocrates populaires	13	
Gauche démocratique et radicaux indépendants	38	
Le Centre		95
FRONT NATIONAL		223
Gauche Indépendante	28	
Radicaux et radicaux-socialistes.........	111	
Union socialiste et républicaine.........	29	
Socialistes S. F. I. O..................	149	
Communistes	72	
RASSEMBLEMENT POPULAIRE		389
ISOLÉS		6
		618

BIBLIOGRAPHY

Parliamentary Debates

Journal Officiel de la République Française. Chambre des Députés, *Débats Parlementaires,* 1933-1939. Paris, Imprimerie des Journaux Officiels.

Journal Officiel de la République Française. Sénat, *Débats Parlementaires,* 1933-1939. Paris, Imprimerie des Journaux Officiels.

French Newspapers and Periodicals: Parisian Press

The so-called *journaux d'information* (or *Grande Presse*) were traditionally composed of the "Big Five": *Le Journal, Le Petit Journal, Le Petit Parisien, Le Matin, L'Echo de Paris* (until 1938); to these were added the three papers of Jean Prouvost: *Paris-Soir, Paris-Midi,* and *L'Intransigeant.* Like the bulk of the press, the so-called *journaux d'opinion,* they presented a definite political viewpoint. The main difference was that the first, having greater circulation, counted more on advertisements to balance their budget (and were thus more or less controlled by the Agence Havas), while the second drew most of their funds from the subvention of the groups they represented; both were often directly controlled by banking or economic interests, such as the Comité des Forges, or, indirectly, by the Agence Havas or the government. The press could also be classified according to the social or political groups they catered to, but a more comprehensive division has been preferred between the newspapers and periodicals representing the position of the Extreme Right and the organs of the *Modérés,* although the line of demarcation is necessarily arbitrary. The *extrémistes Le Jour* and *Le Matin,* for example, could be distinguished from the ultraconservative *L'Echo de Paris* or *L'Intransigeant* only by their greater emphasis on authoritarianism and their sympathy for fascism. Under the broad classification of *Modérés* very different political and social viewpoints have been included, from narrow conservatism to "liberalism."

It is impossible to know the exact circulation of any of the papers, and the figures given (for the years 1936-1938) should be considered only approximate. Only the most important dailies and periodicals are listed here. For a more complete treatment of the subject, see the pioneer study by Carlton J. Hayes in his book *France: A Nation of Patriots* (New York, 1930). It is obvious that many changes have occurred since Professor Hayes made this elaborate analysis of the French press.

PRESS OF THE EXTREME RIGHT: DAILIES

L'Action Française: violently antidemocratic and pro-Fascist; organ of "Integral Nationalism," the authoritarian royalist movement of Charles Maurras; though it used Catholicism as a convenient ally for its authoritarian traditionalism, it was on the Papal Index from December 29, 1926, to July 5, 1939, and did not represent the political views of the French pretender, whose organ was *Le Courrier Royal.* Charles Maurras and Léon Daudet, directors; Maurice Pujo, editor; Jacques Delebecque, specialist on foreign policy; Jacques Bainville, most important contributor. Approximate circulation: from 70,000 in 1936 to 120,000 in 1938(?).

L'Ami du Peuple: authoritarian, *bonapartiste,* pro-Fascist paper of François Coty, the perfume manufacturer. Pierre Taittinger, leader of the Jeunesses Patriotes, director and editor. Approximate circulation in 1936: 150,000; out of circulation in September, 1938.

La Liberté: ultraconservative organ of André Tardieu until May, 1937; then became the mouthpiece of the quasi-Fascist P. P. F. of Jacques Doriot, with Paul Marion editor. Approximate circulation: 40,000 under Tardieu, 90,000 under Doriot.

Le Jour: authoritarian, nationalist paper; owner-editor, Léon Bailby, founder of *L'Intransigeant* and great admirer of Mussolini. A. M. Piétri and Jean Fabry, specialists on foreign policy. Became *Le Jour-Echo de Paris* when the latter was bought in March, 1938. Approximate circulation: 200,000 to 260,000.

Le Matin: ultraconservative, antidemocratic, violently anti-Communist. Maurice Bunau-Varilla, owner; Stéphane Lauzanne, editor. Circulation: 450,000 in 1936; 400,000 in 1938(?).

Le Petit Journal: bought by Colonel de la Rocque from Raymond Patenôtre in 1937; became the main organ of his authoritarian P. P. S. Approximate circulation in 1938: 200,000.

Press of the Extreme Right: Periodicals

Candide: literary and political weekly; traditionalist and authoritarian, politically near *L'Action Française.* Belonged to the publisher Fayard; Jacques Bainville on foreign policy until 1936, then Pierre Gaxotte, former secretary of Charles Maurras.

L'Emancipation Nationale: Fascist mouthpiece for the P. P. F. of Jacques Doriot.

Le Flambeau: organ of the "national reconciliation" of Colonel de la Rocque.

Gringoire: pro-Fascist specialist in slanders; like *Candide* and *Je Suis Partout,* it was read mainly by young men of the middle classes. Horace de Carbuccia, director; numerous contributions from Rightist leaders.

Je Suis Partout: the most open admirer of fascism, politically near *L'Action Française;* Charles Lelca, director of publication; Pierre Gaxotte and Robert Brasillach, editors; belonged to Fayard until 1936, then unknown support.

Revue Hebdomadaire: weekly literary and political magazine. Le Grix, authoritarian pro-Fascist and great admirer of Mussolini, was editor-in-chief and wrote the political section.

Revue Universelle: literary and political bimonthly, clerical and authoritarian. Jacques Bainville, editor; then Henri Massis; among the collaborators were Thierry Maulnier, disciple of Maurras, and R. Brasillach, who wrote for *Gringoire;* Charles Benoist, specialist on domestic politics, and Saint-Brice, specialist on foreign affairs; numerous contributors from the Right.

Press of the *Modérés*: Dailies

L'Aube: organ of the Démocrates Chrétiens; politically and socially liberal. Francisque Gay and Gaston Tenier, directors; Georges Bidault, chief contributor. Circulation: 12,500 in 1936 to 10,000 in 1938.

Bulletin Quotidien; société d'études et d'informations économiques: organ of the Comité des Forges.

La Croix: Catholic conservative paper, designed mainly for the clergy. R. Buteaux, director; Abbé Merklen and J. Guiraud, editors. Circulation: 84,000 in 1936 to 100,000-200,000 in 1938.

L'Echo de Paris (until March, 1938, when absorbed by *Le Jour*): ultraconservative paper of the Catholic bourgeoisie. François Edmond Blanc, controlling stockholder; Henri Simond, director until May, 1937. Henri de Kerillis and Pertinax often disagreed on foreign policy. Circulation: 190,000 to 400,000.

L'Epoque: small conservative daily founded by Henri Simon. Henri de Kerillis, editor-in-chief after he left *L'Echo de Paris* in 1938. Supported Traditional Nationalism. Circulation unknown.

Le Figaro: ultraconservative paper of the *grands bourgeois* and the aristocracy. Francois Coty, owner; then Mme Cotreanu, his ex-wife; Pierre Brinon, editor-in-chief; Wladimir d'Ormesson, specialist on foreign policy. Circulation: 45,000 to 60,000.

L'Information: business paper controlled by the Banque Lazard, as was *L'Agence Economique et Financière.* Fernand de Brinon, specialist on foreign policy. Circulation: 60,000(?).

L'Intransigeant: conservative evening *journal d'information;* belonged to Jean Prouvost, but more to the Right than *Paris-Soir* and *Paris-Midi.* Colonel Fabry, director; A. L. Jeune, editor. Circulation: 500,000 in 1936 to 125,000 in 1938.

Le Journal: conservative *journal d'information.* M. Guimier, owner, formerly on the board of the Agence Havas; De Marsillac, director; Saint Brice, editor. Circulation: 700,000 in 1936; 370,000 in 1938.

Le Journal des Débats: very conservative organ of the *grande bourgeoisie.* Henri de Nalèche, director; André Chaumieux, editor; Pierre Bernus, specialist on foreign policy. Circulation: 20,000.

La Journée Industrielle: clientele of businessmen; controlled by the Confédération Générale du Patronat. C. J. Gignoux, editor-in-chief. Circulation: 20,000.

L'Ordre: small but influential *journal d'opinion,* defending Traditional Nationalism. Emile Buré, director-editor. Circulation: 10,000.

Paris-Midi: paper of Jean Prouvost, more conservative than *Paris-Soir.* Marcel Lucain, editor. Circulation: 100,000.

Paris-Soir: emphasis on news, largest circulation of all French papers. Jean Prouvost, owner; Jules Sauerwein, specialist on foreign policy. Circulation: 1,500,000 to 1,800,000.

Le Petit Journal (until 1937 when bought by Colonel de la Rocque): *modéré journal d'information.* Raymond Patenôtre, owner.

Le Petit Parisien: mildly conservative *journal d'information,* fewer editorials than other Rightist papers. Pierre Dupuy, owner-director; Elie J. Bois, editor; Lucien Bourguès, specialist on foreign policy. Circulation: from 1,100,000 in 1937 to 600,000 in 1938.

La République: although usually considered a paper of the Center Left, it can be classified with the Right for its anti-Marxism and socially conservative policy. In foreign policy combined both the pacifism of the Left and the neo-pacifism of the Right. Emile Roche, director; Pierre Dominique, editor; many contributors, like De Monzie, Marcel Déat, Caillaux, and Paul-Boncour. Circulation: 20,000 to 40,000.

Le Temps: semiofficial mouthpiece of conservative governments, especially on foreign policy; contains a useful "Revue de la Presse"; possibly controlled by the Comité des Forges. Jacques Chastenet and Emile Mireaux, directors; Pierre Reclus, editor-in-chief; Roland de Marès, specialist on foreign policy; many prominent Rightist contributors, often anonymous. Circulation: 70,000.

PRESS OF THE *Modérés*: PERIODICALS

Revue des Deux Mondes: oldest and most "serious" bimonthly of the Right. André Chaumeix, director; René Pinon wrote the "Revue de la Quinzaine" on foreign and domestic policy.

Revue de France: very conservative literary and political bimonthly. Raymond Recouly wrote the political section; numerous contributors from the Right and Extreme Right.

Revue de Paris: conservative, chiefly literary magazine. De Fels, editor.

Vie Intellectuelle, Etudes, Sept, Temps Présent, Politique, Catholic periodicals, may be added to these conservative magazines, although the last three represented a more liberal attitude and could hardly be classified with the Right, since their clientele was limited to the clergy or Catholic intellectuals; their attitude in foreign policy does not indicate that of the Catholic masses.

LEFTIST PRESS: DAILIES

L'Œuvre: organ of the Radical-Socialists. Jean Piot, editor-in-chief; Geneviève Tabouis, specialist on foreign affairs. Circulation: 200,000.

L'Humanité: organ of the Communist party. Marcel Cachin, director; Gabriel Péri, specialist on foreign affairs. Circulation: from 300,000 in 1936 to 450,000 in 1938.

Le Populaire: organ of the Socialist party (S. F. I. O.); Léon Blum, editor-in-chief; then Bracke. Circulation: 250,000.

LEFTIST OR NEUTRAL PRESS: PERIODICALS

L'Europe Nouvelle; revue hebdomadaire des questions extérieures, économiques et littéraires: liberal, representing many political viewpoints, generally Leftist. Fabre-Luce, editor until 1936; then Pertinax; Pierre Brossolette and Pierre Dominique, frequent contributors.

Nouvelle Revue Française: literary and political, covering a wide range of opinions; Drieu la Rochelle and Ramon Fernandez, who were courting fascism, Albert Thibaudet, the philosopher of the Right, and Alain, the philosopher of the Left, all contributed.

Politique Etrangère: monthly periodical published by the Centre d'Études de Politique Etrangère.

Sciences Politiques: published by the Ecole Libre des Sciences Politiques. Could be classified with the Right.

Le Crapouillot: editor, Jean Galtier-Boissière. Literary periodical until 1929; then antiwar, anti-Fascist, and anti-Bolshevist. Opened its pages to men of all political shades at least until 1934; then opposed both by the Extreme Right and Extreme Left.

BOOKS AND PAMPHLETS: FRENCH AUTHORS

Allard, Paul. *Le Quai d'Orsay, son histoire, etc.* Paris, 1938.
   La Guerre du mensonge: comment on nous a bourré le crâne. Paris, 1940.
Bainville, Jacques. *Les Dictateurs.* Paris, 1935.
   La Troisième République. Paris, 1935.
   La Russie et la barrière de l'est. Paris, 1937.
   Histoire de deux peuples, continuée jusqu'à Hitler. Paris, 1938.
Bardoux, Jacques. *Le Drame français: refaire l'état ou subir la force.* Paris, 1934.
   Ni Communiste, ni Hitlérienne: La France de demain. Paris, 1937.
   Les Soviets contre la France. Paris, 1936.
   J'accuse Moscou. Paris, 1936.
   L'Ordre nouveau: face au communisme et au racisme. Paris, 1934.
Berl, Emmanuel. *La Politique et les partis.* Paris, 1932.
   Frère bourgeois, mourez-vous? Ding! Ding! Dong! Paris, 1938.

Bernanos, Georges. *La grande Peur des bien-pensants.* Paris, 1931.
  Les grands Cimetières sous la lune. Paris, 1938.
  Scandale de la vérité. Paris, 1939.
  Lettre aux Anglais. Rio de Janeiro, 1942.
Bonnard, Abel. *Les Modérés.* Paris, 1936.
Borgo, Pozzo di. *La Rocque, fantôme à vendre.* Paris, 1938.
Brinon, Fernand de. *France-Allemagne,* 1918-1934. Paris, 1934.
Carrère, Jean, et Bourgin, Georges. *Manuel des partis politiques en France.* Paris, 1924.
Céline (Louis Ferdinand Destouches). *Bagatelles pour un massacre.* Paris, 1937.
Chevrillon, André. *La Menace allemande.* Paris, 1934.
Creyssel, Paul. *La Rocque contre Tardieu.* Paris, 1938.
Daudet, Léon. *Le Drame franco-allemand.* Paris, 1940.
Dominique, Pierre (Pierre Lucchini). *Veux-tu vivre ou mourir?* Paris, 1936.
  La Guerre qui vient: vous vous réveillerez Allemands. Paris, 1936.
Doriot, Jacques. *La France ne sera pas un pays d'esclaves.* Paris, 1936.
  La France avec nous! Paris, 1937.
  Refaire la France. Paris, 1938.
Drieu la Rochelle. *L'Europe contre les patries.* Paris, 1931.
  Avec Doriot. Paris, 1937.
Duhamel, Georges. *Au chevet de la civilisation.* Paris, 1938.
Eccard, Frédéric. *Moscou à Paris.* Belfort, 1936.
Encyclopédie française, "La Civilisation Ecrite." Vol. XVIII. Paris, 1939.
Fabre-Luce, Alfred. *Le Secret de la république.* Paris, 1938.
  Histoire secrète de la conciliation de Munich. Paris, 1938.
Flandin, Pierre-Etienne. *La Révolution est inutile.* Paris, 1937.
  Paix et liberté: "L'Alliance Démocratique" à l'action. Paris, 1938.
Frédérix, Pierre. *Etat des forces en France.* Paris, 1935.
Fribourg, André. *La Victoire des vaincus.* (Preface by Pétain.) Paris, 1938.
Gauthier, Bertrand. *La Cinquième Colonne contre la paix du monde.* Paris, 1938.
Guéhenno, Jean. *Jeunesse de la France.* Paris, 1936.
  Journal d'une "révolution." Paris, 1939.

Guerdan, Léon. *Je les ai tous connus.* New York, 1942.

Guérin, Daniel. *Fascisme et grand capital.* Paris, 1936.

Halévy, Daniel. *La République des comités.* Paris, 1934.

1938. Une Année d'histoire. Paris, 1938.

Jouvenel, Robert de. *La République des camarades.* Paris, 1914.

La Situation internationale. Paris, 1938.

Kerillis, Henri de. *Laisserons-nous démembrer la France?* Paris, 1939.

La Rocque, François de. *Service public.* Paris, 1934.

The Fiery Cross: The Call to Public Service in France. London, 1936.

Laurent, Raymond. *Face à la Crise.* Paris, 1934.

Lazareff, Pierre. *Deadline.* New York, 1942.

Lefebvre, Henri. *Le Nationalisme contre les nations.* Paris, 1937.

Lévy, Louis. *Vérités sur la France.* New York, 1941.

Lombard, Paul. *Le Chemin de Munich.* Paris, 1938.

Louis-Jaray, Gabriel. *Offensive allemande en Europe.* Paris, 1939.

Marchal, Léon. *Vichy, Two Years of Deception.* New York, 1943.

Marion, Paul. *Programme du P. P. F.* Paris, 1938.

Maritain, Jacques. *A travers le Désastre.* New York, 1941.

Massis, Henri. *Défense de l'Occident.* Paris, 1927.

Maulnier, Thierry. *Au delà du Nationalisme.* Paris, 1938.

La Défaite. Paris, 1941.

Mauriac, François. *Germanisme en marche.* Paris, 1939.

Maurois, André. *Tragedy in France.* New York, 1940.

Maurras, Charles. *Enquête sur la monarchie.* Paris, 1925.

Dictionnaire politique et critique. Paris, 1934.

Mes Idées politiques. Paris, 1937.

La Seule France: chronique des jours d'épreuve. Lyon, 1941.

Maxence, J. P. *Histoire de dix ans.* Paris, 1939.

Millet, Raymond. *Doriot et ses compagnons.* Paris, 1937.

Montherlant, Henri de. *L'Equinoxe de septembre.* Paris, 1938.

Montigny, Jean. *France, libère-toi!* Paris, 1939.

Mordacq, Jean Jules Henri. *Faut-il changer le Régime?* Paris, 1935.

Nizan, Paul. *Chronique de septembre.* Paris, 1939.

Ormesson, Wladimir d'. *L'Europe en danger: le communisme, c'est la guerre.* Paris, 1936.

France. London, 1939.

Perroux, François. *Les Mythes hitlériens.* Lausanne, 1935.

Pertinax (André Géraud). *Les Fossoyeurs.* New York, 1943. 2 vols.

Reynaud, Louis. *La Démocratie en France.* Paris, 1938.

Romains, Jules. *Le Couple France-Allemagne.* Paris, 1935.
Cela dépend de vous. Paris, 1939.
Seven Mysteries of Europe. New York, 1940.
Messages aux Français. New York, 1941.

Saint-Jean, Robert de. *Démocratie, beurre et canons.* New York, 1941.

Siegfried, André. *Tableaux des partis en France.* Paris, 1930.

Simon, Yves. *La grande Crise de la république française.* Montreal, 1941.

Suarez, Georges. *Les Hommes malades de la Paix.* Paris, 1933.
Nos Seigneurs et maîtres. Paris, 1937.

Tabouis, Geneviève. *They Called Me Cassandra.* New York, 1942.
Chantage à la guerre. Paris, 1938.

Tardieu, André. *La Révolution à refaire.* Paris, 1936.
France in Danger! London, 1935.
Alerte aux Français. Paris, 1936.
Notes de semaine 1938. L'Année de Munich. Paris, 1939.

Thibaudet, Albert. *La République des professeurs.* Paris, 1927.
Les Idées politiques de la France. Paris, 1932.

Thomas, Louis. *Histoire d'un jour.* Paris, 1939.

Thorez, Maurice. *Notre Lutte pour la paix.* Paris, 1938.

Tissier, Pierre. *The Government of Vichy.* London, 1942.

Torrès, Henry. *La France trahie: Pierre Laval.* New York, 1941.

Vallin, Charles. *Le P. S. F.* Paris, 1936.

Valois, Georges (Alfred Georges Gressent). *La Révolution nationale: philosophie de la victoire.* Paris, 1924.
Prométhée vainqueur, ou explication de la guerre. Paris, 1940.

Veuillot, François. *La Rocque et son parti comme je les ai vus.* Paris, 1938.

Viance, Georges. *La France veut un chef.* Paris, 1934.

Books and Pamphlets: Anglo-American Authors

Armstrong, Hamilton Fish. *When There Is No Peace.* New York, 1939.
Chronology of Failure: The Last Days of the French Republic New York, 1940.

Brogan, D. W. *France Under the Republic.* New York, 1940.

Buthman, W. C. *The Rise of Integral Nationalism in France.* New York, 1939.

Cameron, Elizabeth R. *Prologue to Appeasement: A Study in French Foreign Policy.* Washington, D. C., 1942.

Chamberlin, William H. *The World's Iron Age.* New York, 1941.

Dingle, Reginald J. *Russia's Work in France.* London, 1938.

Doob, Leonard W. *Propaganda: Its Psychology and Technique.* New York, 1935.

Guérard, Albert. *The France of Tomorrow.* Cambridge, 1942.

Hayes, Carlton J. H. *France: A Nation of Patriots.* New York, 1930.

Hill, Helen. *The Spirit of Modern France.* New York, 1934.

Leeds, Stanton B. *These Rule France.* New York, 1940.

Pickles, Dorothy M. *The French Political Scene.* London, 1938.

Pol, Heinz. *Suicide of a Democracy.* New York, 1940.

Ragatz, L. J. *The Background of the February Riots in Paris.* London, 1934.

Schmitt, Bernadotte. *From Versailles to Munich.* Chicago, 1939.

Seton-Watson, R. W. *Munich and the Dictators.* London, 1939.

Sharp, Walter, *The Government of the French Republic.* New York, 1938.

Taylor, Edmond. *The Strategy of Terror: Europe's Inner Front.* Boston, 1940.

Toynbee, A. J. *Survey of International Affairs.* London, 1934-1939.

Werner, Max. *The Battle for the World.* New York, 1941.

Werth, Alexander. *France in Ferment.* London, 1934.

The Destiny of France. London, 1937.

Which Way France? New York, 1937.

France and Munich: Before and After the Surrender. London, 1939.

Wolfers, Arnold. *Britain and France Between Two Wars: Conflicting Strategies of Peace since Versailles.* New York, 1940.

INDEX

Action Française, L', 15 ff., 33, 42, 56, 73 n., 75 n., 90 ff., 104, 108 n., 109 n., 128 n., 172, 174, 192 n., 206, 209. *See* Maurras

Agence économique et financière, L', 30

Alain, 6, 21 n.

Albania, invasion of, 210 n., 212, 231

Alexander of Yugoslavia, 33 n.

Alliance Démocratique, 67, 127 n., 140 f., 193, 217 n.

Ami du Peuple, L', 26, 30 n., 45, 80 n.

Anschluss, 117, 123, 135 ff., 156 f., 161

Antisemitism, 146 n., 147, 150, 209, 220

Appeasement, 53, 70, 71 n.; *see* Resigned Nationalism

Armbuster, Senator, 104 n., 105 n.

Austria, 45, 72, 78, 125, 135 ff.; *see* Anschluss

Authoritarianism, 19 n.; *see* Fascism, Leagues

Axis, Rome-Berlin, 117, 123, 157, 230

Bailby, 42, 46, 90 f., 145 n., 149, 158 n., 164, 166, 171, 174, 181, 200, 202 n., 204, 209, 211, 216

Bainville, 22 n., 46, 72, 82 n.

Bardoux, 115 n., 121 n., 130 n.

Barrès, Maurice, 16, 20

Barrès, Philippe, 89 n.

Barthélemy, 18, 150 ff., 181, 218

Bastid, Deputy, 76

Belgium, 35, 134, 139, 152, 208

Belin, 185 n.

Bellicism, 2, 41, 61 ff., 90 ff., 96, 102 f., 145 ff., 150, 156, 159 f., 165 f., 171 f., 174, 202, 204, 209 f.

Béraud, 56

Berchtesgaden meeting, with Chamberlain, 161, 164, 167 ff.; with Schuschnigg, 135, 137

Bérenger, Senator, 196 n.

Bergery, Deputy, 116 n., 179, 185 n.

Berl, 18 n., 126 f.

Bernanos, 64 n., 113

Bertrand, 30 n.

Bidault, 55 n., 68 n., 71, 145, 220 n.

Blum, cited, 19, 49 n., 75, 144 n., 150, 153 n., 202 n.; domestic policy, 133, 144 n., 145 ff.; foreign policy, 41, 44, 56 n., 60, 62, 114, 134 n., 147, 170, 176, 191 n.

Bohemia, occupation of, 206 ff.

Bolshevism, *see* Right, attitude toward U. S. S. R. and communism

Bonapartism, 16, 17

Boncour, Paul, 28 n., 92

Bonnard, 18 n.

Bonnet, 171, 175, 179, 197 f., 202 n.

Bordeaux, Henri, 147

Boucher, Le, 91, 98, 165

Bourgeoisie, 2, 14, 18, 19, 115, 122, 204, 224; *see* Right, Modérés

Bourgin, 6

Bourguès, 167

Briand, 22

Brinon, De, 8, 28 n., 30 n., 131 n.,

Brogan, D. W., 16 n., 22, 60

Brossolette, 2, 22, 119, 131, 153 n.

Bucard, 16 n.

Bulletin Quotidien, 8, 125 n.

Buré, 54, 71, 108 n., 149, 219, 220

Cachin, 49 n.

Cagoulards, Les, 133

Caillaux, 72, 196 n.

Candide, 56, 73 n., 84, 90 n., 100, 150, 192 n.; *see* Gaxotte; Bainville

Capital, Le, 184

Carol of Rumania, 190

Carroll, E. M., 4

Cartier, Raymond, 80

Catholicism, 15, 19, 20, 24

Catholics, foreign policy, 55 n., 113, 129

Center, domestic policy, 12 n., 13, 67, 71, 72, 108 n., 127, 131; foreign policy, 30, 69, 71, 137, 140, 142 ff., 146 n., 178, 181

Chamberlain, 136, 141 f., 153 f., 161, 168 ff., 194

Chambre des Députés, debates June, July, 1936, 110, 111, December, 1936, 117 ff., 122 ff., February, 1938, 137 ff., March, 1938, 146 f., October, 1938, 176 ff., January, 1939, 193 ff.; *loi des deux ans,* 49 f.; on Four Power Pact of 1933, 27; on Franco-Soviet Pact, February, 1936, 68 ff., 75 ff., 119 f., 134; on Laval's foreign policy, December, 1935, 53 f., 59 f., 62, 65, 68; on remilitarization of Rhineland, 95, 97; role on public opinion and foreign affairs, 5, 144 n., 196 n.
Chappedelaine, De, Deputy, 180 n.
Chautemps, 133, 135, 137 n.
Choc, 55 n., 73 n., 128 n.
Churchill, 213 n.
Claudel, 113
Clémenceau, 34 n., 205
Comité des Forges, 8, 126 n.
Comité France-Allemagne, 8, 131 n., 199 207 n.
Communism, domestic policy, 13 n., 21, 33, 79, 80, 83 f., 108 ff., 133, 224 ff.; foreign policy, 20, 48 f., 62, 64, 79 ff., 111, 114, 120, 146 f., 176, 179 f., 198 n., 203, 219, 225 f.; *see* Right, attitude toward communism
Confédération Générale du Travail, 41 n., 110, 114, 159, 185 n.
Conservateurs, *see* Extreme-Right
Conservatives, *see* Modérés
Corbin, 148
Cot, 171, 180 n., 201 n.
Coty, 16 n., 30 n.
Counterrevolution, 81, 101 n., 112; *see* Fascism, Extreme-Right
Crapouillot, Le, 21 n., 176
Croix, La, 169 n., 215
Czechoslovakia, 34, 72, 125, 134 ff., 148 ff.; Czech crises, May, 1938, 154 ff., September, 1938, 161 ff.

Daladier, Cabinet I, 24 n., 28 n.; Cabinet II, 16 n.; Cabinet III, 133, 179 f., 202 ff., 220; domestic policy, 109 n., 133, 179, 202 ff., 213, 220; foreign policy, 180, 198, 202, 214
Dantzig, 211
Daudet, 42, 147
Déat, 72, 116, 179, 185 n., 211, 228
Delbos, 65, 114, 116, 134, 137 n., 142
Delcassé, 70

Delebecque, 42, 78
Delmas, 209 n.
Démocrates Populaires, 27 n., 127 n., 129, 146 n.
Desjardins, Senator, 105
Dominique, 30 n., 49 n., 93 n., 95 n., 96 n., 100, 111 n., 131 n., 159
Doob, 7
Doriot, 5, 73, 82, 127 ff., 228
Doumergue, 19, 33, 37 n.
Drieu la Rochelle, 21 n., 25 n., 63 n.

Echo de Paris, see Pertinax, Kerillis
Eden, 136, 142, 153
Elbel, Deputy, 199 n.
Elections législatives, 12 n., 13 n., 108 n.
Emancipation Nationale, 73 n., 129 n.
Epoque, L', 162 n., 169 n.; *see* Kerillis
Ere Nouvelle, L', 203 n.
Ethiopian War, 9, 52 ff., 88, 119, 138, 149
Europe Nouvelle, L', 86, 116, 119, 152, 155 f.
Extreme-Left, *see* Socialists; Communists
Extreme-Right, domestic policy, 15 ff., 33, 108 n., 125 ff., 147 f., 186, 228; foreign policy, 22 f., 30, 34 n., 46, 54, 56 f., 61 ff., 72 ff., 89 ff., 98, 104, 114, 130, 147 ff., 171 f., 186, 209 ff., 216 ff., 228

Fabre-Luce, 57 n., 67 n., 121 n., 178, 214 n., 218
Fabry, Deputy, Senator, 27, 29, 38 n., 41 n., 201 n., 212
Faisceau, Le, 16 n.
Fascism, 15 ff., 61, 63 f., 80 ff., 116, 125 ff., 186, 220, 224 f.
Faure, 185 n., 202 n., 209 n.
Fédération Républicaine, 15 n., 23, 75 n., 76, 127 n., 194
Fernand-Laurent, Deputy, 76 n., 82, 146 f.
Fernandez, 63
Figaro, Le, 92, 192; *see* D'Ormesson, Romier
Finland, 231
Fischer, Louis, 185
Flandin, 33 n., 37 n., 39; domestic policy, 128 f.; foreign policy, 39, 67, 72, 82 n., 122 f., 140 ff., 146, 152, 165, 172, 193 f., 202, 217 n.

Four Power Pact, of 1933, 26 f.; of 1938, 136, 138, 157 ff., 179 n., 180, 192 ff.

France, domestic policy: elections 1936, 108 ff.; general strike of 1938, 204; riots February 6, 1934, 33; sit-down strikes, 110; see Right, Left, Ideology foreign policy: advent of Hitler, 22 f.; *Anschluss,* 135 ff., 144; Barthou's policy, 34 f., 37; Czech crises, 161 ff., 168 ff.; Four Power Pact of 1933, 26; Franco-British guarantees to Eastern Europe, 206; Franco-Soviet Pact, 37 f., 46, 50, 67 ff., 118 ff.; German conscription, 39 ff.; German withdrawal from League, 28 ff.; Italian demands, 198 f., 212; Italo-Ethiopian War, 52 ff.; London conversations, February, 1935, 38; post-Munich policy, 190; remilitarization of Rhineland, 39, 43, 85 ff., 97, 222 f.; Rome agreement, 1935, 38; Spanish Civil War, 114, 116 ff., 190 n.; Stresa Conference, 44 f.

Francistes, 16 n.

Franco, 103 n., 112 f., 118, 159 n., 190, 195

Franco-Soviet Pact, 34 f.; ratification, 67 ff.; signing, 46 ff.

Franklin-Bouillon, Deputy, 27, 29, 41 n.

Free Masons, 62, 102, 105

Frédérix, 6 n., 7 n.

Front Commun, 33, 49

Front de la Liberté, 127, 131 n.

Front National, 83, 93, 100, 102 f., 108 ff., 145 f.

Front Populaire, distintegration, 133 ff., 148, 179, 184 f., 202 ff., 213; domestic policy, 109 ff., 133; foreign policy, 111 ff., 116 ff., 134 ff., 204; formation, 16 n., 79 f., 83, 108 ff., 227

Frossard, Deputy, 185 n.

Galtier-Boissière, 176

Gauche Radicale, 12

Gaxotte, 62, 77, 82 n., 91 n., 100, 114, 147, 150, 214 n.

General Staff, 9 n.

Germain-Martin, 184

Germany, Weimar Republic, 22 f.; advent of Hitler, 24 ff.; *Anschluss,* 135 ff.; conscription, 39 ff.; Czech crises, 154 f., 161 ff., 168 ff.; Franco-German declaration of friendship, 190;

Italo-German *rapprochement,* 117 ff., 123, 156; occupation of Bohemia, 206; rearmament, 32, 38; remilitarization of Rhineland, 85 f.; withdrawal from League, 28 ff.; see Right, attitude toward

Gignoux, 28

Godesberg meeting, 162, 170, 172 f.

Goy, Jean, 30 n., 207 n.

Great Britain, Anglo-German Naval Agreement, 56; *Anschluss,* 136 f.; Barthou's note, April 17, 1934, 33; Czech crises, 154 f., 161 f., 168 ff.; Four Power Pact, 1933, 26, 28 n.; Franco-British Alliance, 154; guarantee to Poland, 206, 210, 213 f.; Italo-Ethiopian War, 52 ff., 55 n.; London conversation, February, 1935, 38, 39; remilitarization of Rhineland, 85, 95 ff.; Spanish Civil War, 118 ff., 153 ff.; Stresa Conference, 44 f.; see Right, attitude toward

Gringoire, 56, 73 n., 90 n., 128 n., 150, 192 n.

Grix, Le, 62, 64, 73, 82 n., 116, 128, 142, 147, 150, 186

Grumbach, Deputy, 201 n.

Halévy, 14 n.

Halifax, Lord, 159 n.

Hamp, 15 n.

Harcourt, D', 169 n.

Henderson, Sir Nevile, 154

Henlein, 161, 168

Henriot, Deputy, 81 n., 196 f., 200 n., 202 n.

Héraud, Deputy, 76 n.

Hermant, 26

Herriot, 34 n., 82 f., 100 n., 202 n.

Hitler, 2, 24 f., 29 ff., 37, 39, 41, 75 n., 85, 89, 91, 100, 103, 115, 123, 135, 144, 149, 159 ff., 185, 190, 206, 210, 215, 218

Hoare, Sir Samuel, 52, 55 n.

Holland, 152, 208

Humanité, L', 41

Ideology, influence: on domestic policy, 79 ff., 99, 100, 108 ff., 125 ff., 145 ff., 179 f., 184 ff., 201 ff.; on foreign policy, 61 ff., 74, 79 ff., 88 ff., 99 ff., 106, 111 ff., 118 ff., 131 f., 158 ff., 184 ff., 201 ff., 208 ff., 224 ff., 229 ff.

Information, L', 8

Isolationism, *see* Nationalism (resigned)
Italy, propaganda, 9; colonial demands, 198, 212; Ethiopian War, 52 ff.; Four Power Pact, 1933, 26; Italo-German *rapprochement,* 117 ff., 123 f., 156 ff.; Rome agreements, 1935, 38; Stresa conference, 43 ff.; *see* Right, attitude toward

Japan, 122, 207, 228
Jaurès, 176
Je Suis Partout, 56, 73 n., 97 n., 150, 192 n., 220
Jeune, A. L., 93
Jeunesses Patriotes, 16 n., 65
Jouhaux, 41 n.
Jour, Le, 29, 56, 73 n.; *see* Bailby
Journal, Le, 175, 192
Journal des Débats, 8, 30, 79
Journée Industrielle, La, 28
Jouvenel, Bertrand de, 75 n., 130 n.
Jouvenel, Robert de, 6 n.

Kaiser, Jacques, 30 n.
Kerillis, De, 54, 58, 71, 74, 80, 82 n., 91, 102, 103, 108, 111, 118, 131, 144, 146 n., 148, 162 n., 163, 176 f., 191, 198 n., 201, 219

Lasteyrie, De, Deputy, 76 n.
Lauzanne, 43, 48, 56, 87, 163, 175 f., 186, 192, 208
Laval, cabinet, 52 ff., 69; cited, 33 n., 67, 69 n., 133, 149, 157, 228; foreign policy, 37, 46, 48 f., 52 f., 59 f., 68
League of Nations, condemns German coup 1935, 43, 45 f.; entry of U. S. S. R., 34, 37; loss of prestige, 119, 134, 136 f., 141; Rhineland coup, 85, 87 ff., 98; sanctions against Italy, 52 ff.; withdrawal of Germany from, 28 f.; *see* Right, attitude toward
Leagues, 16, 125 ff.; *see* Croix de Feu, *L'Action Française*
Left, domestic policy before 1936, 12 ff., 33, 80; end of Popular Front, 133, 148, 179 f., 185 n., 202 ff.; Popular Front Government, 108 ff., 145 ff.
foreign policy before 1933, 2, 19 ff.; *Anschluss,* 143, 145 ff.; Four Power Pact, 1933, 27; Franco-German *rapprochement,* 72; Italo-Ethiopian War, 53, 60 ff.; *loi des deux ans,* 41; Munich, 170, 176, 178 ff.; remilitari-

zation of Rhineland, 100 f.; Spanish Civil War, 114, 116 f.; Stresa conference, 44; *see* Right, attitude toward
Lémery, Senator, 105, 196 f., 216
Liberalism, 15, 16 n., 18
Liberté, La, 55 n., 73 n., 128 n., 150, 172
Litvinov, 69
Locarno Pact, 22, 45, 85, 88 n., 90, 95 114, 151

MacDonald, 26, 28 n.
Maginot Line, 85, 97 n., 137, 142, 146 n., 162 n., 222
Mandel, 29, 71, 86, 108 n., 146 n., 162 n., 202 n.
Maritain, 55 n., 113
Marquet, 179, 185 n.
Marxism, 17, 18 n., 49 n., 125, 126 n., 127 n., 130 n., 202 f., 224 ff.; *see* Right, attitude toward Communism
Matin, Le, 29, 56, 63 n., 81 n., 136, 184, 208, 210 n.; *see* Lauzanne
Maulnier, Thierry, 16, 18, 224
Mauriac, 55 n., 113
Maurras, 16 f., 20, 22 n., 40, 75 n., 77 ff., 91 f., 101 n., 145, 148, 171 f., 174, 181 f., 209, 211, 217, 224, 228
Maxence, 75 n., 126 n., 224
Millerand, 104, 203 n.
Mistler, Deputy, 179 n.
Modérés, domestic policy, 15, 17 f., 35, 108 ff., 125 ff., 133, 203 n., 227; foreign policy, 22 f., 35, 46 ff., 54 ff., 61 ff., 68, 73 f., 82 n., 93, 101 ff., 184, 186, 228; *see* Conditional Nationism
Molotov, 216 n.
Montigny, 69, 72, 77, 97 n., 110 n., 111, 130 n., 137, 139 f., 181, 193, 202 n., 207 n., 217 n.
Monzie, De, Deputy, 179 n., 185 n., 202 n.
Moutet, Deputy, 75
Munichois, 67, 152, 180, 185 n., 190 ff., 212
Munich Pact, 2, 103, 161 f., 174 ff., 190 ff., 206 f., 215, 220
Mussolini, 19, 26, 37, 60, 64, 100, 123 f., 138, 149 f., 156 ff., 185

Nation, La, 153 n.
National Socialism, 16 n., 19, 24 f., 30, 179, 228

Nationalism: conditional, 73 f., 93, 101 ff., 122, 131, 137 ff., 153 ff., 159, 166 ff., 172 f., 186, 192, 194 ff., 205, 207 f., 215 f., 228
resigned, 71 ff., 89 ff., 98 n., 101, 130 f., 139 ff., 145 ff., 163 ff., 171 f., 186, 192 ff., 204, 208 ff., 213 n., 215 ff., 228
traditional, 19 ff., 26 f., 53 ff., 70 f., 88, 136 n., 137, 142 ff., 162 f., 170, 191, 201, 219 f., 228
Neo-pacifism, see Pacifism
Neo-socialism, 18, 72, 185
Nouvelle Revue Française, 6 n., 15 n.

Oberkirch, Deputy, 75 n., 195 f.
Oeuvre, L', 211
Ordre, L', 162, 169 n., 170; see Buré
Ormesson, D', 21, 24, 25 n., 31, 41, 58, 69, 82 n., 88 n., 96 n., 115 n., 120 f., 145, 154, 157, 160 n., 169 n., 173, 191, 198 n., 202 n., 203 n., 207, 213, 215

Pacifism, 2, 20, 41, 75, 170, 176 ff., 222 f.; neo-pacifism, 40, 58 ff., 74 f., 88 ff., 94 ff., 105 f., 117, 150 ff., 163 ff., 169 ff., 175 ff., 202 ff., 208 ff., 217 ff., 223 ff.
Papen, 24
Paris Midi, 93
Paris Soir, 75 n.
Parti Agraire, 127 n.
Parti Populaire Français, 127 ff.
Parti Républicain National et Social, 127 n.
Parti Social Français, 15 n., 126 ff., 139, 195, 200 n.
Péri, Deputy, 64, 140 ff., 159, 211
Pertinax, 29, 44, 54 f., 68 n., 71, 72 n., 87, 88 n., 137 n., 144, 145 n., 152, 155 f., 162, 165, 231 n.
Pétain, 147
Petit Journal, Le, 4, 68 n., 127 n., 174, 218; see La Rocque
Petit Parisien, Le, 4, 45, 68 n., 146 n., 167, 208
Pezet, Deputy, 55, 59 n., 65, 71, 119, 123 n., 137 n., 146 n., 191, 197
Pichot, 30 n., 207 n.
Pinon, 25 f., 31 f., 35, 43, 57, 94 n., 109 n., 110, 112 n., 122, 160, 172, 184, 192 n., 194, 196 n., 206, 207 n., 212 n., 215

Piot, 30 n.
Poincaré, 33
Poland, 34, 37, 53, 72, 76, 120, 130, 134, 140, 144, 196, 206, 209, 211, 214, 216 f., 220
Politique, 55 n.
Politique Étrangère, 55 n., 162 n.
Pomaret, Deputy, 185 n.
Populaire, Le, 41 n., 44, 101 n., 170, 191 n., 209 n.
Potemkin, 46
Prade, 184 n.
Preparedness (France's), 77 f., 91, 94 ff., 139, 151 n., 182 f., 212
Press, 5 ff.; see Bibliography and individual newspapers
Propaganda, 9, 83, 160, 224 f.
Prouvost, 175
Public opinion, 3 ff.
Pujo, 92

Quai d'Orsay, 8, 28 n.; see France, foreign policy
Queipo de Llano, 113 n.

Radical Socialists, domestic policy, 12 n., 13, 33, 37 n., 72, 90, 108 n., 109, 129, 133, 151 n., 179, 186 n., 202, 203 n.; foreign policy, 21 n., 24 n., 30 n., 41, 53 n., 67, 72, 83, 178 ff., 202 n.
Rapprochement, 22, 28 f., 65, 72 f., 73, 75; see Right, foreign policy
Rassemblement Populaire, see Front Populaire
Realism, in foreign policy, 45, 54 ff., 60 ff., 76 ff., 94 ff., 99, 106 f., 139 ff., 151 f., 154, 182 ff., 191 ff., 217 f., 223
Recouly, 24, 39, 48, 88 n., 94 n., 109 n., 112, 115, 123 n., 124, 166, 183, 199 n., 201, 208, 212 n.
Reibel, Senator, 193 n., 203 n.
République, La, 72, 159, 169 n., 192 n.
Retrenchment, see Nationalism (resigned)
Revue Bleue, 184 n.
Revue de France, see Recouly
Revue des Deux Mondes, see Pinon
Revue Hebdomadaire, see Le Grix
Revue Universelle, 56, 73 n.
Reynaud, cited, 41 n., 108 n., 125, 134, 137, 146 n., 159, 162 n., 202 n., 224; foreign policy, 55, 71, 95, 111, 115, 119 f., 142 f.
Rhineland, remilitarization of, 78, 85 ff., 183

Ribbentrop, 204

Right: attitude toward: communism, 62, 79 ff., 83 f., 89, 99, 109 ff., 120 f., 126, 131, 146 f., 158, 184, 202 f., 213, 225 f.; Fascism, 15 ff., 61, 63 f., 80 f., 83, 100, 111, 116, 125 ff., 186, 220, 224 f., 228; Left, 12 ff., 61 ff., 69, 91 f., 99 ff., 108 ff., 114 ff., 121, 125 ff., 145 ff., 172, 184 f., 202 f., 226 ff.

attitude toward: Germany, see Nationalism, Modérés, Extreme-Right; Great Britain, 56 ff., 88, 90, 95 ff., 119, 122 ff., 138, 141 ff., 153 ff., 167, 173, 181, 193 ff., 208, 213 f., 222 f.; League, 22 f., 43, 45, 53 ff., 87 f., 90 ff., 97 ff., 110, 119, 141, 151, 181; Italy, 26 f., 53 ff., 88, 90, 98 f., 102, 110, 123 f., 134, 138 ff., 153, 156 ff., 194 f., 197 ff., 209 ff., 222; Soviet Russia, 35, 67 ff., 89 ff., 98 ff., 104 f., 114 ff., 118 ff., 130 f., 140 ff., 146, 149, 158 ff., 164 ff., 171, 183 ff., 193 ff., 209 ff., 213 ff., 219 f., 224 f.

domestic policy: until 1933, 2, 12 ff.; success of Popular Front, 108 ff., 125 ff., 226 ff.; end of Popular Front, 133, 145 ff., 179 f., 226 ff.

foreign policy: until 1933, 2, 19 ff.; advent of Hitler, 24 f.; Anschluss, 137 ff.; Barthou's policy, 34 f.; Czech crises, May, 1938, 148 ff., September, 162, 168 ff.; Four Power Pact of 1933, 26 f.; Franco-Soviet Pact, 46 ff., 67 ff., 72 ff., 76 ff., 110 n., 111, 118 ff., 124; German withdrawal from League, 28 ff.; Italo-Ethiopian War, 53 ff.; occupation of Prague, 206 ff.; Rhineland coup, 87 ff., 97 ff.; Spanish Civil War, 112 ff., 201 n., 227, 230

Roche, 30 n., 163 f., 173

Rochefoucault, De la, 30 n.

Rocque, De la, 5, 15 n., 92, 126 ff., 138, 153, 166, 172 ff., 184, 210 n., 218

Rollin, Deputy, 110 f.

Romains, 72 n.

Romier, 14, 18, 93, 158 n., 167 n., 192

Roosevelt, 80, 175

Royalists, see L'Action Française

Rumania, 34, 76, 134, 190, 196, 206 f., 209

Runciman, Lord, 156, 162, 166, 169, 179 n.

Saar plebiscite, 37

St. Brice, 34, 54, 97 n.

Sanctions, see League of Nations

Sarraut, 67, 69 n., 86, 90, 92

Scapini, Deputy, 199

Schleicher, Von, 24

Schlumberger, 30

Schuschnigg, Von, 135

Sciences Politiques, 129 n., 131 n.

Security: collective, 37 ff., 43, 53 ff., 60 f., 70 ff., 76 ff., 86 ff., 97 ff., 117 ff., 168, 181, 191 ff., 206 ff., 222 ff.; French, 22 f., 33 ff., 37 ff., 45 ff., 70 ff., 76 ff., 86 ff., 97 ff., 119, 177, 181 f., 192 ff., 206 ff.

Senate, on Four Power diplomacy, 196 f., 198 n.; on Franco-Soviet Pact, 103 ff.; role on public opinion and foreign affairs, 5, 196 n.

Sept, 55 n.

Seyss-Inquart, 135

S. F. I. O., see Socialists

Siegfried, 13, 19

Siegfried Line, 151, 209

Simon, Deputy, 146 n.

Simon, Sir John, 28 n., 42

Socialist party, domestic policy, 33, 67, 108 n., 129, 133 n., 148, 185 n., 203 f., 226, 231; foreign policy, 20 n., 24 n., 56 n., 60 ff., 82, 114, 178 ff., 185 n., 198 n., 203, 209 n., 230; see Blum; Right, attitude toward Left

Solidarité Française, 16 n.

Soviet Russia, see U. S. S. R.

Spain, 111 ff., 149 f.

Spanish Civil War, see Spain

Stalin, 48, 49 n., 69, 80, 91, 125 n., 211 n., 226

Stavisky scandal, 33

Stresa conference, 44 f., 50; see Right, attitude toward Italy

Strikes, of 1936, 110 f.; of 1938, 198, 204

Suarez, 30 n., 101, 136

Sudeten Germans, 151, 160 ff.

Taittinger, Deputy, 16 n., 65, 73, 75, 76 n., 84, 118, 123 n.

Tardieu, 29 n., 34 n., 128, 133

Temps, Le, 8, 19, 27 f., 39, 44 f., 47 f., 58, 63 n., 75 n., 89, 109, 110, 123 n., 145, 150, 152, 153 n., 157 n., 166,

168 n., 169 n., 199, 206, 207 n., 208 n., 210 n.

Thellier, Deputy, 54 n.

Thibaudet, 5, 12, 13 n., 14 f., 62 n.

Third International, *see* Right, attitude toward Soviet Russia; Communism

Torrès, Deputy, 68

Toynbee, 60, 63 n.

Trotsky, 226

Ukraine, 194, 196 n.

Union Nationale, 145 ff.

Union Républicaine, 104

Union Socialiste Républicaine, 178, 185 n., 198 n.

U. S. S. R., entry into League, 34, 37; Four Power Pact policy, 184, 189, 201, 215 f., 219; Franco-Soviet Pact, 34 f., 37, 45 ff., 67 ff., 76 ff.; Laval's trip to Moscow, 48 f.; Munich, 164, 171;

Spanish Civil War, 114 ff., 118 ff.; *see* Right, attitude toward

United States of America, 167, 226

Vallat, Deputy, 76, 78, 147, 196 n., 200

Vallin, 126 n., 129 n., 131 n.

Valois, 16 n.

Versailles Treaty, 20, 32, 36, 39, 85 f., 104

Veuillot, 127 n., 129 n.

Vichy régime, 228

Vignaux, 55 n., 113

Volonté, La, 30 n.

Werth, 49 f., 128, 133, 137 n.

Wolfers, 22 n.

Ybarnégaray, Deputy, 123 n., 126, 131, 137 ff., 176, 218

Yugoslavia, 134, 140, 190, 208

Zay, Deputy, 65 n.